PENGUIN HANDBOOKS
PH 33
THE PENGUIN KNITTING BOOK
JAMES NORBURY

This book is written for the experienced knitter as well as the beginner.

As well as telling you how to knit, the author gives a large number of patterns for knitted fabrics, and then goes on to suggest what you can knit for every member of the family. Babies' coats, pullovers for father, sweaters for the teenager, dresses, jumpers, coats, and cardigans, you will find them all in this aid to better knitting, illustrated with many drawings and photographs of the stitches and garments.

One exciting feature of the Penguin Handbook on Knitting is the Fashion Supplement, containing a selection of designs that reflect the fashion trends of the moment. In future editions of the book this section will be changed from time to time to keep the *Penguin Knitting Book* to the forefront of current knitwear fashion.

Cover design by Heather Standring

D1514194

James Norbury

THE PENGUIN KNITTING BOOK

A Reissue of the Original Book

PENGUIN BOOKS

PENGUIN BOOKS

Published by the Penguin Group
Penguin Books Ltd, 80 Strand, London WC2R 0RL, England
Penguin Group (USA) Inc., 375 Hudson Street, New York, New York 10014, USA
Penguin Group (Canada), 90 Eglinton Avenue East, Suite 700, Toronto, Ontario, Canada M4P 2Y3
(a division of Pearson Penguin Canada Inc.)
Penguin Ireland, 25 St Stephen's Green, Dublin 2, Ireland (a division of Penguin Books Ltd)
Penguin Group (Australia), 707 Collins Street, Melbourne, Victoria 3008, Australia
(a division of Pearson Australia Group Pty Ltd)
Penguin Books India Pvt Ltd, 11 Community Centre, Panchsheel Park, New Delhi – 110 017, India
Penguin Group (NZ), 67 Apollo Drive, Rosedale, Auckland 0632, New Zealand
(a division of Pearson New Zealand Ltd)
Penguin Books (South Africa) (Pty) Ltd, Block D, Rosebank Office Park,
181 Jan Smuts Avenue, Parktown North, Gauteng 2193, South Africa

Penguin Books Ltd, Registered Offices: 80 Strand, London WC2R 0RL, England

www.penguin.com

First published by Penguin Books 1957
Reissued in its original format 2014
001

Copyright © James Norbury, 1957, 2014
All rights reserved

The moral right of the author has been asserted

Printed in Great Britain by Clays Ltd, St Ives plc

ISBN: 978-0-241-97125-3

www.greenpenguin.co.uk

For

BRYAN CLAYDEN

A slight token of friendship

... for a great fashion designer to come into being, talent alone is not enough: the designer must have the absolute and authoritative genius to impose his or her vision of the needs of the times on the times themselves, so that fashions which a year previously would have been considered outrageous are suddenly a necessity. It is the genius who creates the need, though that need must reflect the unconscious wishes of the moment if the genius is to be accepted, at least by his contemporaries.

CECIL BEATON: *The Glass of Fashion*

CONTENTS

LIST OF PLATES

Stitches

Garments

Fashion Supplement

The photographs of the different stitches were taken by John Dyson, those of the garments by Peter Clark and John Dyson, and those for the Fashion Supplement by Michael Dunne. The line drawings were made by Pamela Cox.

ABBREVIATIONS

K – knit

P – purl

KB – Knit into back of stitch

PB – Purl into back of stitch

st – stitch

sl – slip

wf – wool forward

yf – yarn forward

wft – wool front, bring wool to front of needle

wb – wool back, take wool to back of needle

wrn – wool round needle

won – wool on needle

psso – pass slipped stitch over

tog – together

tbl – through back of loop

inc – increase by working into front and back of stitch

dec – decrease by working 2 stitches together

beg – beginning

alt – alternate

rep – repeat

patt – pattern

incl – inclusive

ins – inches

dc – double crochet

o – no sts

M1   – Make 1, by picking up loop that lies between st just worked and following st, and working into back of it.

M1K – Make 1 knitwise by picking up loop that lies between st just worked and following st and *knitting* into back of it.

M1P – Make 1 purlwise by picking up loop that lies between st just worked and following st and *purling* into back of it.

MB   – Make Bobble by P1, K1, P1, K1, P1 into next st thus making 5 sts out of next st, turn, K5, turn, P5, slip 2nd, 3rd, 4th, and 5th sts over first st.

C2F – Cable 2 Front by working across next 4 sts as follows: Slip next 2 sts on to cable needle and leave at *front* of work, knit next 2 sts, then knit 2 sts from cable needle.

C2B	– Cable 2 Back as C2F, but leave sts at *back* of work in place of front.
C3F	– Cable 3 Front by working across next 6 sts as follows: Slip next 3 sts on to cable needle and leave at *front* of work, knit across next 3 sts then knit 3 sts from cable needle.
C3B	– Cable 3 Back as C3F, but leave sts at *back* of work in place of front.
C4F	– Cable 4 front by working across next 8 sts as follows: Slip next 4 sts on to cable needle and leave at *front* of work, knit across next 4 sts then knit 4 sts from cable needle.
Tw2	– Twist 2 by knitting the next 2 sts together, but do not slip off left-hand needle, knit into the first of these sts again, then slip both sts off needle.
Tw2P	– Twist 2 purlwise by purling the next 2 sts together but do not slip off left-hand needle, purl into the first of these sts again, then slip both sts off needle.
Tw3	– Twist 3 by inserting point of right-hand needle knitwise into front of 3rd st keeping point of this needle at *front* of work, knit the st in the ordinary way; work the 2nd st in the same manner, now knit into front of the 1st st then slip all 3 sts off left-hand needle together.

LP – Lace panel
B – Blue
BG – Bottle green
C – Contrast
D – Dark
G – Ground shade
L – Light
LN – Light natural
M – Medium
PY – Pale yellow
S – Scarlet
Y – Yellow
W – White

CHAPTER 1

Once Upon a Time

KNITTING fills a fascinating page in the human story. It is one of those by-ways of social history that, although lying off the main track along which man has travelled down the ages, has still contributed a great deal to the economic, social, and aesthetic life of civilization. In spite of many years' research it has been impossible to track down this ancient craft to its earliest beginnings.

In ancient times a nomadic people wandered about the desert places, living in small communities in the oasis where they had their habitations. Thus some of the nomads became village dwellers. These people were the first knitters. The craft was carried out entirely by the men-folk. The women spun the flax into linen thread and the various animal fibres into woollen yarns. The men took the threads and knitted them into garments.

During this first phase of knitting the work was probably carried out on simple frames. These consisted of long narrow pieces of wood into which wooden or bone pegs had been driven to form a simple rake frame on which the knitting was done. The working method was much the same as in the bobbin work that many of us did when we were children.

The earliest examples of knitted fabric were done in a twisted stocking stitch and when worked on these frames created a firm and durable fabric.*

The origin of knitting needles is completely unknown. Netting, using a long bone tool, was one of man's very early crafts and hooks have been discovered that suggest that our earliest ancestors had some knowledge of looped fabrics made with hooks. Some Egyptologists claim that they have found in the tombs of the Pharaohs long bone pins that may have been used for knitting. There is another piece of evidence. That is a knitted doll in the Victoria and Albert Museum. This was found in one of the tombs, proving that knitting was an established craft at the time of Cleopatra.

* Fragments of fabric knitted in crossed stocking stitch in silk yarn have been discovered with a tension of 36 stitches to the inch.

Among the earliest examples of knitting preserved for us to-day are sandal socks. These have been found in various parts of the desert places in Arabia, and specimens of them can be seen in museums in all parts of the world.

The most exciting fragment of fabric was a piece of Arabic knitting in several colours in the collection of Dr Fritz Ikle, who was a German authority on all kinds of textile fabrics. His world-famous collection disappeared before the war under the Nazi régime. The date of this fragment is somewhere between the fifth and seventh centuries. Its interest for us to-day is in the fact that it is a piece of stranded colour knitting in stocking stitch, a technique that was to inspire the craftsmen of the later Middle Ages and early Renaissance to develop knitting during the golden age of the Craft Guilds. These men were the friends of Kings and Courtiers, and designed and knitted elaborate coats in silk fibres and gold and silver threads of which there are several specimens in the Victoria and Albert Museum.

The importance of knitting to the economic life of the community cannot be over-estimated. For centuries it was one of the basic industries not only in England but also in France and Italy. The Florentine knitters have left us a legacy of heavily brocaded knitting, while the Guild of Stocking Knitters in Paris has bequeathed to us lovely lace hose. A pair of stockings of French workmanship were copied by Mrs Montague and presented by her to the first Queen Elizabeth.

When the craft was in its heyday the apprentices to the Knitting Guilds served an arduous apprenticeship that lasted six years. For the first three years they were taught the rudiments of the craft, and for the second three years they travelled extensively all over the continent studying the work of the master knitters there. At the end of the six years the apprentice was ready to apply for entry into the Guild, when he could proudly call himself a master craftsman and set up in business on his own account. Before this privilege was granted to him the young man who had served his apprenticeship honestly had to complete in thirteen weeks a knitted carpet in a coloured design containing flowers, foliage, birds, and animals, approximately six feet by five feet; to knit and felt a woollen beret; to knit himself a woollen shirt and a pair of hose with Spanish Clocks.

16

It is interesting to note that in some of the Guilds the stockings were to be made after the English style, proving that in those days the people of this country were well known for their knitted hosiery.

The carpet, however, was the masterpiece. The apprentice first submitted a colour design, swearing that the design was entirely his own work. He was then placed in the workroom of one of the master craftsmen where he had to knit the carpet himself.

When all his test pieces were completed they had to be submitted to the Council of the Guild and if they received the approval of the Council the title of Master Knitter was bestowed upon him.

The silk shirt worn by King Charles I on the day of his execution, and to-day in the London Museum, is a fine example of the work of a Master Knitter of that period and has another point of interest for us in that it reflects in the design the influence of Dutch embossed knitting.

It is difficult to discover the types of knitted garments worn in those early days. There are one or two pointers in England's story. An Act of Parliament passed in 1488 during the reign of King Henry VII mentions knitted caps; while another Act of 1553, passed during the reign of King Edward VI, mentions knitted petticoats, gloves, sleeves, and hose. The significance of these Acts of Parliament is that they prove that knitting had already established itself as an industry that was important enough to be protected by law.

The year 1589 saw a revolution in knitting. William Lee, a Cambridgeshire clergyman, invented the first stocking frame machine, thus laying the foundations of the hosiery industry that was to grow and thrive in Nottinghamshire and Leicestershire where it is one of the basic industries of to-day. Mistress Lee, William Lee's wife, was herself an ardent knitter and plied her needles day by day, thus helping to maintain the family with her earnings. It was watching his wife working all hours from daylight to rushlight that inspired William Lee to invent a machine which was to breathe new life into knitting, not only in this country but also all over the continent. So we see that a couple of centuries before the Industrial Revolution took place its first faint rumblings were heard during the Elizabethan Age.

In England the knitting of hosiery had become a staple industry. In France and Belgium lace knitting flourished. In Germany and Austria heavy cable and bobble fabrics were produced. In Holland embossed knitted fabrics created wonderful effects, animals, birds, and flowers being worked in reverse stocking stitch on a stocking stitch foundation.

Another page of the story was being written in Scandinavia, where the peasants copied in knitting, on gloves and coats, the reindeer and pine trees that were the natural background to their everyday life.

Colour knitting bequeathed to Europe from its Arabic sources by the early Phoenician traders, travelled from Spain to Fair Isle. The Spanish tradition still lingers there, for in all genuine Fair Isle garments one of the basic motifs is the 'Armada Cross'. The influence of Christianity can also be seen in the patterns used in Fair Isle knitting. Their very names, the 'Rose of Sharon', the 'Sacred Heart', the 'Crown of Glory', all speak to us of the golden age of Christendom itself.

Shetland lace knitting is another fascinating aspect of a world-wide story. The practice of lace knitting in Shetland was derived from needle-made laces. In the early part of the nineteenth century a Mrs Jessie Scanlon visited Shetland, taking with her a wonderful collection of laces she had gathered together in all parts of Europe. The Shetlanders, who were already ardent knitters, mainly following the Scandinavian tradition which had been taken to the islands by the Norse settlers in the ninth century, were soon busy plying their needles and wool copying the intricate patternings from Mrs Scanlon's laces.

By the end of the first Elizabethan age London ceased to be a small collection of villages clustered round the city itself and became transformed into the banking and trading centre of England. Knitting was driven farther and farther North, finally establishing itself as a home industry among the hand knitters of the Yorkshire Dales.

The men and women of the Dales became famous for their hand-knitted stockings and until the beginning of the eighteenth century were able to earn a good livelihood by plying their needles and wool.

The Crimean War marked the final phase in this part of our

story. The last burst of prosperity came to the knitters of the Dales through the making of Balaclava helmets, which were worn by the British troops in that campaign. Lord Cardigan gave his name to the well-known knitted garment that is worn to-day by both men and women.

The beginning of the Victorian Age at first seemed destined to sound the death knell of this ancient craft. That knitting resurrected itself was largely due to the women's magazines, which made their first appearance in the middle period of Queen Victoria's reign. Mrs Beeton seems to have had a finger in this pie as well, but probably the credit ought to go to Mrs Weldon, who founded her *Ladies' Journal*. These magazines encouraged the ladies of leisure to devote their time to handicrafts, and although we may shudder at the ugliness of many of the Victorian knick-knacks or look at them merely as bizarre curiosities collected for us in museums, it was due to these things that knitting was kept alive during what might have been its last lingering twilight.

In 1854 a Mrs Gaugain published in Edinburgh *The Lady's Assistant*, 'for,' as she tells us, 'executing useful and fancy designs in knitting, netting, and crochet work.' This interesting little book, sold at 5/6d, soon ran into seven editions, and among the list of patronesses and subscribers we find such imposing names as 'Her Majesty The Queen Dowager, and Their Royal Highnesses The Duchess of Gloucester, The Duchess of Cambridge, and the Princess Augusta Carolina'.

Not only did Mrs Gaugain produce a second volume of *The Lady's Assistant* in the same year, but she seems to have been her own advertising agent. On the fly-leaf of Volume Two we find the following paragraph:

Many Ladies having found great difficulty in procuring the proper Wool for the Fine Shetland Shawl, page 105; the Alpine Knit Scarf, page 331; the Barege Fichu, page 226; the Square Shawl with Shaded Border, page 369; also for the Triangular Shawl, page 370, &c.; MRS GAUGAIN begs to intimate that she can forward the Wool to any Post Town in Great Britain. Through the medium of the post, Material for the largest piece of Knitting mentioned above, may be sent, postage included, for 6s. 3d.; all other Materials may be forwarded, in the same way, at an extra charge of 2d. postage on every ounce.

The First World War saw women once more busy with their knitting needles, making comforts for the troops. The emancipation of women in 1920 produced the 'Sweater Girl' who, wearing her long, loose, knitted sack-like tunic, became the symbol of the 'Roaring Twenties'. Chanel, the world famous *couturier*, was then the reigning queen of *haute couture* in Paris and her collections always contained specimens of knitted sweaters, thus placing them in the forefront of fashion. To-day Lola Prussac and Anny Blatt are the leading exponents of *couture* knitwear, while recently Christian Dior himself has entered the field. The classic tailored lines dominate knitwear to-day.

CHAPTER 2

Ways and Means

I KNOW of no home-craft that enjoys the universal popularity of hand-knitting. Watching knitters at work in France and Germany, in Scandinavia and Italy, in Shetland and on Fair Isle – in fact in all the countries where my journeys have led me during the past twenty-five years, I often wonder what gives the craft its wide appeal.

The answer is the ease and simplicity with which knitted fabrics can be produced and the cheapness of the tools and materials used for carrying out the various stitches and techniques used in knitting.

Fibres for Knitting

Almost any fibre is suitable for knitting. Cotton, silk, the new nylon yarns, rayons, and wool all have their right use and proper purpose in the pursuit of the craft.

The right purpose is the important thing. Always buy the type of wool or fibre recommended on the knitting instructions you are using. Knitting wools fall into two main groups – these are known as botanies and cross-breds. In the main, cross-breds are harder wearing and will stand up to more rough and tumble than the softer botanies. For babies' wear soft botanies are ideal, while for hardwearing school jerseys and pullovers a good cross-bred should be selected.

The wool and nylon mixtures on the market are very suitable for socks, while for women's fashion garments you can use either a good botany or a good cross-bred.

Classification of Knitting Wools

Knitting wools fall mainly into the following groups:

(a) 1 Ply. This is a very fine spun yarn suitable for garments that will not be subject to hard wear.

(b) 2 Ply. An ideal yarn for light-weight underwear and summer garments.

21

(c) 3 Ply. One of the best all-purpose knitting wools that can be obtained, as it is equally suitable for men's, women's, or children's garments where a fairly fine fabric is desired.

(d) 4 Ply. The 4-ply weights are another useful all-purpose yarn; for men's cardigans and pullovers, women's coats, children's school garments, and lightweight sports jumpers and sweaters this is the perfect wool to use.

(e) Double knitting. This wool is approximately double the thickness of 3-ply and is the perfect medium for heavy sweaters and coats.

Fancy Wools and Mixtures

In addition to the above wools there is always a wide variety of fancy yarns on the market. Some of these are mixtures of wool and rayon, others mixtures of various fibres and wool. There is also crepe wool and bouclet. Both these wools were well known before the war and are slowly regaining popularity among discriminating knitters. Crepe wool has a tighter twist than an ordinary fingering and creates a very firm and attractive fabric. Bouclet is spun with a series of little bumps or loops that create in stocking stitch, when the reverse side is used, almost the appearance of a woven fabric.

In buying knitting wools select a good make that has a reputation, as although this may cost you a little more at the outset it will prove well worth while when you have knitted your garment.

Knitting Needles

Knitting needles are made in various lengths and sizes and can be obtained in either metal, bone, or plastic. I prefer the metal type of needle covered with an alloy, as this has a smooth knitting surface that helps to produce a smooth fabric.

You can obtain pairs of knitting needles with knobs on the end in lengths varying from ten inches to fourteen inches, while sets of four, pointed at both ends used for knitting in the round, can be obtained in lengths varying from six inches to twelve inches.

In addition to the standard needles you can also obtain cable needles in various sizes. These are short needles with points at both ends and are used mainly for working cable patterns.

The best knitting is always done on long needles. The end of the right-hand needle is tucked firmly under the arm thus enabling you to hold the right-hand needle rigid while working with the left-hand needle. This helps to ensure an even tension throughout the fabric. I know that to some of you this may seem an old wives' tale, but for centuries knitters always used either a sheath or a pouch and long steel needles. One end of the needle was stuck into the sheath that was fastened into the belt or into the pad on the pouch that had a belt attached to it in order to keep the needle completely rigid. You will still find knitting pouches in daily use in Shetland, and the Shetland knitters are still among the finest craftsmen in the world.

Another point to watch for in selecting knitting needles is that the point is not too long and tapering. A good knitter always works as near to the points of the needles as possible, and a long tapering point can cause variation of tension throughout the fabric.

SIZE OF KNITTING NEEDLES. Most knitting needles are stamped with the size (this is called the gauge of needle). The sizes of English, and Continental and American, knitting needles differ, as there has been no agreed standardization for these three types of needles. The following table gives you the comparative sizes of English, and Continental and American, knitting needles:

English	Continental and American
1	13
2	12
3	11
4	10
5	9
6	8
7	7
8	6
9	5
10	4
11	3
12	2
13	1
14	

23

The sizes given in this table for the Continental and American needles are approximate, as there is a very slight variation in the diameters of the needles.

You can easily adjust this, however, by carefully checking the tension before commencing to work a garment if you are knitting from a Continental or American pattern and using English knitting needles.

The Knitter's Work Basket

The wise knitter's work basket will also contain two or three stitch-holders. These are very simple gadgets on to which stitches

that are not being worked can be put. Another useful item is a bell gauge for measuring the sizes of knitting needles. These gauges are made in cardboard, plastic, or metal, and have holes

punched in them the exact circumference of the appropriate sizes of knitting needles. Each hole is marked with a number, the gauge of the needle. If your needles get mixed up in your work basket it is a simple matter to check the size by using a gauge of this type for the purpose.

For making up the pieces of fabric into a finished garment you should always use a blunt pointed tapestry needle. Keep a packet of these in your work basket. A few safety pins are also very useful, as you can use these to slip the stitches on when you are knitting front bands that later have to be incorporated in neck-bands.

Another useful accessory is a row counter. There is one on the market to-day that you slip on to the end of the knitting needle, rotating a round disc at the end of the counter that brings numbers into view in the little round windows on the front of the counter itself. A gadget of this kind is particularly useful for matching the front and back of a garment or the length of the sleeves. It enables you to be quite sure you have done exactly the same number of rows on each piece of the garment up to a given point.

These simple things all add to the tailored finish of your work and give to home knitting the master touch that every woman longs for in her home knitted garments.

Tension

From knitting needles and gauges we turn naturally to the all-important question of tension. This seems to be the nigger in every knitter's wood pile. Most complaints about garments not being the correct size are almost entirely due to the knitter's failure to work to the correct tension.

Tension is a very simple matter. It simply means that to every square inch of fabric there will be a given number of stitches to the inch across the width of the fabric and a given number of rows to the inch down the length of the fabric. All good knitting instructions give you a working tension at the beginning of the pattern. Here is a list giving you the standard tensions for 2-, 3-, and 4-ply, and double knitting on knitting needles ranging from size 5 to size 14:

25

Needles	2-ply		3-ply		4-ply		Double knitting	
	Sts	Rows	Sts	Rows	Sts	Rows	Sts	Rows
5	5½	7½	5	7	4½	6½	4¾	6
6	6	8	5½	7½	5	7	5	6½
7	6½	8½	6	8	5½	7½	5¼	7
8	7	9	6½	8½	6	8	5½	7½
9	7½	9½	7	9	6½	8½	5¾	7¾
10	8	10	7½	9½	7	9	6	8
11	8½	10½	8	10	7½	9½	6¾	9
12	9	11	8½	10½	8	10	7¼	10
13	9½	11½	9	11	8½	10½		
14	10	12	9½	11½	9	11		

All these tensions are given in stocking stitch. If you work to the correct tension in this fabric the fancy patterns and fabrics you knit will also be at the right tension.

Persevere with your tension before commencing to knit any design. Cast on sufficient stitches to knit a two inch square of fabric. This means that if you are working in 3-ply wool on size 11 needles you will cast on sixteen stitches. Now work a sufficient number of rows for two inches. This means working with the same 3-ply wool on the same 11 needles you will work twenty rows. Cast off the stitches and then lightly press this square of fabric on the wrong side, using a warm iron and damp cloth. If your tension is correct the piece of fabric should be exactly two inches square.

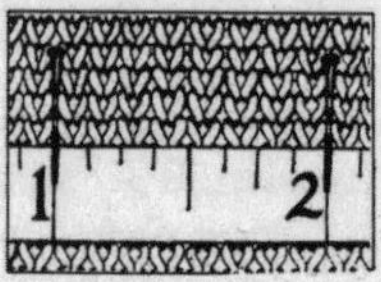

Rough Hands and Rubbed Wool

The care of the hands plays an important part in producing perfect knitted fabrics. To-day many women do their own chores. Soap powders and detergents are being widely advertised and used. That is why your hands may get slightly rough, and when you are knitting please do take that little extra care of your hands. Rub a good cream into them occasionally to keep them smooth, or if the fingers seem very slightly rough pour a little icing sugar into the palm of the hand and rub it all over the hands themselves. This will act like a very fine sandpaper and smooth off the roughened ends of the fingers.

The reason for this advice is that some women complain that knitting wool always rubs up. Rough fingers, even when the roughness is hardly visible to the naked eye, are one of the main causes of this trouble.

Always wrap up your knitting in a soft cloth before putting it away. If you spread this cloth on your knee when you are working it will protect the wool from becoming roughened as it rubs against the fabric of your skirt or dress. The fabric may have an uneven weave, giving it a rough texture, and your wool will suffer unless you protect it from direct contact.

Look After Your Wool

If you buy the wool in skeins wind it loosely into balls. Slip two fingers between the ball and the wool as you are winding it,

as this will help to keep the wool soft and pliable. Tightly wound wool robs the yarn of its natural softness and may even stretch it, thus ruining the garment before you have begun to knit.

Always buy sufficient wool to complete the garment you propose making, otherwise you may obtain the same colour that has come out of two different batches of dyeing. No matter how careful the spinner may be there may be a slight variation in tone in the same shade in different dye-lots.

CHAPTER 3
Plains and Purls

ONE piece of practical advice I always give to the beginner is 'Master the basic stitches before you start to knit any design.' This is a down-to-earth remark that may seem obvious to everybody. Alas, so many knitters tend to use the bull-at-the-gate technique before getting the first principles right, and then wonder why their finished fabric lacks the smoothness and evenness that is the hall-mark of perfect knitting.

Obviously the first thing one must learn to do is to cast on stitches. The method I am giving you here is casting on between the stitches. This is one of the best all round ways of casting on and is used for nearly every type of garment. This cast on has a firm but elastic edge that is essential if a garment is to stretch sufficiently at the lower edge without the cast-on row breaking.

Casting On Between Stitches

(a) Place the right-hand needle under the right arm. Make a small loop at the end of the ball of wool and place this loop on the point of the left-hand needle.

(b) Insert the point of the right-hand needle through the loop on the point of the left-hand needle. The wool you are working

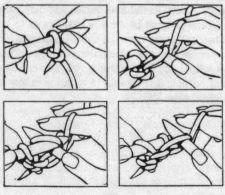

28

from is held in the right hand, as follows: Place the wool between the second and third fingers, now take it round the third finger and up in front of the second finger, take it behind the first finger so that it lies loosely between the first finger and the thumb. Wrap the wool round the point of the right-hand needle and draw a second loop through the loop on the left-hand needle.

(c) Place the loop thus formed on to the point of the left-hand needle, thus you will have two stitches on the left-hand needle.

(d) * Place the point of the right-hand needle between the two stitches on the left-hand needle. Wrap the wool round the point of the right-hand needle again, draw a loop between the two stitches and place the loop thus formed on to the left-hand needle.

(e) Repeat from * between the last two stitches on the left-hand needle until all the stitches have been cast on.

There is another method of casting on that every practical knitter should know. It is used to form a looped edge on the cast-on foundation of the fabric. This looped edge is used for knitting up with the stitches already on the needle when you are making a hem in knitting.

Casting On Through the Stitches

(a) Place the right-hand needle under the right arm. Make a loop at the end of the length of wool and place this loop on the left-hand needle.

(b) * Place the point of the right-hand needle through the loop on the left-hand needle. Holding the wool as for the first method of casting on, wrap the wool round the point of the right-hand needle, draw a second loop through the loop on the left-hand needle and place this loop on the point of the left-hand needle.

(c) Repeat from * through the last stitch on the left-hand needle until the correct number of stitches have been cast on.

Knitting stitches consists of working the stitches from the left-hand needle on to the right-hand needle. This is done as follows:

Knitting a Stitch

(a) Holding the right-hand needle under the right arm, place the point of the right-hand needle through the first stitch on the left-hand needle.

(b) Holding the wool as before wrap it round the point of the right-hand needle.

(c) Draw a loop through the first stitch on the left-hand needle, then drop the stitch, through which the loop has been drawn off the left-hand needle. Repeat this action across all the stitches.

Purling stitches is identical in action to knitting them, except that while in knitting the wool always lies at the back of the work, in purling the wool lies at the front of the work.

Purling a Stitch

(a) Holding the right-hand needle under the right arm and keeping the wool to the front of the work, place the point of the right-hand needle through the front of the first stitch on the left-hand needle.

(b) Wrap the wool round the point of the right-hand needle, draw a loop through the first stitch on the left-hand needle, then drop the stitch through which the loop has been drawn off the left-hand needle. Repeat this action all across the row.

These two stitches, knitting and purling, are the basic stitches used in all knitted fabrics.

Casting Off

Knit the first two stitches in the ordinary way, now slip the point of the left-hand needle under the second stitch (the first stitch knitted) on the right-hand needle and draw this stitch over the other stitch on the right-hand needle; knit the next stitch, there now being two stitches on the needle again and repeat this action until all the stitches are cast off.

Garter Stitch (*sometimes called plain knitting*)

This is produced by knitting every row in the fabric when you are working on two needles. If you are knitting in rounds, garter stitch is produced by working as follows:

1st round: Knit.
2nd round: Purl.

Repeat this action for the length required.

Stocking Stitch (*sometimes called jersey fabric*)

This is produced on two needles as follows:
1st row: Knit.
2nd row: Purl.
Repeat these two rows throughout the fabric.

When you are working in rounds, stocking stitch is produced by knitting every round.

Ribbings

Ribbing is used for welts and cuffs on jumpers and jerseys and also to create decorative effects in garments. It is worked by alternating knit and purl stitches so that they form vertical ridges of stocking stitch and reverse stocking stitch. This means that ribbed fabrics are always reversible.

K 1, P 1 Rib

Using two needles cast on an even number of stitches:

1st and every row: * K I, P I, repeat from * to end.

When working K I, P I, rib in rounds, cast on an even number of stitches and work every round:

* K I, P I, repeat from * to end.

K 2, P 2 Rib

Using two needles cast on a number of stitches divisible by four:

1st row: K I, * P2, K2, repeat from * to last 3 stitches, P2, K I.

2nd row: P I, * K2, P2, repeat from * to last 3 stitches K2, P I.

Repeat these two rows for the length required.

When working K2, P2 rib in rounds, cast on a number of stitches divisible by four and work every round:

* K2, P2, repeat from * to end of round.

Moss Stitch

This is a fabric formed by alternating throughout the position of one knit and one purl stitch all over the fabric. This fabric is exactly the same on both sides.

Using two needles (four needles if working in the round) cast on an odd number of stitches:

1st and every row or round: * K I, P I, repeat from * to last stitch, K I.

I have given all the above fabrics in rows or rounds as they are the ones generally used for articles or garments worked on four needles. The remainder of the fabrics are worked on two needles throughout.

Check Patterns

These are worked by alternating groups of knit and groups of purl stitches. A simple example of this is a three and three check.

SIMPLE CHECK PATTERN. Using two needles cast on a multiple of 6 sts:

1st to 4th rows: * K3, P3, repeat from * to end.

5th to 8th rows: * P3, K3, repeat from * to end.

ELONGATED CHECK PATTERN. Cast on a multiple of 4 sts plus 2:

1st row: * K2, P2, repeat from * to last 2 sts K2.
2nd row: * P2, K2, repeat from * to last 2 sts P2.
3rd to 6th rows: Repeat 1st and 2nd rows twice more.
7th row: * P2, K2, repeat from * to last 2 sts P2.
8th row: * K2, P2, repeat from * to last 2 sts K2.
9th to 12th rows: Repeat the 7th and 8th rows twice more.
(Plate 1a).

BROKEN CHECK PATTERN. Cast on a multiple of 8 sts plus 4:
1st row: * K4, P4, repeat from * to last 4 sts K4.
2nd row: Purl.
3rd to 8th rows: Repeat 1st and 2nd rows 3 times more.
9th row: * P4, K4, repeat from * to last 4 sts P4.
10th row: Purl.
11th to 16th rows: Repeat 9th and 10th rows 3 times more.
(Plate 1b).

Embossed Fabrics

These fabrics are worked by alternating knit and purl stitches so that they form geometrical shapes on the surface of the fabric.

TRIANGULAR STITCH. Cast on a multiple of 7 sts:
1st row: * P6, K1, repeat from * to end.
2nd row: * P2, K5, repeat from * to end.
3rd row: * P4, K3, repeat from * to end.
4th row: * P4, K3, repeat from * to end.
5th row: * P2, K5, repeat from * to end.
6th row: * P6, K1, repeat from * to end.
These 6 rows form the patt. (Plate 1c).

VANDYKE PATTERN. Cast on a multiple of 6 sts:
1st row: * K5, P1, repeat from * to end.
2nd row: * K2, P4, repeat from * to end.
3rd row: * K3, P3, repeat from * to end.
4th row: * K4, P2, repeat from * to end.
5th row: * K1, P5, repeat from * to end.
6th row: * K4, P2, repeat from * to end.
7th row: * K3, P3, repeat from * to end.
8th row: * K2, P4, repeat from * to end.
These 8 rows form the patt. (Plate 2a).

VANDYKE AND CHECK PATTERN. Cast on a multiple of 8 sts:

1st row: Knit.

2nd row: * K4, P4, repeat from * to end.

3rd row: * P1, K4, P3, repeat from * to end.

4th row: * K2, P4, K2, repeat from * to end.

5th row: * P3, K4, P1, repeat from * to end.

6th row: * P4, K4, repeat from * to end.

7th row: Knit.

8th to 11th rows: * K4, P4, repeat from * to end.

12th row: Purl.

13th row: * P4, K4, repeat from * to end.

14th row: * K1, P4, K3, repeat from * to end.

15th row: * P2, K4, P2, repeat from * to end.

16th row: * K3, P4, K1, repeat from * to end.

17th row: * K4, P4, repeat from * to end.

18th row: Purl.

19th to 22nd rows: * P4, K4, repeat from * to end.

These 22 rows form the patt. (Plate 2b).

Working into the Back of a Stitch

Another principle that is frequently used in knitting is called 'working into the back of the stitches'. This method of knitting is derived from early Arabic sources, and produces, when it is used in stocking stitch, a fabric referred to as twisted stocking stitch. The loops on the front surface of the work are crossed at the bottom, giving a very decorative effect to the finished fabric.

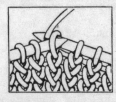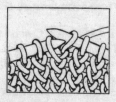

(a) Slip the point of the right-hand needle through the stitch on the left-hand needle, placing the point through the back instead of the front of the stitch.

(b) Now work the stitch off (knitting or purling, as the case may be) in the ordinary way.

34

Diagonal Striped Pattern

Here is a delightful pattern forming a diagonal striped effect. It is made by using the 'working into the back of the stitch' technique on the stocking stitch stripes that lie on the front surface of the work.

Cast on a multiple of 8 sts:

1st row: * Knit into the back of 4 sts, P4, repeat from * to end.
2nd row: * K4, Purl into the back of 4 sts, repeat from * to end.
3rd row: * P1, Knit into the back of 4 sts, P3, repeat from * to end.
4th row: * K3, Purl into the back of 4 sts, K1, repeat from * to end.
5th row: * P2, Knit into the back of 4 sts, P2, repeat from * to end.
6th row: * K2, Purl into the back of 4 sts, K2, repeat from * to end.
7th row: * P3, Knit into the back of 4 sts, P1, repeat from * to end.
8th row: * K1, Purl into the back of 4 sts, K3, repeat from * to end.
9th row: * P4, Knit into the back of 4 sts, repeat from * to end.
10th row: * Purl into the back of 4 sts, K4, repeat from * to end.

These 10 rows form the diagonal movement of the patt. (Plate 2c).

Why Not Knit a Shawl?

One of the most interesting facts about fashion is that we are always coming back to the point from which we started. Shawls were extremely popular during the latter part of the Regency Period. They came into fashion again with the Victorian Age and during Edwardian times once more made their appearance in my lady's wardrobe. To-day to wear a shawl for beach or evening occasions is again very much *à la mode*.

Shawls can be either square or triangular in shape. The heavier types are worked in double knitting, using a size 8 needle to give you a really chunky fabric. For a light-weight wrap use a 3-ply wool and a size 10 needle. Any of the stitches from the check pattern on page 32 to the diagonal striped pattern on this page can be used for either square or triangular shawls.

For a square shawl simply cast on the number of stitches to make the shawl the required size. This should be a multiple of the number of stitches required for the pattern, plus six edge stitches. Work in pattern with garter stitch borders until a square has been completed, knitting six rows at the beginning and five rows before casting off.

Let us presume you are going to knit a shawl in diagonal stripe pattern. You will need one approximately thirty-six inches square without the fringe.

The tension of double knitting on size 8 needles is five and a half stitches to the inch. Thus you will need approximately 198 stitches. Subtract six stitches from 198 for the three stitch garter stitch borders, thus leaving you with 192 stitches. Divide 192 by eight and you will find that it goes into this number exactly twenty-four times, thus 198 stitches are exactly the number required for this shawl.

To make the shawl, cast on stitches and knit six rows. Now, knitting three stitches at each end of every row, proceed in diagonal striped pattern as on page 35, repeating rows one to ten of the pattern throughout until a square has been knitted.

Knit five rows, cast off.

Contrasting fringes give a charming touch to these shawls. To make a fringe, cut your contrasting wool into eight-inch lengths. Take four eight-inch lengths, fold in half, insert a crochet hook through the edge of the shawl, draw the four loops of the fringe through the edge, insert the crochet hook under the eight strands, draw these through the loops on the hook and pull the ends into a tight knot.

Continue fringing in this manner all round the shawl.

Triangular shawls are very easy to make. Commence by casting on the number of stitches required for the width of the shawl along the straight edge. Work in pattern, decreasing at both ends of second and every following third row until two stitches remain. Cast off.

As an example of a triangular shawl, if you are using the simple check pattern on page 32, you will need a multiple of six stitches. Using 4-ply wool and size 9 needles, for a shawl forty inches along the top edge of the triangle you will need 260 stitches. Six goes into 260, forty-three times and two over, thus giving you one stitch to knit at each end of every row on the shawl.

Using No 9 needles, cast on 260 stitches and knit two rows. Now, knitting the stitch at each end of every row, proceed in simple check pattern, decreasing inside the knit stitch edge on second and every following third row as follows:

1st row: K I, work in check pattern to last st, K I.
2nd row: K I, work 2 tog, check patt. to last 3 sts, work 2 tog, K I.
3rd and 4th rows: K I, work in check patt to last st, K I.
5th row: As 2nd row.
6th and 7th rows: As 3rd and 4th.

Continue decreasing in this manner on next and every following third row until two stitches remain. Cast off.

Fringe with contrasting colour as on square shawl on the two short sides of shawl.

To give the top edge a perfect finish, using contrast, work one row of double crochet all across top edge.

The principle outlined in the above triangular shawl can be applied to any stitch or pattern you like.

CHAPTER 4

Increasing and Decreasing

HAVING mastered the first principles of knitting and learned to produce fabrics based on knitting and purling, we are now ready to consider increasing and decreasing. This consists of making stitches for the increases and losing stitches for the decreases.

Simple increases and decreases are used mainly for the shaping of garments. They are also used in the production of certain types of embossed fabrics that will be dealt with later in this chapter.

Increasing on a Knit Row

The principle here is making two stitches out of one, to do this:

(a) Insert the point of the right-hand needle into the stitch that is to be increased in on the left-hand needle. Knit this stitch in the ordinary way but do not slip it off the left-hand needle.

(b) Now insert the point of the right-hand needle through the back of the same stitch on the left-hand needle. Knit another stitch through this stitch then slip the stitch off the left-hand needle. You will now have formed two stitches out of one stitch.

Double Increase on a Knit Row

This is similar to a single increase except that three stitches instead of two are made out of one.

(a) Repeat actions (a) and (b) above but do not slip the stitch off the left-hand needle when the second stitch has been knitted up.

(b) Insert the point of the right-hand needle through the front of the stitch on the left-hand needle. Knit another stitch through the first stitch on the left-hand needle, thus making three stitches out of one. Slip the stitch off the left-hand needle.

Increases are worked in exactly the same way on the purl side of the fabric except that the actions are performed purlwise instead of knitwise.

Increasing by Making a Stitch Out of the Fabric

Another type of increase, used mainly to produce tailored shapings in the garment itself, is worked by making stitches not out of a stitch, but out of the fabric itself. This is done as follows:

Stitches made in this way are always worked between two stitches.

(a) Knit the stitch before the point where the stitch is to be made.

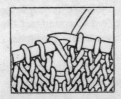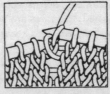

(b) Using the point of the left-hand needle pick up the loop that lies between the stitch you have just knitted and the following stitch. Knit into the back of this loop, thus twisting it and closing up the gap in the fabric where the loop was picked up.

A stitch can be made in the same way on the purl side of the fabric by purling a stitch before the stitch to be made, picking up the loop on the point of the left-hand needle as before and purling into the back of the loop.

Increasing by Wrapping the Wool Round the Needle

The third method of increasing consists of wrapping the wool over the needle between two stitches. This method forms holes in the fabric and is mainly used for lace patternings.

(a) Knit a stitch. Bring the wool forward from the back of the work to the front.

(b) Take the wool over the right-hand needle and knit the following stitch.

(c) When this 'wrapping the wool round the needle' action is performed between a purl and a knit stitch, simply take the wool from the front to the back of the needle, allowing it to lie over the top of the right-hand needle before knitting the following stitch.

(d) When this action is to be carried out between two purl stitches, purl a stitch, then take the wool over the top of the right-hand needle, bring it under the right-hand needle to the front of the work again and purl the following stitch.

In most knitted patterns where this 'over' principle for making stitches is used, decreases are worked to counteract the stitches formed by the overs. This keeps the number of stitches stable on every row.

Decreasing means losing one or more stitches. In shaping a piece of fabric or in producing a lace pattern, it is done by working two or three stitches together. There are several ways in which decreases of this type are worked.

Ordinary Decrease

This consists of knitting two stitches together and is worked as follows:

(a) Insert the point of the right-hand needle through the two stitches to be knitted together on the left-hand needle.

(b) Wrap the wool round the point of the right-hand needle,

draw a stitch through the two stitches on the point of the left-hand needle and then drop the two stitches off the left-hand needle.

The same action can be worked purlwise. The point of the right-hand needle is inserted purlwise through the two stitches to be purled together on the left-hand needle.

Decrease Working into the Back of the Stitches

This decrease is usually carried out at the beginning of a row. When this is done it lines up with the ordinary decrease at the other end of the row. It is used mainly in tailored shapings.

(a) Slip the point of the right-hand needle through the back of the two stitches on the left-hand needle.

(b) Wrap the wool round the point of the right-hand needle, draw a stitch through the two stitches on the left-hand needle, and then drop the two stitches off the left-hand needle.

Double Decrease

This means losing two stitches instead of one. A double decrease is worked by either knitting three stitches together, or by slipping a stitch, knitting two together and then passing the slipped stitch over.

Ordinary Double Decrease (K3 tog)

(a) Insert the point of the right-hand needle through the three stitches on the left-hand needle that are to be knitted together.

(b) Wrap the wool round the point of the right-hand needle, draw a stitch through the three stitches on the left-hand needle then drop the three stitches off the left-hand needle.

To work a double decrease on the purl side, insert the point of

the right-hand needle through the three stitches purlwise, wrap the wool round the point of the right-hand needle draw a stitch through and drop the stitches off the left-hand needle.

Slip Stitch Decrease (sl1, K2 tog, psso)

(a) Slip the first stitch of the three stitches that are used in the double decrease on to the point of the right-hand needle without knitting it.

(b) Insert the point of the right-hand needle through the next two stitches, wrap the wool round the point of the right-hand needle, draw a stitch through the two stitches, then drop the two stitches off the right-hand needle.

(c) Now insert the point of the left-hand needle through the second stitch from the point on the right-hand needle (the stitch that was slipped). Lift this stitch over the first stitch, then drop it off the left-hand needle.

The same action can be worked on the purl side of the fabric. Keep the wool at the front of the work. Slip the first stitch purlwise on to the right-hand needle. Purl the next two stitches together, then pass the slipped stitch over the first stitch on the right-hand needle as before.

Let us now look at some of the interesting fabrics that can be created by using these various methods of increasing and decreasing.

Embossed Diamond Stitch
(incorporating the simple increases and decreases)

Cast on a multiple of 7 sts:

1st row: * P3, K1, P3, rep from * to end.

2nd row: * K3, inc 3 purlwise into next st by purling into the front, back, front of the st, K3, rep from * to end.

3rd row: * P3, K3, P3, rep from * to end.

4th row: * K3, inc once in next st by purling into front and back of it, P1, inc once in next st by purling into back and front of it, K3, rep from * to end.

5th row: * P3, K5, P3, rep from * to end.

6th row: * K3, inc once purlwise in next st as before, P3, inc once purlwise into next st as before, K3.

7th row: * P3, K7, P3, rep from * to end.

8th row: * K3, inc once purlwise in next st as before, P5, inc once purlwise in next st as before, rep from * to end.

9th row: * P3, K9, P3, rep from * to end.

10th row: * K3, P2 tog, P5, P2 tog through back of loops, K3, rep from * to end.

11th row: * P3, K7, P3, rep from * to end.

12th row: * K3, P2 tog, P3, P2 tog tbl, K3, rep from * to end.

13th row: * P3, K5, P3, rep from * to end.

14th row: * K3, P2 tog, P1, P2 tog tbl, K3.

15th row: * P3, K3, P3, rep from * to end.

16th row: * K3, P3 tog, K3, rep from * to end.

17th row: * P3, K1, P3, rep from * to end.

18th row: K.

19th row: P.

20th row: K.

These 20 rows form the patt. (Plate 3a).

Embossed Ribbed Pattern

MIP stands for make one purlwise, this is done by picking up the loop that lies between the stitch just worked and the following stitch and purling into the back of it.

Cast on a multiple of 18 sts plus 1:

1st row: * P1, K3, P11, K3, rep from * to last st, P1.

2nd row: K1, * P3, K11, P3, K1, rep from * to end.

3rd row: * P1, MIP, K3, P2 tog, P7, P2 tog, K3, MIP, rep from * to last st, P1.

4th row: K2, * P3, K9, P3, K3, rep from * ending K2 instead of K3.

5th row: P2, * MIP, K3, P2 tog, P5, P2 tog, K3, MIP, P3, rep from * ending P2, instead of P3.

6th row: K3, * P3, K7, P3, K5, rep from * ending K3 instead of K5.

7th row: P3, * MIP, K3, P2 tog, P3, P2 tog, K3, MIP, P5, rep from * ending P3 instead of P5.

8th row: K4, * P3, K5, P3, K7, rep from * ending K4 instead of K7.

9th row: P4, * MIP, K3, P2 tog, P1, P2 tog, K3, MIP, P7, rep from * ending P4 instead of P7.

10th row: K5, * P3, K3, P3, K9, rep from * ending K5 instead of K9.

11th row: P5, * MIP, K3, P3 tog, K3, MIP, P9, rep from * ending P5 instead of P9.

12th row: K6. * P3, K1, P3, K11, rep from * ending K6 instead of K11.

13th row: P4, * P2 tog, K3, MIP, P1, MIP, K3, P2 tog, P7, rep from * ending P4 instead of P7.

14th row: K5, * P3, K3, P3, K9, rep from * ending K5 instead of K9.

15th row: P3. * P2 tog, K3, MIP, P3, MIP, K3, P2 tog, P5, rep from * ending P3 instead of P5.

16th row: K4, * P3, K5, P3, K7, rep from * ending K4 instead of K7.

17th row: P2, * P2 tog, K3, MIP, P5, MIP, K3, P2 tog, P3, rep from * ending P2 instead of P3.

18th row: K3, * P3, K7, P3, K5, rep from * ending K3 instead of K5.

19th row: * P1, P2 tog, K3, MIP, P7, MIP, K3, P2 tog, rep from * to last st, P1.

20th row: K2, * P3, K9, P3, K3, rep from * ending K2 instead of K3.

21st row: P2 tog, * K3, MIP, P9, MIP, K3, P3 tog, rep from * ending P2 tog instead of P3 tog.

22nd row: K1, * P3, K11, P3, K1, rep from * to end.

Rows 3–22 incl form the patt. (Plate 3b).

44

Embossed Bell Pattern

The principle in this pattern is casting on the stitches that form the basis of each bell and losing these stitches in a series of graded decreases as the pattern proceeds.

Cast on a multiple of 4 sts:

1st row: * P2, cast on 8 stitches as follows: wrap a loop round the left thumb, insert the point of the needle in the loop, slip the loop on to the needle and draw the wool up tight, rep this action 7 times more, P2, rep from * to end.

2nd row: * K2, P8, K2, rep from * to end.

3rd row: * P2, K8, P2, rep from * to end.

4th row: As 2nd row.

5th row: * P2, K2 tog tbl, K4, K2 tog, P2, rep from * to end.

6th row: * K2, P6, K2, rep from * to end.

7th row: * P2, K2 tog tbl, K2, K2 tog, P2, rep from * to end.

8th row: * K2, P4, K2.

9th row: * P2, K2 tog tbl, K2 tog, P2, rep from * to end.

10th row: * K2, P2, K2, rep from * to end.

11th row: * P2, K2 tog, P2, rep from * to end.

12 row: * K2, P1, K2, rep from * to end.

13th row: * P2, K2 tog, P1, rep from * to end.

14th row: K.

15th row: P.

16th row: K.

These 16 rows form the patt. (Plate 3c).

Diamond Eyelet Pattern

Cast on a multiple of 10 sts plus 4:

1st row: K2, wf, K2 tog tbl, * K1, K2 tog, (wf) twice, K2 tog tbl, rep from * to last 5 sts K1, K2 tog, wf, K2.

2nd and every alternate row: P (purling into front and back of 'wool forward twice' of previous row throughout).

3rd row: K2, * K2 tog, wf, K6, wf, K2 tog tbl, rep from * to last 2 sts, K2.

5th row: K3, * K2 tog, wf, K4, wf, K2 tog tbl, K2, rep from * to end, ending row K3, instead of K2.

7th row: K4, * K2 tog, wf, K2, wf, K2 tog tbl, K4, rep from * to end.

9th row: K2, wf, K2 tog tbl, * K1, K2 tog, (wf) twice, K2 tog tbl, rep from * to last 5 sts, K1, K2 tog, wf, K2.

11th row: K5, * wf, K2 tog tbl, K2 tog, wf, K6, rep from * to end, ending K5 instead of K6.

13th row: K4, * wf, K2 tog tbl, K2, K2 tog, wf, K4, rep from * to end.

15th row: K3, * wf, K2 tog tbl, K4, K2 tog, wf, K2, rep from * to end, ending K3 instead of K2.

16th row: P.

These 16 rows form the patt. (Plate 4a).

Crown of Glory Pattern

This is a traditional Shetland pattern and is beautiful for shawls and dressing wraps knitted in fine lace wools.

Cast on a multiple of 14 sts plus 5:

1st row: K3, * K2 tog tbl, K9, K2 tog, K1, rep from * to last 2 sts, K2.

2nd row: P2, * P1, P2 tog, P7, P2 tog tbl, rep from * to last 3 sts, P3.

3rd row: K3, * K2 tog tbl, K2, (wf) 3 times, K3, K2 tog, K1, rep from * to last 2 sts, K2.

4th row: P2, * P1, P2 tog, P2, now make 5 sts out of the 3 wool forwards on the previous row by working (K1, P1) twice, K1 into the large loop formed by the 3 wool forwards, P1, P2 tog tbl, rep from * to last 3 sts, P3.

5th row: K3, * K2 tog tbl, K6, K2 tog, K1, rep from * to last 2 sts, K2.

6th row: P2, * P1, P2 tog, P6, rep from * to last 3 sts, P3.

7th row: K3, * K1, (wf, K1) 6 times, K1, rep from * to last 2 sts, K2.

8th row: P.

9th row: K.

10th row: P.

11th and 12th rows: As 9th and 10th rows.

These 12 rows form the patt. (Plate 4b).

Feather Pattern

Cast on a multiple of 7 sts:

1st row: K2 tog, K1, wf, * K1, wf, K1, K2 tog tbl, K2 tog, K1, wf, rep from * to last 4 sts, K1, wf, K1, K2 tog tbl.

2nd row: P.

These 2 rows form the patt. (Plate 4c).

Beech Leaf Pattern

Cast on a multiple of 14 sts plus 1:

1st row: * K1, wf, K5, wf, slip 1, K2 tog, psso, wf, K5, wf, rep from * to last st, K1.

2nd row: P.

3rd row: * K1, wf, K1, K2 tog, P1, K2 tog tbl, K1, wrn, P1, won, K1, K2 tog, P1, K2 tog tbl, K1, wf, rep from * to last st, K1.

4th row: P1, * (P3, K1) 3 times, P4, rep from * to end.

5th row: * K1, wf, K1, K2 tog, P1, K2 tog tbl, K1, P1, K1, K2 tog, P1, K2 tog tbl, K1, wf, rep from * to last st, K1.

6th row: P1, * P3, K1, (P2, K1) twice, P4, rep from * to end.

7th row: * (K1, wf) twice, K2 tog, P1, K2 tog tbl, P1, K2 tog, P1, K2 tog tbl, wf, K1, wf, rep from * to last st, K1.

8th row: P1, * P4, (K1, P1) twice, K1, P5, rep from * to end.

9th row: * K1, wf, K3, wf, slip 1, K2 tog, psso, P1, K3 tog, wf, K3, wf, rep from * to last st, K1.

10th row: P.

These 10 rows form the patt. (Plate 5a).

CHAPTER 5

Twists, Cables, and Bobbles

SOME of the most interesting and decorative effects in knitting are obtained by working over-patterning on the fabric. These over-patternings are generally carried out on a ribbed foundation.

The first group of these fabrics are produced by what are known as twists in the stitches. The action here is quite simple. It consists of twisting 2, 3, or 4 stitches together and running 1 or 2 purl stitches up each side of the group of stitches that have been twisted.

Purl 1 Twist 2 Pattern

Cast on a multiple of 3 sts plus 1:

1st foundation row: * P1, K2, rep from * to last st, P1.

2nd foundation row: * K1, P2, rep from * to last st, K1.

Having established the ribbed base we now are ready to work the twist st patt.

1st row: * P1, twist 2 sts as follows: Slip the point of the right-hand needle into the second st on the left-hand needle knitwise, K the st but do not slip it off the needle. Now insert

the point of the right-hand needle knitwise into the first st on the left-hand needle. Knit the st then slip the first and second st off the left-hand needle together, rep from * to last st, P1.

2nd row: * K1, P2, rep from * to last st, K1.

These 2 rows form the patt. (Plate 5b).

The next patt is worked on the same basis except that 3 sts are twisted between the 2 P sts.

Purl 1 Twist 3 Pattern

Cast on a multiple of 4 sts plus 1:

1st row: * P1, K3, rep from * to last st, P1.

2nd row: * K1, P3, rep from * to last st, K1.

3rd row: (Twist row): * P1, twist the next 3 sts on the left-hand needle as follows: slip the point of the right-hand needle knit-wise into the third st on the left-hand needle, knit a st through this st but do not slip it off the needle, rep the same action through the second st on the left-hand needle, rep the same action through the first st on the left-hand needle, then slip the 3 sts off the left-hand needle together, rep from * to last st, P1.

4th row: * K1, P3, rep from * to last st, K1.

These 4 rows form the patt. (Plate 5c).

A 4 st twist is worked in exactly the same manner, the number of sts cast on being a multiple of 5 plus 1.

CABLE PATTERNS

Cabling in knitting, that is the forming of rope-like vertical stripes on the fabric, is worked by crossing one group of stitches

either in front or behind a second group of stitches. A purl stitch or garter stitch rib is worked up each side of the stitches that have been cabled to give the proper emphasis to the pattern itself. When you are working cable patterns you need a short needle pointed at both ends, called a cable needle. In order to avoid stretching the stitches, as this would give an unevenness to the fabric, it is advisable to use a cable needle one size finer than the needles on which the knitting itself is being worked.

Single Cable Pattern (*with four stitch cable*)

Cast on a multiple of 5 sts plus 1:

1st row: * P1, K4, rep from * to last st, P1.

2nd row: P.

3rd and 4th rows: As 1st and 2nd.

5th row: * P1, now work the cable action across the next 4 sts as follows: Sl the next 2 sts on to the cable needle and leave these at the front of the work. Now K across the next 2 sts, the second 2 of the group of 4, in the ordinary way, now

take the cable needle back and K across the 2 sts on the cable needle, thus crossing 2 sts in front of two sts, rep from * to last st, P1.

6th row: P.

By working the cable 2 front as on the fifth row throughout the patt you will create the effect of a narrow twisted rope running in vertical stripes throughout the fabric. (Plate 6a).

A variation of this patt is worked by alternating the cable movement from the front to the back of the work on the fifth and every following sixth row. This is called a wave cable and is worked as follows:

Wave Cable Pattern

Cast on a multiple of 5 sts plus 1:

Rows 1–6: As in Single Cable Pattern.

Rows 7–10: As rows 1–4 in Single Cable Pattern.

11th row: * P1, now work the cable action across the next 4 sts as follows, *noting* that this time the action is at the back instead of the front of the work. Sl the next 2 sts on to a cable needle and leave at the back of the work, K across the following 2 sts, bring the cable needle forward and K across the 2 sts on the cable needle, rep from * to last st, P1.

12th row: P.

These 12 rows form the patt. (Plate 6b).

Bolder cable effects can be worked over groups of 6, 8, 10, or 12 sts. To work the cable sl half the total number of sts on to the cable needle, and, working the cable action at the front or back of the work as desired, proceed in exactly the same way as in the cable patt given above.

Where you are working on 6 sts the cable movement will be on the 7th and every following 8th row. Where you are working across 10 sts the cable action will be on the 11th and every following 12th row. Where you are working across 12 sts the cable action will be on the 13th and every following 14th row.

Let us now consider various cable patternings embodying the principles of cabling already outlined in this chapter. The first variation is called double rope cable and is worked as follows:

Double Rope Cable Pattern

Cast on a multiple of 11 sts plus 2:

1st row: * P2, K9, rep from * to last 2 sts, P2.

2nd row: * K2, P9, rep from * to last 2 sts, K2.

3rd and 4th rows: As 1st and 2nd.

5th row: * P2, cable 3 front across the next 6 sts, K3, rep from * to last 2 sts, P2.

6th row: As 2nd row.

7th–10th rows: Rep 1st and 2nd rows twice more.

11th row: * P2, K3, cable 3 back across the next 6 sts, rep from * to last 2 sts, P2.

12th row: * K2, P9, rep from * to last 2 sts, K2.

These 12 rows form the patt. (Plate 6c).

The second variation is known as branch cable pattern. It is worked in exactly the same way as the double rope cable pattern, except that the cabling action is reversed on the 5th and 11th rows, as follows:

Branch Cable Pattern

Cast on a multiple of 11 sts plus 2:

1st–4th rows: As rows 1–4 double rope cable pattern.

5th row: * P2, cable 3 back K3 across the next 9 sts, rep from * to last 2 sts, P2.

6th–10th rows: As rows 6–10 double rope cable pattern.

11th row: * P2, K3, cable 3 front across the next 6 sts, rep from * to last 2 sts, P2.

12th row: * K2, P9, rep from * to last 2 sts, K2.

These 12 rows form the patt. (Plate 7a).

The next group of cable patternings are worked by alternating reverse movements of cable over groups of sts. The first is called medallion cable pattern and is worked as follows:

Medallion Cable Pattern

Cast on a multiple of 15 sts plus 2:

1st row: * P2, K13, rep from * to last 2 sts, P2.

2nd row: * K2, P13, rep from * to last 2 sts, K2.

3rd and 4th rows: As 1st and 2nd.

5th row: * P2, cable 3 front across the next 6 sts, K1, cable back across the next 6 sts, rep from * to last 2 sts, P2.

6th row: As 2nd row.

7th–12th rows: Rep 1st and 2nd rows 3 times more.

13th row: * P2, cable 3 back across the next 6 sts, K1, now cable 3 front across the next 6 sts, rep from * to last 2 sts, P2.

14th row: As 2nd row.

15th and 16th rows: As 1st and 2nd.

These 16 rows form the patt. (Plate 7b).

Another interesting variation in cable is wheat ear cable. It is worked as follows:

Wheat Ear Cable Pattern

Cast on a multiple of 15 sts plus 2:

1st and 2nd rows: As 1st and 2nd rows of medallion cable pattern.

3rd row: * P2, cable 3 back across the next 6 sts, K1, cable 3 front across the next 6 sts, rep from * to last 2 sts, P2.

4th row: * K2, P13, rep from * to last 2 sts, K2.

These 4 rows form the patt. (Plate 8a).

A delightful all-over fabric is known as cable check pattern, and this is worked as follows:

Cable Check Pattern

Cast on a multiple of 12 sts plus 6:

1st row: * P6, K6, rep from * to last 6 sts, P6.

2nd row: * K6, P6, rep from * to last 6 sts, K6.

3rd and 4th rows: As 1st and 2nd.

5th row: * P6, cable 3 front across next 6 sts, rep from * to last 6 sts, P6.

6th–9th rows: Rep 2nd and 3rd rows twice.

10th row: * P6, K6 rep from * to last 6 sts, P6.

11th row: * K6, P6, rep from * to last 6 sts, K6.

12th and 13th rows: As 10th and 11th rows.

14th row: * Cable 3 back purlwise across the next 6 sts as follows: Sl the first 3 sts on to the cable needle and leave at back of work, P across the next 3 sts. Bring the cable needle forward and P across the sts on the cable needle, K6, rep from * to last 6 sts, then cable 3 back purlwise as before across these 6 sts.

15th–18th rows: Rep 11th and 12th rows twice.

These 18 rows form the patt. (Plate 8b).

The final variation of cable patterning I am giving you creates an embossed effect on a stocking stitch foundation. It is known as diagonal wave pattern. It is worked as follows:

Diagonal Wave Pattern

Cast on a multiple of 6 sts plus 3:

1st row: K.

2nd row: P.

3rd row: * Cable 3 back across the next 6 sts, rep from * to last 3 sts, K3.

4th row: P.

5th and 6th rows: As 1st and 2nd.

7th row: K 3, * cable 3 back across the next 6 sts, rep from * to end of row.

8th row: P.

These 8 rows form the patt. (Plate 8c).

BOBBLE STITCHES

Bobbles, consisting of large, knot-like formations on the front surface of the fabric, are made by increasing in the stitch that is to form the bobble. The work is done in reverse stocking stitch across the increase stitches for the number of rows required. These will depend on the size of the bobble. When the piece of reverse stocking stitch has been completed, the stitches that have been increased are slipped over the first stitch again.

Let us take as our example a four stitch bobble. To make the bobble, increase into the stitch in which the bobble is to be made by knitting into the front and back of the same stitch twice. This gives you four stitches made out of one stitch. Turn the work round and knit across these four stitches; turn it round again and purl across these four stitches. Repeat these two rows once more. To complete the bobble, slip the second, third, and fourth stitch on the left-hand needle over the first stitch on the left-hand needle, then slip this stitch on to the right-hand needle. On the next row purl into the back of the stitch out of which the bobble has been made, as this locks the bobble at the front of the fabric.

Simple Bobble Pattern

Cast on a multiple of 8 sts plus 3:

1st row: K.

2nd row: P.

3rd and 4th rows: As 1st and 2nd.

5th row: K 1, * Make 4 st bobble in the next st as follows: K into the front and back of the next st twice, turn the work round and K across the 4 sts that have been made out of the one st, turn again and purl across these 4 sts, turn again and K across these 4 sts, turn again and P across these 4 sts. Now slip the

2nd, 3rd, and 4th st on the left-hand needle over the 1st st, K7, rep from * to last 2 sts, make 4 st bobble, K1.

6th row: P1, * P into back of the next st, P7, rep from * to last 2 sts, PB1, P1.

7th row: K.

8th row: P.

9th–12th rows: Rep 7th and 8th rows twice.

13th row: K5, * make 4 st bobble, K7, rep from * to last 6 sts, make 4 st bobble, K5.

14th row: P5, * PB1, P7, rep from * to last 6 sts, PB1, P5.

15th row: K.

16th row: P.

These 16 rows form the patt. (Plate 9a).

By clustering the bobbles in triangular groups of three you form what is known as Trefoil Bobble Pattern. It is worked as follows:

Trefoil Bobble Pattern

Cast on a multiple of 8 sts plus 3:

1st–6th rows: As 1st–6th rows of Simple Bobble Pattern.

7th row: K1, * K1, make 4 st bobble, K5, make 4 st bobble, rep from * to last 2 sts, K2.

8th row: P2, * PB1, P5, PB1, P1, rep from * to last st, P1.

9th–14th rows: As 9th–14th rows of Simple Bobble Pattern.

15th row: K1, * K3, make 4 st bobble, K1, make 4 st bobble, K2, rep from * to last 2 sts, K2.

16th row: P2, * P2, PB1, P1, PB1, P3, rep from * to last st, P1.

These 16 rows form the patt. (Plate 9b).

Cables and bobbles can be used very effectively to produce attractive knitted fabrics. These are always worked on a rib base, thus emphasizing the decorative stripes formed by the cable and bobble action. Here is a combination of medallion cable stitch and bobble pattern:

Fancy Cable Pattern

Cast on a multiple of 18 sts plus 3:

1st row: * P1, KB1, P1, K15, rep from * to last 3 sts, P1, KB1, P1.

2nd row: * K1, PB1, K1, P15, rep from * to last 3 sts, K1, PB1, K1.

3rd row: * P1, KB1, P1, now cable 3 back across the next 6 sts, K3, now cable 3 front across the next 6 sts, rep from * to last 3 sts, P1, KB1, P1.

4th row: As 2nd row.

5th and 6th rows: As 1st and 2nd.

7th row: * P1, KB1, P1, K7, make 4 st bobble in next st, K7, rep from * to last 3 sts, P1, KB1, P1.

8th row: * K1, PB1, K1, P7, PB1, P7, rep from * to last 3 sts, K1, PB1, K1.

9th–12th rows: Rep 7th and 8th rows twice more.

13th and 14th rows: Rep 1st and 2nd rows.

15th row: * P1, KB1, P1, now cable 3 front across the next 6 sts, K3, now cable 3 back across the next 6 sts, rep from * to last 3 sts, P1, KB1, P1.

16th row: As 2nd row.

17th and 18th rows: As 1st and 2nd.

19th–24th rows: Rep 7th and 8th rows 3 times more.

These 24 rows form the patt. (Plate 9c).

CHAPTER 6

It's the Finish that Counts

ONE of the most interesting, in fact the most revolutionary, advance in home knitting to-day is the development of the tailored line.

From the sack-like sweater which Chanel introduced in the twenties, to the slick Italian fully-fashioned sweaters of to-day, has been one of the most interesting phases in the history of knitting.

The daily press, the women's weekly papers, the fact that high fashion can be bought in shops at moderate prices, all these are varying aspects of one theme. The smart woman of to-day knows that 'It's the line that tells the tale'.

The tailored line is achieved in knitting by finishing properly the pieces of fabric that go to make up the completed garment.

It is no longer a case of threading a darning needle with a length of wool and joining the pieces into the semblance of a jumper or a cardigan. Each seam must bear the tailored imprint of the tailored line. It must be flattering to the figure. Above all it must take away the home-made look from your knitting.

Let us now examine step by step the make-up of your home knitteds. When you have completed the knitting of the separate pieces, they must all be blocked, pressed, and seamed together.

BLOCKING THE PIECES

To block out pieces of knitted fabric properly, you need a thick blanket under an ordinary ironing sheet, a box of pins, and an inch tape.

Study the measurements carefully and block out each piece to its correct measurements.

Let us take as an example the front of a jumper. First of all pin out the garment at the armhole shaping – if this is a thirty-four inch jumper the width here should be seventeen and one quarter inches.

(a) Place the front of the jumper (the wrong side facing) on the ironing sheet. Place a pin along the side edge of the front just below the armhole shaping. Now place an inch tape by the pin and measure seventeen and one quarter inches across the front of the jumper to the same point below the second armhole shaping at

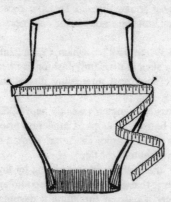

the other side. Place a second pin at this point so that the front of the garment measures seventeen and one quarter inches at the bust line.

(b) Now take another pin, and flattening out the fabric carefully, place it at the centre of the shoulder. Place the end of the inch tape against the pin and pin out to the length stated for the garment in the instructions, in the same way as you pinned out the

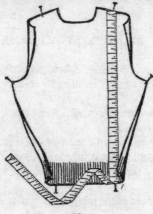

width at the bust line. Repeat this action from the centre of the second shoulder. You have now roughly blocked out the piece of fabric.

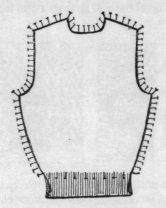

To complete the blocking process, pin out the front all round from the top of the ribbing, round the sides, armholes, and neck, easing it into shape. The pins should be approximately half an inch apart. The pins you placed at the lower edge when you commenced the blocking operation are left in position at this stage. Now pin out carefully across the top of the ribbing, then remove the pins from the bottom edge. The ribbing itself is never pressed, as this may rob it of some of its natural elasticity.

Using a warm iron and damp cloth, omitting the ribbing, lightly press the blocked piece of fabric.

Each piece of the garment is blocked out in exactly the same manner.

Fair Isle and colour knitting is blocked out in exactly the same way, but when pressing the pieces use a hot iron and a wet cloth.

MAKING UP THE GARMENT

Although some people advocate making up hand knitteds on a sewing machine, I do not recommend this method at all.

The garment must be made up with the same wool in which it has been knitted. Two seams only are used. A back-stitched seam for all parts of the garment except ribbing and a flat seam for the ribbing.

I advise you to tack the pieces together before commencing the actual make-up as this will give you a firm foundation for the final work.

Using a back-stitch seam join all the pieces of fabric (apart from the ribbing), working the back-stitch one and a half stitches in from the side edge throughout.

Using a flat seam join the ribbing.

Finally press all seams.

Facing Front Bands

When making up cardigans I advise you to stitch a ribbon facing on the wrong side of the front bands. This will strengthen the front edge and help you to avoid the floppiness that often spoils the straight line of a garment of this type.

Prepare the ribbon facing by marking buttonholes (to match the buttonholes on the knitted front band) on the piece of ribbon with which you are going to line the right front band of the cardigan (for a man's cardigan it should be the left front band). Cut the buttonholes, using a pair of ordinary buttonhole scissors for this purpose. To complete the preparation of the band, buttonhole round the slits you have made, using ordinary buttonhole twist. Neatly stitch the facing to the right front band of the cardigan, taking care to match buttonhole for buttonhole. You can face the left front band (right front band for a man) in the same way if you wish to do so, omitting the buttonholes.

Picot Edges

When you knit a picot edge round the neck or sleeves of a garment, you will find that this consists of a piece of either stocking stitch or reverse stocking stitch with a row of holes formed by a 'wool forward knit two together' action all along the centre row of the picot edge. Fold the piece of fabric over at the row of holes, then, using a flat seam, neatly stitch down the

cast-off edge to the knitted up edge on the wrong side of the garment. Lightly press the picot edge when you have seamed the cast-off stitches to the knitted up stitches.

WASHING YOUR WOOLLENS

One of the most pertinent questions I am asked by women is 'What is the best way to wash hand knitted garments?' The practical answer is 'Use ordinary care in washing, pressing, and re-blocking and then you will have no worries'.

Let us deal stage by stage with washing hand-knitted garments:

(a) Use good soapflakes or detergent. If you use a detergent (i.e., one of the many soapless powders for home washing), read the instructions on the packet carefully, as most detergents in common use give special instructions for washing woollens. If there is no mention of woollens on the packet, I advise you not to use this particular powder as it may damage your garment.

(b) Mix the soapflakes or powder in a small quantity of hot water, making sure the medium is thoroughly dissolved before adding sufficient water (lukewarm for soap flakes, cool for powders) in which to immerse the garment.

(c) Immerse the garment in the solution and leave it soaking for three or four minutes as this will loosen the dirt.

(d) Squeeze the dirt out of the garment, using a motion rather like kneading bread. Be sure to keep the garment thoroughly immersed in the water, as if you lift it in and out of the water you may stretch the fabric out of shape. Avoid rubbing, as this causes felting.

(e) When the dirt has been thoroughly worked out of the garment, rinse it thoroughly in clean lukewarm water. I strongly advise two or three rinsings. The important thing here is to remove all trace of soap from the fabric. If you are using a powder where the manufacturer tells you rinsing is unnecessary, I still advise rinsing as this is a precaution against damaging the fabric in any way.

(f) Lift the garment out of the bowl. Squeeze out as much surplus water as possible.

(g) Fold the sleeves inside the garment, then fold the garment over at the centre. Run it through a wringer, thus getting the remainder of the surplus water out of the garment. The more water you can get out of the garment at this stage the easier it is to dry and re-block.

White Woollens

A practical hint that will prove very useful in home washing is to soak white garments in a bowl of lukewarm water to which a tablespoonful of household ammonia has been added. After soaking remove the garment from the ammonia solution and wash in the ordinary way.

Drying the Garment

The ideal way to dry knitted garments after they have been washed is to lay them flat, as this avoids any possibility of stretching. You can buy string hammocks that fit over an ordinary bath and these are ideal for drying woollens.

If you hang it on a clothes-horse or rack, hang the garment at the centre (across the bust line) and then fold the sleeves over the clothes-horse or rack again to prevent them dangling. If they hang loosely, the remaining weight of water will seep down into the ends of the sleeves, causing them to stretch.

Re-blocking the Garment

When the garment is thoroughly dry, re-block it into shape on an ironing sheet in the same way as you blocked the pieces before making up the garment. Lightly press on the wrong side, using a warm iron and damp cloth.

If you wash, dry, and re-block your garments in this way, you should certainly have no trouble with them and they will wear like new each time they have been washed.

Special care must be taken in the washing, drying, and re-blocking of fine lacy garments. It is always advisable to dry them flat, as the texture of the fabric is more liable to cause this type of garment to stretch than any other.

If you leave buttons on the garment when you are washing it, be sure to fold the buttons in carefully to protect them when the garment is going through the wringer. The golden rule is to remove the buttons before washing and sew them on again when you have re-blocked the garment.

LOOKING AFTER YOUR HAND KNITTEDS

The way I have seen some women treat their knitteds fills me with dismay. I find myself wondering if women think they can maltreat them as much as they like without harm.

I have seen jumpers flung across a chair. I have shuddered at cardigans hanging from an ordinary hook behind a door. The idea seems to be 'oh it's only a woolly so it doesn't matter'.

When you are not wearing your knitted garments fold them neatly and place them in a drawer. Use a good moth preventive as this will prevent these little pests from finding their way into your jumpers and cardigans and laying their eggs, that will later develop into grubs on the surface of the wool, as it is these which cause all the damage.

You can get a perfectly safe moth powder from any chemist and the easiest way is to sprinkle it lightly on the garment before placing it in the drawer. The powder will shake off when you take the garment out again.

If you are storing lightweight summer woollies away for the winter after washing them, fold them, wrap them in a newspaper, and seal the newspaper with ordinary adhesive tape. This is another way of defending them from the attacks of moths.

Here's another useful tip. If the ribbing seems to be getting rather loose and out of shape, bunch the garment up in the hand just above the ribbing, close the hand round the lower edge of the ribbing and gently pull it back into shape. If you do this after you have washed the garment while it is still wet, it will help to preserve the natural elasticity of the ribbing.

Sometimes when sleeves do not shrink they creep up slightly. You may find after you have worn a jumper or cardigan for some time the sleeves seem to be shorter than they were when you first knitted and wore it. Keep any oddments of wool left over from the knitting in your work-basket. To lengthen the sleeves draw a thread at the centre of the edge above the ribbing. Cut the thread, thus releasing the stitches at the top of the ribbing and commencement of the sleeve. Place the set of stitches on a spare needle. Slip the stitches at the top of the ribbing on to a needle the same size as was used for originally knitting the sleeve above the ribbing. Knit on the extra length you require and then graft the two sets of stitches together as follows: with wrong sides of work outside * insert darning needle knitwise through first stitch on each needle, slip first stitch off back needle, draw wool through, insert darning needle purlwise through first stitch on each needle, slip first stitch off front needle, draw wool through, rep from * until all stitches are worked off.

If you use a back-stitch seam on the shoulders, you should have no trouble with the shoulders sagging and stretching when the garment is in wear. If the shoulders should stretch slightly, before you wash the garment cut two lengths of tape the width of the shoulder, neatly stitch these tapes on the inside along the shoulder seam, easing the shoulder of the garment on to the tape if necessary. This will hold the shoulder quite firmly and give a new look to the garment itself.

EMBROIDERY ON KNITTING

Embroidery is used on knitting mainly for peasant coats that reflect the gaiety of the Austrian Tyrol. Ordinary classics can often be brightened up with embroidered motifs on the yoke or on the neckband.

The secret of working embroidery on knitted fabric is to use a simple stitch. Be sure to use wool that is fast to washing, otherwise the colours may bleed on to the fabric of the garment itself when it is washed, thus ruining the jumper or the cardigan.

A wool one ply thicker than the actual wool used for the knitting is ideal for embroidery. Thus on a 2-ply you would use a 3-ply; on a 3-ply a 4-ply; and on a 4-ply a double knitting. On fabrics knitted in double knitting the same thickness of wool as used for the garment is sufficient to give you the bold effects that this type of garment demands. If you want a heavier type of embroidery you can use 4-ply double.

The following simple working diagrams give you the type of embroidery stitches that are the most useful for working on a knitted fabric.

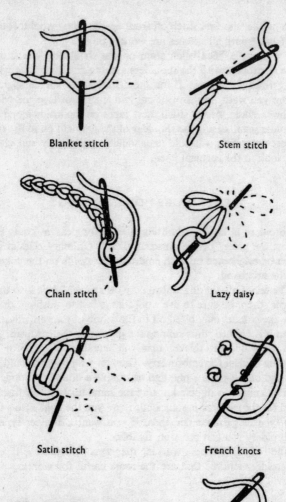

Blanket stitch

Stem stitch

Chain stitch

Lazy daisy

Satin stitch

French knots

Herringbone

Fly stitch

CHAPTER 7

Knitwear for the Family

BABY'S LAYETTE
Illustrated in Plates 10 and 11a

Lace Pattern, (14 sts plus 1) *Used in Coat, Bonnet, Mitts, Bootees.*
1st row: K2 tog, wf, * K3, wf, K1, sl1, K2 tog, psso, K1, wf, K3, wf, sl1, K2 tog, psso, wf, rep from * to last 13 sts, K3, wf, K1, sl1, K2 tog, psso, K1, wf, K3, wf, sl1, K1, psso.
2nd row: P.
3rd row: K2 tog, wf, * K4, wf, sl1, K2 tog, psso, wf, rep from * to last 6 sts, K4, wf, sl1, K1, psso.
4th row: P.
These 4 rows form the patt.

Coat

3 oz Baby Wool. Two No 10 needles. Three buttons. Length, 11½ ins. Width, 18½ ins. Sleeve, 5 ins.

This garment must be worked at a tension of 7½ sts and 9½ rows to one square inch on No 10 needles measured over stocking stitch.

BACK

Cast on 113 sts. K8 rows.

Work rows 1–4 incl of lace patt.

Continue in lace patt until work measures 6¾ ins, finishing at end of a P row.

Next row: K1, * (K2 tog) twice, K3 tog, rep from * to last 7 sts, (K2 tog) 3 times, K1 (50 sts).

K7 rows.

Next row: Inc in first st, (K2, inc in next st) 6 times, (K1, inc in next st) 6 times, (K2, inc in next st) 6 times, K1 (69 sts).

Next row: K1, P to last st, K1.

Work 2 rows in stocking st.

Continue in stocking stitch, *shaping armholes* by casting off 3 sts at beg of next 2 rows. Dec 1 st at both ends of next 3 rows then every alt row until 53 sts remain.

Continue on these sts until work measures 3¾ ins from beg of armhole shaping.

Shape shoulders by casting off 8 sts at beg of next 4 rows. Cast off.

RIGHT FRONT

Cast on 62 sts. K 8 rows.

Keeping a border of 5 sts in garter stitch (every row K) at front edge and working remaining sts in lace patt proceed as follows:

1st row: K5, work as first row of lace patt to end.

2nd row: K1, P to last 5 sts, K5.

3rd row: K5, work as third row of lace patt to end.

4th row: As 2nd row.

Continue in this manner until work measures 6¾ ins, finishing at front edge.

Next row: K7, (K2 tog, K3 tog) 10 times, K2 tog, K3 (31 sts). K 3 rows.

Next row: K2, wf, K2 tog (for buttonhole), K to end. K 3 rows.

Next row: K7, (inc in next st, K3) 6 times, (37 sts).

Next row: K1, P to last 5 sts, K5.

Keeping border correct, work 3 rows in stocking stitch, working a buttonhole as before on 3rd row.

Shape armhole by casting off 3 sts at beg of next row. Dec 1 st at armhole edge on next 3 rows then on every alt row until 29 sts remain, *noting* that the 3rd buttonhole should be worked on last row of armhole shaping.

Next row: K1, P to last 5 sts, K5.

Commence front slope as follows:

Next row: K5, K2 tog tbl, K to end.

Work 2 rows.

Next row: K1, P to last 7 sts, P2 tog tbl, K5.

Work 2 rows.

** Continue in this manner, dec 1 st inside 5 border sts on next and every following 3rd row until 21 sts remain. Continue on these sts until work measures same as back up to shoulder shaping, finishing at armhole edge.

68

Shape shoulder by casting off 8 sts at beg of next and alt row. Continue in garter stitch on remaining 5 sts for 1¼ ins. Cast off.

LEFT FRONT

Cast on 62 sts. K 8 rows.

Keeping a border of 5 sts in garter stitch at front edge and working remaining sts in lace patt proceed as follows:

1st row: Work in lace patt to last 5 sts, K5.

2nd row: K5, P to last st, K1.

3rd row: Work in lace patt to last 5 sts, K5.

4th row: As 2nd row.

Continue in this manner until work measures 6¾ ins from beg, finishing at side edge.

Next row: K3, K2 tog, (K3 tog, K2 tog) 10 times, K7.

K 7 rows.

Next row: (K3, inc in next st) 6 times, K7 (37 sts).

Next row: K5, P to last st, K1.

Work 2 rows.

Shape armhole by casting off 3 sts at beg of next row, dec 1 st at armhole edge on next 3 rows then every alt row until 29 sts remain.

Work 2 rows.

Commence front slope as follows:

Next row: K to last 7 sts, K2 tog, K5.

Work 2 rows.

Next row: K5, P2 tog, P to last st, K1.

Work 2 rows.

Complete as right front, working from ** to end.

SLEEVES

Cast on 29 sts. K 14 rows.

Next row: (K2 tog, K2) 7 times, K1 (22 sts).

Next row: K.

Next row: Inc twice in first st, then inc once in each of next 21 sts (45 sts).

Next row: K1, P to last st, K1.

Proceed in stocking stitch, inc 1 st at both ends of 9th and every following 8th row until there are 51 sts. Continue on these sts until work measures 5 ins from beg.

Shape top by casting off 1 st at beg of every row until 35 sts remain, then 2 sts at beg of every row until 23 sts remain.
Cast off, working 2 tog all across row to last st, cast off last st.

MAKE UP

Press on wrong side using a warm iron and damp cloth. Using a back-stitch seam join shoulder seams. Using a flat seam, join side and sleeve seams, and stitch sleeves into position. Join cast-off sts of border and stitch into position at back of neck. Attach buttons. Press seams.

Bonnet

1 oz Baby Wool. Two No 11 and two No 10 needles. Length of ribbon.
Width all round brim slightly stretched, 12 ins.
This garment must be worked at a tension of 7½ sts and 9½ rows to 1 square inch on No 10 needles measured over stocking stitch.
Using No 11 needles, cast on 85 sts. K 4 rows.
Work rows 1–4 incl of lace patt 5 times.
Work in K1, P1 rib for 17 rows.
Next row: K12, (inc in next st, K19) 3 times, inc in next st, K to end (89 sts).

Change to No 10 needles.
Next row: K1, P to last st, K1.
Proceed in stocking stitch until work measures 6¾ ins from beg finishing at end of a P row.

Shape crown as follows:
1st row: (K9, K2 tog) 8 times, K1.
2nd and alt rows: K.
3rd row: (K8, K2 tog) 8 times, K1.
5th row: (K7, K2 tog) 8 times, K1.
Continue in this manner working 1 st less between dec on every alt row until 17 sts remain.

70

Next row: (K2 tog) 8 times, K1.

Break off wool, run end through remaining sts and fasten off securely.

MAKE UP

Press on wrong side using a warm iron and damp cloth. Using a flat seam join seam from centre of crown to ½ inch past crown shaping. Press seam. Turn back front edge and make rosettes and stitch into position at sides of bonnet.

Baby's Mitts (both alike)

1 oz Baby Wool. Two No 11 and two No 10 needles. Length 4¾ ins.

Tension – as Coat.

Using No 11 needles, cast on 43 sts. K 2 rows.

Work rows 1–4 incl of lace patt 3 times.

Change to No 10 needles.

Next row: K21, K2 tog, K20 (42 sts).

Commencing with a P row, work 19 rows in stocking stitch.

Shape top as follows:

1st row: (K1, K2 tog tbl, K15, K2 tog, K1) twice.
2nd and alt rows: P.
3rd row: (K1, K2 tog tbl, K13, K2 tog, K1) twice.
5th row: (K1, K2 tog tbl, K11, K2 tog, K1) twice.
7th row: (K1, K2 tog tbl, K9, K2 tog, K1) twice.
8th row: As 2nd row.
Cast off.

MAKE UP

Using a flat seam join seam. Press seam. Make a twisted cord and thread through top row of holes of lace patt. Attach a small tassel to each end of cord.

Bootees (both alike)

1 oz Baby Wool. Two No 12 needles.

This garment must be worked at a tension of 8½ sts and 10½

rows to one square inch on No 12 needles measured over stocking stitch.

Cast on 43 sts. K 2 rows.

Work rows 1–4 incl of lace patt 8 times.

Divide work as follows:

1st row: K29, turn.

2nd row: K1, P13, K1.

Knitting 1 st at both ends of every row work 14 rows in stocking stitch on these 15 sts. Break off wool.

With right side of work facing, commencing where sts were left and using same needle *knit up* 15 sts evenly along one side of instep, K across 15 sts on needle, *knit up* 15 sts from other side of instep, K remaining 14 sts (73 sts).

K15 rows.

Shape foot as follows:

1st row: K1, K2 tog, K31, K2 tog, K1, K2 tog, K31, K2 tog, K1.

2nd row: K32, K2 tog, K1, K2 tog, K32.

3rd row: K1, K2 tog, K28, K2 tog, K1, K2 tog, K28, K2 tog, K1.

4th row: K29, K2 tog, K1, K2 tog, K29.

5th row: K1, K2 tog, K25, K2 tog, K1, K2 tog, K25, K2 tog, K1.

Cast off.

MAKE UP

Press lightly on wrong side. Join seam. Make a twisted cord and thread through last row of holes of lace patt. Attach a small tassel to each end of cord.

Dress

3 oz Baby Wool. Two No 10 needles. Five buttons.

Length, 15 ins. Width, 18 ins. Sleeve, 1½ ins.

Tension – as Coat.

FRONT

Cast on 126 sts. K 8 rows.

Proceed in lace panels as follows:

1st row: K9, * wf, sl1, K2 tog, psso, wf, K18, rep from * to last 12 sts, wf, sl1, K2 tog, psso, wf, K9.

2nd row: K1, P to last st, K1.

Rep these 2 rows until work measures 10½ ins from beg, finishing at end of a P row.

Next row: K1, * (K2 tog) twice, K3 tog, rep from * to last 6 sts, (K2 tog) twice, K2 (56 sts).

K 6 rows.

Next row: K3, (inc in next st, K4) 10 times, inc in next st, K to end (67 sts). **

Proceed in stocking stitch and continue lace panel as follows:

1st row: K25, wf, sl1, K2 tog, psso, wf, K3, wf, K1, sl1, K2 tog, psso, K1, wf, K3, wf, sl1, K2 tog, psso, wf, K25.

2nd row: K1, P to last st, K1.

3rd row: K25, wf, sl1, K2 tog, psso, wf, K4, wf, sl1, K2 tog, psso, wf, K4, wf, sl1, K2 tog, psso, wf, K25.

4th row: K1, P to last st, K1.

These 4 rows form the patt.

Keeping patt correct, *shape armholes* by casting off 3 sts at beg of next 2 rows. Dec 1 st at both ends of next and every alt row until 51 sts remain.

Continue on these sts until work measures 2¼ ins from beg of armhole shaping, finishing at end of a P row.

Shape neck as follows:

Work 20 sts, cast off 11 sts, work to end.

Continue on *each* group of sts, dec 1 st at neck edge on every row until 15 sts remain.

Continue on these sts until work measures 3½ ins from beg of armhole shaping, finishing at armhole edge.

Shape shoulder as follows:

1st row: Cast off 7 sts, work to end.

2nd row: Work all across, cast off.

BACK

Work as Front until ** is reached. Work 2 rows in stocking stitch.

Divide work as follows:

Next row: K34, turn.

Continue on this group of sts as follows:

73

Next row: K I, P to last st, K I.

*** *Shape armhole* by casting off 3 sts at beg of next row. Dec I st at armhole edge on every alt row until 26 sts remain. Continue on these sts until work measures same as Front up to shoulder shaping, finishing at armhole edge.

Shape shoulder as follows:

1st row: Cast off 7 sts, work to end.

2nd row: Work all across.

3rd row: Cast off 8 sts, work to end.

4th row: Work all across.

Cast off.

Rejoin wool to sts on needle.

Cast on 4 sts for underflap and knitting these 4 sts on every row, work 3 rows.

Complete as first half of Back working from *** to end, *noting* that there will be 29 sts in place of 26 sts after completion of armhole shaping.

SLEEVES (BOTH ALIKE)

Cast on 39 sts. K 8 rows.

Next row: K 3, (inc in next st, K I) 17 times, K 2 (56 sts).

Next row: K I, P to last st, K I.

Continue in stocking stitch until work measures $1\frac{1}{2}$ ins from beg.

Shape top by casting off 3 sts at beg of next 2 rows, dec I st at both ends of next and every alt row until 32 sts remain.

Cast off working 2 tog all across row.

NECKBAND

Using a back-stitch seam join shoulders of back and front.

With right side of work facing *knit up* 55 sts round neck.

K 4 rows.

Cast off.

MAKE UP

Press on wrong side using a warm iron and damp cloth. Using a flat seam join side and sleeve seams and stitch sleeves into position. Stitch down end of underflap. Attach buttons to left side of back opening, work button-loops to correspond. Press seams.

Vest

2 oz Baby Wool. Two No 9 needles. Length of ribbon. Width, 16 ins, Length, 9 ins.

This garment must be worked at a tension of 7 sts and 9 rows to one square inch on No 9 needles, measured over stocking stitch.

RIGHT FRONT

Cast on 43 sts. K 56 rows.

Make slot as follows:

Next row: K 33, turn.

K 6 rows on these 33 sts.

Break off wool and rejoin to group of 10 sts.

K 7 rows on these 10 sts.

Next row: K all across.

** *Shape neck and sleeve* as follows:

1st row: Cast off 9 sts, K to end.

2nd row: K to end.

3rd row: K 3, K 2 tog, K to last 2 sts, inc in next st, K 1.

4th–11th rows: Rep 2nd and 3rd rows 4 times.

12th row: Cast on 8 sts, K to end (42 sts).

13th row: K 3, K 2 tog, K to end.

14th row: K to end.

15th row: K 3, K 2 tog, K to last 3 sts, turn.

16th row: K to end.

17th row: K 3, K 2 tog, K to end.

18th row: K to end.

Rep rows 13–18 incl twice, then 13th and 14th rows once.

Next row: K to last 3 sts, turn.

Next row: K to end. **

K 8 rows on these 32 sts.

Slip sts on to a length of wool and leave.

LEFT FRONT AND BACK

Cast on 43 sts. K 64 rows.

Work as right front from ** to **.

K 7 rows.

Next row: K to end, cast on 15 sts for back of neck, slip sts from right front on to left-hand needle (neck edge at point of needle), K across these sts (79 sts).

K 2 rows.

Proceed as follows:

1st–4th rows: K to end.

5th and 6th rows: K to last 3 sts, turn.

Rep these 6 rows 3 times.

K 2 rows.

Shape sleeves by casting off 8 sts at beg of next 2 rows. Dec 1 st at both ends of next and every alt row until 53 sts remain.

K 66 rows.

Cast off.

MAKE UP

Using a flat seam join side and sleeve seams. Attach a length of ribbon to corner of each front and to corresponding position on side seams. Press seams.

Pilch

1 oz Baby Wool. Two No 9 needles. Length of elastic. Length at centre front, $8\frac{1}{2}$ ins.

Tension – as Vest.

Commencing at front, cast on 52 sts.

1st row: K2, * P1, K1, rep from * to end.

Rep this row 3 times.

Next row: K2, * wf, K2 tog, P1, K1, rep from * to last 2 sts, wf, K2 tog.

Rep 1st row 7 times.

Next row: K6, (inc in next st, K12) 3 times, inc in next st, K6 (56 sts.).

K 61 rows.

Divide sts for legs as follows:

1st row: K18, turn.

2nd row: K1, K2 tog, K15.

3rd row: K14, K2 tog, K1, turn.

4th row: K1, K2 tog, K13.

Continue dec in this manner until 2 sts remain.

Next row: K 2 tog. Fasten off.

Rejoin wool and K across 38 sts on needle.

Proceed as follows:

1st row: K 15, K 2 tog, K 1, turn.

2nd row: K 1, K 2 tog, K 14.

3rd row: K 13, K 2 tog, K 1, turn.

4th row: K 1, K 2 tog, K 12.

Continue dec in this manner until 2 sts remain.

Next row: K 2 tog. Fasten off.

Rejoin wool and K 11 rows on remaining 20 sts.

Inc once at both ends of next and every alt row until there are 56 sts on needle.

K 79 rows.

Shape back as follows:

1st and 2nd rows: K to last 3 sts, turn.

3rd and 4th rows: K to last 6 sts, turn.

5th and 6th rows: K to last 9 sts, turn.

7th and 8th rows: K to last 12 sts, turn.

9th and 10th rows: K to last 15 sts, turn.

11th and 12th rows: K to last 18 sts, turn.

13th and 14th rows: K to end.

15th row: K 6, (K 2 tog, K 12) 3 times, K 2 tog, K 6.

16th row: K 2, * P 1, K 1, rep from * to end.

Rep 16th row 6 times.

Next row: K 2, * wf, K 2 tog, P 1, K 1, rep from * to last 2 sts, wf, K 2, tog.

Rep 16th row 4 times.

Cast off in rib.

MAKE UP

Using a flat seam join side seams as far as shaping.

Thread elastic through holes at waist

CHILD'S CARDIGAN IN THREE SIZES
Illustrated in Plate 11b

3/3/4 oz 3-ply. Two No 12 and two No 10 needles.

Five/six/seven buttons.

Length, $10\frac{1}{2}$/12/$13\frac{1}{2}$ ins. Width, 20/22/24 ins. Sleeve, 8/9/10 ins.

This garment must be worked at a tension of $7\frac{1}{2}$ sts and $9\frac{1}{2}$ rows to one square inch measured over stocking stitch on No 10 needles.

RIGHT FRONT

Using No 12 needles cast on 34/38/42 sts.

Work in K1, P1 rib for 2/$2\frac{1}{4}$/$2\frac{1}{2}$ ins, inc 1 st at beg of last row (35/39/43 sts).

Change to No 10 needles and proceed in stocking stitch with fancy panel as follows:

1st row: K9/11/13, (P1, K2) twice, K2 tog, wf, K1, wf, K2 tog tbl, (K2, P1) twice, K9/11/13.

2nd and alt rows: P.

3rd row: K9/11/13, P1, K2, P1, K1, K2 tog, wf, K3, wf, K2 tog tbl, K1, P1, K2, P1, K9/11/13.

5th row: K9/11/13, (P1, K2) twice, K1, wf, sl1, K2 tog, psso, wf, K1, (K2, P1) twice, K9/11/13.

7th row: K9/11/13, (P1, K2) twice, K5, (K2, P1) twice, K9/11/13.

8th row: P.

These 8 rows form the patt.

Keeping patt correct continue until work measures $6\frac{1}{4}$/$7\frac{1}{2}$/$8\frac{3}{4}$ ins from beg, finishing at side edge.**

Shape armhole and front slope as follows:

1st row: Cast off 3/4/5 sts, work to end.

2nd row: K2 tog, work to last 2 sts, K2 tog.

*** Continue dec at armhole edge on every alt row until 5 more dec have been worked at armhole edge, *at the same time* dec 1 st at front edge on every 4th row from previous dec (23/26/29 sts).

Continue without further dec at armhole edge, but still dec at front slope on 2nd row following and every following 6th row until 19/21/23 sts remain.

Continue on these sts until work measures $4\frac{1}{4}$/$4\frac{1}{2}$/$4\frac{3}{4}$ ins from beg of armhole shaping, finishing at armhole edge.

Shape shoulder as follows:

1st row: Cast off 6/7/8 sts, work to end.

2nd row: Work all across.

Rep these 2 rows once.
Cast off.

LEFT FRONT

Work as right front until ** is reached.

Shape armhole and front slope as follows:
1st row: Cast off 3/4/5 sts, work to end.
2nd row: P to end.
3rd row: K2 tog, work to last 2 sts, K2 tog.
Complete as right front working from *** to end.

BACK

Using No 12 needles, cast on 74/82/90 sts. Work in K1, P1 rib for 2/2½/2½ ins, inc 1 st at end of last row (75/83/91 sts).

Change to No 10 needles and proceed in stocking stitch with fancy panels as follows:
1st row: K9/11/13, * (P1, K2) twice, K2 tog, wf, K1, wf, K2 tog tbl, (K2, P1) twice, * K23/27/31, rep from * to * once, K9/11/13.
2nd and alt rows: P.
3rd row: K9/11/13, * P1, K2, P1, K1, K2 tog, wf, K3, wf, K2 tog tbl, K1, P1, K2, P1, * K23/27/31, rep from * to * once, K9/11/13.
5th row: K9/11/13, * (P1, K2) twice, K1, wf, sl1, K2 tog, psso, wf, K1, (K2, P1) twice, * K23/27/31, rep from * to * once, K9/11/13.
7th row: K9/11/13, * (P1, K2) twice, K5, (K2, P1) twice, * K23/27/31, rep from * to * once, K9/11/13.
8th row: P.
Continue in patt until work measures same as fronts up to armhole shaping.

Shape armholes by casting off 3/4/5 sts at beg of next 2 rows. Dec 1 st at both ends of next and every alt row until 57/63/69 sts remain.
Continue on these sts until work measures same as fronts up to shoulder shaping.

Shape shoulders by casting off 6/7/8 sts at beg of next 4 rows;

79

7 sts at beg of following 2 rows.
Cast off.

SLEEVES

Using No 12 needles, cast on 40/42/44 sts.

Work in K I, P I rib for 2/2¼/2½ ins.

Next row: Rib 4/5/6, (inc in next st, rib 7) 4 times, inc in next st, rib to end (45/47/49 sts).

Change to No 10 needles and proceed in stocking stitch, inc 1 st at both ends of 7th/5th/3rd row and every following 10th row until there are 55/59/63 sts.

Continue on these sts until work measures 8/9/10 ins from beg.

Shape top by casting off 3/4/4 sts at beg of next 2 rows. Dec 1 st at both ends of next and every alt row until 25/25/25 sts remain; both ends of every row until 15/15/15 sts remain. Cast off.

FRONT BAND

Using No 12 needles, cast on 9 sts.

1st row: K 2, (P I, K I) 3 times, K I.

2nd row: (K I, P I) 4 times, K I.

3rd row: Rib 4, cast off 2, rib to end.

4th row: Rib 3, cast on 2, rib to end.

Continue in rib working a buttonhole as on 3rd and 4th rows on following 13th and 14th rows from previous buttonhole until 5/6/7 buttonholes *in all* have been worked.

Continue without further buttonholes until band measures 23/26/29 ins (not stretched) from beg.

Cast off in rib.

MAKE UP

Omitting ribbing, block and press. Using a back-stitch seam join shoulder, side and sleeve seams and stitch sleeves into position.

Using a flat seam stitch on front band. Attach buttons. Press seams.

CHILD'S JERSEY (3–6 YEARS)

Illustrated in Plate 11b

4 oz 3-ply. Two No 12 and two No 10 needles. A cable needle.

Four buttons.

Width, 23/25 ins. Length, 12½/14¼ ins. Sleeve, 9/11 ins.

This garment must be worked at a tension of 7½ sts and 9½ rows to one square inch on No 10 needles measured over stocking stitch.

FRONT

Using No 12 needles, cast on 78/86 sts.

Work 21/23 rows in K 1, P 1 rib.

Next row: Rib 3/7, (inc in next st, rib 7) 9 times, inc in next st, rib to end (88/96 sts).

Change to No 10 needles and proceed in *all-over* patt *with centre cable panel* as follows:

1st row: (K2, P2), 9/10 times, K4, C2B, C2F, K4, (P2, K2) 9/10 times.

2nd row: P.

3rd row: (K2, P2) 9/10 times, K2, C2B, K4, C2F, (K2, P2) 9/10 times, K2.

4th row: P.

5th row: K.

6th row: P.

These 6 rows form the patt.

Continue in patt until work measures 8/9½ ins from beg, finishing at end of a P row.

Keeping patt correct, *shape armholes* by casting off 5/6 sts at beg of next 2 rows. Dec 1 st at both ends of next and every alt row until 66/70 sts remain.

Continue on these sts until work measures 3¼ ins from beg of armhole shaping, finishing at end of a P row.

Shape neck as follows:

Next row: Patt 26/28, cast off 14 sts, patt to end.

Continue on *each* group of sts dec 1 st at neck edge on every row until 21/23 sts remain.

Continue on these sts until work measures 4½/4¾ ins from beg of armhole shaping, finishing at armhole edge.

Shape shoulder as follows:
1st row: Cast off 7/8 sts, work to end.
2nd row: Work all across.
Rep these 2 rows once.
Cast off.

BACK

Using No 12 needles, cast on 78/86 sts.
Work 21/23 rows in K I, P I rib.
Next row: Rib 3/7, (inc in next st, rib 9) 7 times, inc in next st, rib to end (86/94 sts).

Change to No 10 needles and proceed in *all-over* patt as follows:
1st row: * K2, P2, rep from * to last 2 sts, K2.
2nd row: P.
3rd and 4th rows: As 1st and 2nd.
5th row: K.
6th row: P.
These 6 rows form the patt.
Continue in patt until work measures same as Front up to armhole shaping.

Shape armholes by casting off 5/6 sts at beg of next 2 rows. Dec I st at both ends of next and every alt row until 64/68 sts remain.
Continue on these sts until the work measures same as Front up to shoulder shaping, finishing so that right side of work will be facing when working next row.
Next row: Cast off 7/8 sts, work to end.
Next row: Cast off 7/8 sts, P 15/16 (16/17 sts now on left-hand needle) turn.
** Continue in stocking stitch on this group of 16/17 sts, dec I st at neck edge on next 2 rows.
Work 4 rows in stocking stitch on remaining 14/15 sts for underflap. Cast off.**
Rejoin wool to sts on needle.
Cast off 18/18 sts, P to end.
Work as first half from ** to **.

SLEEVES

Using No 12 needles, cast on 42/46 sts.

Work 21/23 rows in K 1, P 1 rib.

Next row: Rib 4/6, (inc in next st, rib 10) 3 times, inc in next st, rib to end (46/50 sts).

Change to No 10 needles and proceed in *all-over* patt as on Back inc 1 st at both ends of 7th and every following 9th/11th row until there are 60/64 sts.

Continue on these sts until work measures 9/11 ins from beg.

Shape top by casting off 3 sts at beg of next 4 rows. Dec 1 st at both ends of next and every following 3rd row until 40/42 sts remain; every alt row until 36/38 sts remain, every row until 24/26 sts remain. Cast off 4 sts at beg of next 4 rows. Cast off

FRONT NECKBAND

Using No 12 needles, with right side of work facing *knit up* 54/58 sts round neck.

Work 5 rows in K 1, P 1 rib.

Cast off in rib.

BACK NECKBAND

Using No 12 needles, commencing at corner of right underflap *knit up* 36/36 sts round back of neck, finishing at corner of left underflap.

Work 5 rows in K 1, P 1 rib.

Cast off in rib.

MAKE UP

Omitting ribbing, block and press. Using a back-stitch seam join side and sleeve seams. Join first group of cast-off shoulder sts on back and fronts. Stitch underflap into position on wrong side. Stitch sleeves into position. Work 2 buttonholes on each shoulder. Attach buttons. Press seams.

BOY'S OR GIRL'S POLO NECK SWEATER
Illustrated in Plate 12a

13/14/15 oz Double Knitting. Two No 8 and two No 10 needles. Set of four No 10 needles with points at both ends. A cable needle. Width, 28/30/32 ins. Length, 17½/19/20½ ins. Sleeve, 13½/15/16½ ins.

This garment must be worked at a tension of 5½ stitches and 7½ rows to one square inch on No 8 needles measured over stocking stitch.

FRONT

Using No 10 needles, cast on 78/84/88 sts.

Work in K 1, P 1 rib for 2¾/3/3¼ ins.

Next row: Rib 6/9/11, (inc in next st, rib 5) 11 times, inc in next st, rib to end (90/96/100 sts).

Change to No 8 needles and proceed in stocking stitch with cable as follows:

1st row: K 17/19/20, (C 2B) twice, K 12/13/14, (C 2B) twice, (C 2F) twice, K 12/13/14, (C 2F) twice, K 17/19/20.

2nd and alt rows: P.

3rd row: K.

5th row: K 17/19/20, (C 2F) twice, K 12/13/14, (C 2F) twice, (C 2B) twice, K 12/13/14, (C 2B) twice, K 17/19/20.

7th row: K.

8th row: P.

These 8 rows form the patt.

Continue in patt until work measures 11/12¼/13½ ins from beg.

Shape armholes by casting off 4/5/6 sts at beg of next 2 rows. Dec 1 st at both ends of next and every alt row until 72/76/78 sts remain. Continue on these sts until work measures 4½/4½/4¾ ins from beg of armhole shaping, finishing at end of a P row.

Divide for neck as follows:

Next row: Patt 28/30/31 sts, turn.

Continue on this group of sts, dec 1 st at neck edge on every alt row until 23/24/25 sts remain.

Continue on these sts until work measures 6½/6¾/7 ins from beg of armhole shaping, finishing at armhole edge.

Shape shoulder as follows:
1st row: Cast off 8 sts, work to end.
2nd row: Work all across.
Rep these 2 rows once.
Cast off.
Slip first 16 sts left on needle on to a length of wool and leave. Rejoin wool to sts on needle and complete to match other half of neck.

BACK

Work as Front until armhole shaping is completed (72/76/78 sts). Continue on these sts until work measures 5½/5½/5¾ ins from beg of armhole shaping, finishing at end of a P row.

Divide for neck and complete as on Front but *noting* that dec at neck edge should be worked on *every* row instead of every alt row.

SLEEVES

Using No 10 needles, cast on 38/40/42 sts.
Work in K 1, P 1 rib for 2¾/3/3¼ ins.
Next row: Rib 2/3/4, (inc in next st, rib 2) 11 times, inc in next st, rib to end (50/52/54 sts).

Change to No 8 needles and proceed in stocking stitch with cable as follows:
1st row: K 17/18/19, (C2B) twice, (C2F) twice, K 17/18/19.
2nd and alt rows: P.
3rd row: K.
5th row: K 17/18/19, (C2F) twice, (C2B) twice, K 17/18/19.
7th row: K.
8th row: P.
Keeping patt correct, inc 1 st at both ends of next and every following 7th/8th/8th row until there are 70/74/76 sts on needle, working extra sts in stocking stitch. Continue on these sts until work measures 13½/15/16½ ins from beg.

Shape top by casting off 4/5/6 sts at beg of next 2 rows. Dec 1 st at both ends of every alt row until 30 sts remain.

85

Cast off 4 sts at beg of next 4 rows.
Cast off.

POLO NECK

Using a back-stitch seam join shoulders of back and front. Using
set of No 10 needles with right side of work facing *knit up*
86/92/98 sts round neck. Work in rounds of K1, P1, rib for
5/5½/6 ins.
Cast off in rib.

MAKE UP

Omitting ribbing, block and press work on wrong side using a
warm iron and damp cloth. Using a back-stitch seam join side
and sleeve seams and stitch sleeves into position. Press
seams.

PULLOVER WITH V NECK FOR BOY OR GIRL
Illustrated in Plate 12a

9/10/11 oz 4-ply Fingering. Two No 12 and two No 10 needles.
Set of four No 12 needles with points at both ends. Chest 30/32/
34 ins. Length 18½/19½/20½ ins. Sleeve, 15½/16½/17½ ins.

This garment must be worked at a tension of 7 sts and 9 rows
to one square inch on No 10 needles measured over stocking
stitch.

FRONT

** Using No 12 needles, cast on 98/102/106 sts.
Work in K1, P1 rib for 3/3¼/3½ ins.
Next row:

Small size only: Rib 9, (inc in next st, rib 9) 8 times, inc in next st,
rib to end (107 sts).

Middle size only: Rib 5, (inc in next st, rib 6) 12 times, inc in next
st, rib to end (115 sts).

Large size only: Rib 4, (inc in next st, rib 6) 14 times, inc in next
st, rib to end (121 sts).

All sizes:

Change to No 10 needles and proceed in stocking stitch until work measures 12/12½/13 ins from beg, finishing at end of a P row. **

Shape armholes and divide for V Neck as follows:

Next row: Cast off 6/7/7, K to last 54/58/61 sts, cast off 1, K to end.

Next row: Cast off 6/7/7, P 46/49/52 sts.

*** Continue on this group of 47/50/53 sts, dec 1 st at armhole edge on next and every alt row until 7/8/9 dec *in all* have been worked at armhole edge, *at the same time* dec 1 st at neck edge on next and every following 4th row until armhole shaping is completed.

Continue without further shaping at armhole edge but still dec at neck edge on every 4th row from previous dec until 26/27/28 sts remain.

Continue on these sts until work measures 6½/7/7½ ins from beg of armhole shaping, finishing at armhole edge.

Shape shoulder as follows:

1st row: Cast off 9, work to end.

2nd row: Work all across.

Rep these 2 rows once.

Cast off.

Rejoin wool to remaining group of 47/50/53 sts.

Next row: P.

Complete as for other half of Front working from *** to end.

BACK

Work as Front from ** to **.

Shape armholes by casting off 6/7/7 sts at beg of next 2 rows. Dec 1 st at both ends of next and every alt row until 81/85/89 sts remain.

Continue on these sts until work measures same as Front up to shoulder shaping.

Shape shoulders by casting off 9 sts at beg of next 4 rows, 8/9/10 sts at beg of following 2 rows.

Cast off.

SLEEVES

Using No 12 needles, cast on 52/56/60 sts.

Work in K1, P1 rib for 3 ins.

Next row: Rib 6/8/10, (inc in next st, rib 9) 4 times, inc in next st, rib to end (57/61/65 sts).

Change to No 10 needles and proceed in stocking stitch, inc 1 st at both ends of 3rd and every following 8th/8th/9th row until there are 83/87/91 sts.

Continue on these sts until work measures 15½/16½/17½ ins from beg.

Shape top by casting off 2 sts at beg of next 6 rows. Dec 1 st at both ends of every row until 61/65/69 sts remain; every alt row until 25 sts remain; every row until 15 sts remain.

Cast off 3 sts at beg of next 4 rows.

Cast off.

NECKBAND

Using a back-stitch seam join shoulders of back and front.

Using set of No 12 needles, with right side of work facing, commencing at top of left shoulder, *knit up* 59/63/67 sts to centre V, *knit up* 1 st at centre V, then *knit up* 59/63/67 sts along other side of neck, finally *knit up* 29/31/33 sts across back of neck (148/158/168 sts).

Dec 1 st at each side of centre st on every round, work 9 rounds in K1, P1 rib.

Cast off loosely in rib.

MAKE UP

Omitting ribbing, block and press on wrong side using a warm iron and damp cloth. Using a back-stitch seam, join side and sleeve seams. Stitch sleeves into position. Press all seams.

GIRL'S CABLE AND ALL-OVER PATTERNED CARDIGAN
Illustrated in Plate 11b

15/16/17 oz Double Knitting. Two No 10 and two No 8 needles. One cable needle. 7/7/8 buttons.

Bust, 30/32/34 ins. Length, 18½/19½/20½ ins. Sleeve, 15½/16½/17½ ins.

This garment must be worked at a tension of $5\frac{1}{2}$ sts and $7\frac{1}{2}$ rows to one square inch on No 8 needles measured over stocking stitch.

RIGHT FRONT

Using No 10 needles, cast on 40/42/44 sts.

Work in K1, P1 rib for $3/3\frac{1}{2}/3\frac{1}{2}$ ins, inc 1 st at both ends of last row (42/44/46 sts).

Change to No 8 needles and proceed in *cable and all-over patt* as follows:

Next row: (K1, P1) 3 times, P1, K8, P1, (P1, K1) 13/14/15 times.

2nd and every alt row: P to last 16 sts, K1, P8, K1, P to end.

3rd row: (P1, K1) 3 times, P1, K8, P1, (K1, P1) 13/14/15 times.

5th row: (K1, P1) 3 times, P1, C4F, P1, (P1, K1) 13/14/15 times.

7th row: As 3rd row.

8th row: P to last 16 sts, K1, P8, K1, P to end.

These 8 rows form the patt.

** Keeping patt correct continue on these sts until work measures $12/12\frac{1}{2}/13$ ins from beg, finishing so that right side of work will be facing when working next row.**

Commence *front slope* as follows:

Next row: Patt 16, work 2 tog, patt to end.

Shape armhole by casting off 4/5/6 sts at beg of next row. *** Dec 1 st at armhole edge on next and every alt row until 6 dec *in all* have been worked at armhole edge, *at the same time* dec 1 st inside cable border as before on every 4th row from previous dec until armhole shaping is completed.

Continue without further shaping at armhole edge but still dec at front edge on every 6th row from previous dec until 23/24/25 sts remain.

Continue on these sts until work measures $6\frac{1}{2}/7/7\frac{1}{2}$ ins from beg of armhole shaping, finishing at armhole edge.

Shape shoulder as follows:

1st row: Cast off 7/8/8, work to end.

2nd row: Work all across.

Rep these 2 rows once.

Cast off.

LEFT FRONT

Work rib as on Right Front (42/44/46 sts).

Change to No 8 needles and proceed in *cable and all-over patt* as follows:

1st row: (K1, P1) 13/14/15 times, P1, K8, P1, (P1, K1) 3 times.

2nd and every alt row: P6, K1, P8, K1, P to end.

3rd row: (P1, K1) 13/14/15 times, P1, K8, P1, (K1, P1) 3 times.

5th row: (K1, P1) 13/14/15 times, P1, C4B, P1, (P1, K1) 3 times.

7th row: As 3rd row.

8th row: P6, K1, P8, K1, P to end.

These 8 rows form the patt.

Work as Right Front from ** to **.

Shape armhole and commence front slope as follows:

Next row: Cast off 4/5/6, patt to last 18 sts, work 2 tog, patt to end.

Complete as for Right Front working from *** to end.

BACK

Using No 10 needles, cast on 78/84/90 sts.

Work in K1, P1 rib for 3/3¼/3½ ins.

Next row: Rib 9/12/15, (inc in next st, rib 14) 4 times, inc in next st, rib to end (83/89/95 sts).

Change to No 8 needles and proceed in *all-over patt* as follows:

1st row: * K1, P1, rep from * to last st, K1.

2nd row: P.

3rd row: * P1, K1, rep from * to last st, P1.

4th row: P.

These 4 rows form the patt.

Continue in patt until work measures same as Fronts up to armhole shaping.

Shape armholes by casting off 4/5/6 sts at beg of next 2 rows. Dec 1 st at both ends of next and every alt row until 63/67/71 sts remain.

Continue on these sts until work measures same as Fronts up to shoulder shaping.

Cast off all across.

SLEEVES

Using No 10 needles, cast on 38/42/44 sts.

Work in K 1, P 1 rib for 3 ins.

Next row: Rib 3/5/6, (inc in next st, rib 7) 4 times, inc in next st, rib to end (43/47/49 sts).

Change to No 8 needles and proceed in *all-over patt* as on Back, inc 1 st at both ends of 5th and every following 7th/8th/8th row until there are 67/71/73 sts.

Continue on these sts until work measures 15½/16½/17½ ins from beg.

Shape top by casting off 2 sts at beg of next 8 rows. Dec 1 st at both ends of next and every alt row until 23/23/21 sts remain. Work 1 row.

Cast off 3 sts at beg of next 4 rows.

Cast off.

FRONT BAND

Using No 10 needles, cast on 9 sts.

1st row: K 2, (P 1, K 1) 3 times, K 1.

2nd row: (K 1, P 1) 4 times, K 1.

3rd row: Rib 3, cast off 3, rib to end.

4th row: Rib 3, cast on 3, rib to end.

Continue in rib, working a buttonhole as on 3rd and 4th rows on following 17th and 18th/17th and 18th/15th and 16th rows from previous buttonhole until 7/7/8 buttonholes *in all* have been worked.

Continue without further buttonholes until work measures 41/43/45 ins (not stretched) from beg.

Cast off in rib.

MAKE UP

Block and press work on wrong side using a warm iron and damp cloth. Using a back-stitch seam join shoulder, side, and sleeve seams, stitch sleeves into position. Using a flat seam stitch front band into position. Attach buttons to correspond with buttonholes. Press all seams.

LUMBER JACKET
Illustrated in Plate 12a

17 oz Double Knitting. Two No 10 and two No 8 needles. One 20-inch open-ended zipp fastener. Two buttons. Bust, 32/34/36 ins. Length, 21/21/21 ins. Sleeve seam, 17/17½/18 ins.

This garment must be worked at a tension of 5½ sts and 7½ rows to one square inch on No 8 needles measured over stocking stitch (6 sts and 8 rows over patt).

POCKET TOPS

Using No 8 needles, cast on 19 sts. K 4 rows.
Next row: K9, wf, K2 tog, K to end.
K 4 rows.
Break off wool. Slip sts on to a length of wool and leave.

RIGHT FRONT

Using No 10 needles, cast on 48/50/54 sts.
1st row: K5, * P1, K1, rep from * to last st, P1.
2nd row: * K1, P1, rep from * to last 6 sts, K6.
Rep these 2 rows 16 times, inc 1 st at beg of last row on *middle size* only (48/51/54 sts).

Change to No 8 needles and proceed in *all-over* patt as follows:
1st row: K5, P to end.
2nd row: K.
3rd row: K5, * P2, K1, rep from * to last st, P1.
4th row: K1, * P1, K2, rep from * to last 5 sts, K5.
These 4 rows form the patt.
Continue in patt until work measures 13½/13¼/13 ins. from beg finishing at side edge.

Shape armhole by casting off 6/6/7 sts. Dec 1 st at armhole edge on next and every alt row until 36/38/40 sts remain.
Continue on these sts until work measures 2½/2¾/3 ins from beg of armhole shaping, finishing at front edge.

Place pocket top as follows:
Next row: K5, patt 6/7/8, cast off 20 sts, patt to end.
Next row: Patt 6/7/8, slip sts from pocket top on to left-hand

needle with wrong side of work facing, work in patt across these sts, patt to last 5 sts, K5.

Continue in patt until work measures 20 ins along front edge, finishing at front edge.

Shape neck by casting off 6/7/8 sts at beg of next row then dec 1 st at neck edge on every row until 23/25/26 sts remain.

Continue on these sts until work measures $7\frac{1}{2}/7\frac{3}{4}/8$ ins from beg of armhole shaping, finishing at armhole edge.

Shape shoulder as follows:

1st row: Cast off 7/8/8 sts, work to end.

2nd row: Work all across.

Rep these 2 rows once.

Cast off.

LEFT FRONT

Complete to match Right Front, reversing all shapings, *noting* that the first two rows of rib will be:

1st row: * P1, K1, rep from * to last 6 sts, P1, K5.

2nd row: K6, * P1, K1, rep from * to end;

and the first 4 rows of patt will be:

1st row: P to last 5 sts, K5.

2nd row: K.

3rd row: P1, * K1, P2, rep from * to last 5 sts, K5.

4th row: K5, * K2, P1, rep from * to last st, K1.

BACK

Using No 10 needles, cast on 90/96/102 sts.

Work 33 rows in K1, P1 rib.

Next row: Rib 5/8/11, (inc in next st, rib 15) 5 times, inc in next st, rib to end (96/102/108 sts).

Change to No 8 needles and proceed in patt as follows:

1st row: P.

2nd row: K.

3rd row: P1, * K1, P2, rep from * to last 2 sts, K1, P1.

4th row: K1, * P1, K2, rep from * to last 2 sts, P1, K1.

These 4 rows form the patt.

Continue in patt until work measures same as Fronts up to armhole shaping.

Shape armholes by casting off 6/6/7 sts at beg of next 2 rows. Dec 1 st at both ends of next and every alt row until 72/76/80 sts remain.

Continue on these sts until work measures same as Fronts up to shoulder shaping.

Shape shoulders by casting off 7/8/8 sts at beg of next 4 rows, 9/9/10 sts at beg of following 2 rows.

Cast off.

SLEEVES

Using No 10 needles, cast on 46 sts.

Work in K1, P1 rib for 3 ins.

Next row: Rib 2, (inc in next st, rib 5) 7 times, inc in next st, rib to end (54 sts).

Change to No 8 needles and proceed in patt as on Back, inc 1 st at both ends of 5th and every following 9th/8th/7th row until there are 76/80/84 sts on needle.

Continue on these sts until work measures 17/17½/18 ins from beg.

Shape top by casting off 3 sts at beg of next 6 rows, 2 sts at beg of next 6 rows. Dec 1 st at both ends of every alt row until 24/26/28 sts remain.

Cast off 4/5/5 sts at beg of next 4 rows.

Cast off.

POCKETS

Using No 8 needles, cast on 19 sts.

Work in stocking stitch for 3/3¼/3½ ins.

Cast off.

COLLAR

Using a back-stitch seam join shoulders of Back and Fronts.

Using No 10 needles, with right side of work facing, *knit up* 77/81/85 sts round neck.

1st row: K2, * P1, K1, rep from * to last st, K1.

2nd row: * K1, P1, rep from * to last st, K1.

Rep these 2 rows until work measures 2 ins from beg.

Change to No 8 needles and continue until work measures 3/3¼/3½ ins from beg.
Cast off in rib.

MAKE UP

Omitting ribbing, block and press. Using a back-stitch seam join side and sleeve seams and stitch sleeves into position. Using a flat seam stitch zipp into position. Stitch pockets into position on wrong side of work. Attach buttons to correspond with buttonholes. Press all seams.

CHILD'S FAIR ISLE BERET AND GLOVES
Illustrated in Plate 12b

Beret

1 oz Light Natural, small oddments of Blue, Yellow, Pale Yellow, Bottle Green, Scarlet, and White Fair Isle Fingering. Set of four No 11 needles (with points at both ends).
Diameter, 8 ins. Head-band (when slightly stretched) 17 ins.

This garment must be worked at a tension of 8 sts and 10 rows to one square inch on No 11 needles measured over stocking stitch.

Using Light Natural, cast on 104 sts (36 sts on first needle and 34 sts on each of 2nd and 3rd needles).

Work 8 rounds in K 1, P 1 rib.

Next round: * K 1, inc in next st knitwise, rep from * to end of round (156 sts).

K 2 rounds.

Proceed to work *Fair Isle patt* (every round K) joining in and breaking off colours as required.

1st round: * 2 LN, 1 B, 1 LN, rep from * to end of round.

2nd round: * 1 LN, 3 B, rep from * to end of round.

3rd round: Using Blue K.

4th round: * 2 B, 2 Y, 1 B, 2 Y, 3 B, 1 Y, 1 B, rep from * to end of round.

5th round: * 2 B, 5 Y, 2 B, 3 Y, rep from * to end of round.

6th round: * 2 PY, 1 BG, 3 PY, 1 BG, 2 PY, 1 BG, 1 PY, 1 BG, rep from * to end of round.

7th round: * 3PY, 1BG, 1PY, 1BG, 3PY, 3BG, rep from * to end of round.

8th round: * (1S, 3W) twice, 2S, 1W, 1S, rep from * to end of round.

9th–15th rounds: As rounds 7–1 in backward rotation i.e., 7, 6, 5, 4, etc.

16th and 17th rounds: Using LN, K.

18th round: * 3LN, 3BG, rep from * to end of round.

19th round: * 3S, 3LN, rep from * to end of round.

20th round: As 18th round.

21st and 22nd rounds: Using LN, K.

23rd–37th rounds: As 1st–15th.

38th round: Using LN, * K1, (K2 tog, K2) 6 times, K1, rep from * to end of round (120 sts).

39th round: Using LN, K.

40th round: * (2Y, 1B) 3 times, 1Y, (1B, 2Y) 3 times, 1B, rep from * to end of round.

41st round: * 1Y, (1B, 2Y) 3 times, 1Y, (1B, 2Y) 3 times, rep from * to end of round.

42nd round: * (1B, 2Y) 6 times, 1B, 1Y, rep from * to end of round.

43rd round: * (2Y, 1B) 3 times, 2B, (2Y, 1B) 3 times, rep from * to end of round.

44th round: * 1Y, (1B, 2Y) twice, 1B, sl1, K2 tog Y, psso, (1B, 2Y) 3 times, rep from * to end of round (108 sts).

45th round: * (1BG, 2PY) three times, 1PY, (1BG, 2PY) twice, 1BG, 1PY, rep from * to end of round.

46th round: * (2PY, 1BG twice, 1PY, sl1, K2 tog PY, psso, 1PY, (1BG, 2PY) twice, 1BG, rep from * to end of round (96 sts).

47th round: * 1PY, (1BG, 2PY) 5 times, rep from * to end of round.

48th round: * (1S, 2W) twice, sl1, K2 tog S, psso, (2W, 1S) twice, 1W, rep from * to end of round (84 sts).

49th round: * (2W, 1S) twice, 2S, (2W, 1S) twice, rep from * to end of round.

50th round: * 1W, 1S, 2W, 1S, sl1, K2 tog S, psso, (1S, 2W) twice, rep from * to end of round (72 sts).

51st round: * 1S, 2W, 5S, 2W, 1S, 1W, rep from * to end of round.

1a. Elongated check pattern (p. 32)

1b. Broken check pattern (p. 33)

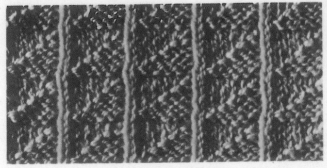

1c. Triangular stitch (p. 33)

2a. Vandyke pattern (p. 33)

2b. Vandyke and check pattern (p. 34)

2c. Diagonal striped pattern (p. 35)

3a. Embossed diamond stitch (p. 43)

3b. Embossed ribbed pattern (p. 43)

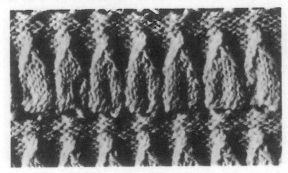

3c. Embossed bell pattern (p. 45)

4a. Diamond eyelet pattern (p. 45)

4b. Crown of glory pattern (p. 46)

4c. Feather pattern (p. 47)

5a. Beech leaf pattern (p. 47)

5b. Purl 1 twist 2 pattern (p. 48)

5c. Purl 1 twist 3 pattern (p. 49)

6a. Single cable pattern (p. 50)

6b. Wave cable pattern (p. 50)

6c. Double rope cable pattern (p. 51)

7a. Branch cable pattern (p. 52)

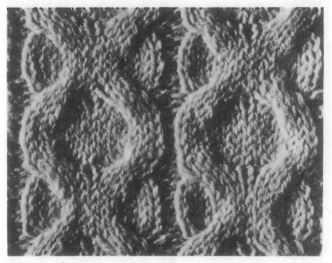

7b. Medallion cable pattern (p. 52)

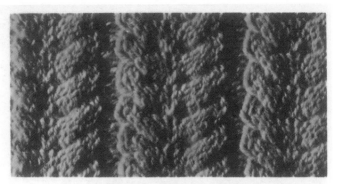

8a. Wheat ear cable pattern (p. 52)

8b. Cable check pattern (p. 53)

8c. Diagonal wave pattern (p. 53)

9a. Simple bobble pattern (p. 54)

9b. Trefoil bobble pattern (p. 55)

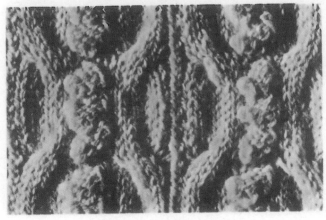

9c. Fancy cable pattern (p. 55)

10. Baby's layette: Coat, bonnet, mitts, and bootees (p. 67)

11a. Baby's layette: Dress, vest, and pilch (p. 72)

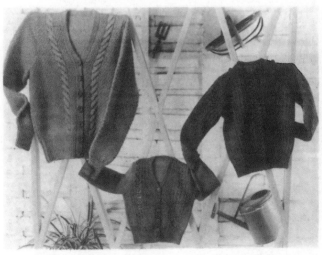

11b. Child's cardigan in three sizes (p. 77), Child's jersey (p. 81), Girl's cable and all-over patterned cardigan (p. 88)

12a. Lumber jacket (p. 92). Polo neck sweater (p. 84).
Pullover with V neck (p. 86), for boys or girls

12b. Child's Fair Isle beret and gloves (p. 95),
Man's Fair Isle scarf and gloves (p. 167)

13a. Lady's vest (p. 99), Lady's lace knickers (p.103) Lady's knickers in rib and lace (p.101)

13b. Two-ply jumper with square neck (p. 103)

14a. Classic twin set (p. 107)

14b. Classic cardigan with low V neckline (p. 113)

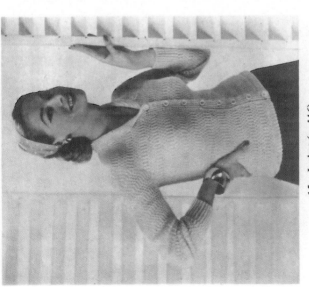

16a. Lady's outsize twin set (p. 124)

16b. Basic suit in three sizes (p. 133),
Dog's coat (p. 182)

52nd round: * 2W, 2S, sl I, K2 tog S, psso, 2S, 2W, I S, rep from * to end of round (60 sts).

53rd round: * 2PY, 5BG, 2PY, I BG, rep from * to end of round.

54th round: * 2PY, I BG, sl I, K2 tog BG, psso, I BG, 2PY, I BG, rep from * to end of round (48 sts).

55th round: * 2PY, 3BG, 2PY, I BG, rep from * to end of round.

56th round: * 2PY, sl I, K2 tog BG, psso, 2PY, I BG, rep from * to end of round (36 sts).

57th round: * 2Y, I B, rep from * to end of round.

58th round: * I Y, sl I, K2 tog B, psso, I Y, I B, rep from * to end of round (24 sts).

59th round: * sl I, K2 tog B, psso, I B, rep from * to end of round (12 sts).

60th round: * K2 tog B, rep from * to end of round (6 sts).

Slip wool through remaining sts and fasten off securely.

To finish: Fasten off all ends.

Cut a circle of cardboard 8 ins in diameter, insert this into beret and using a hot iron and wet cloth press work on right side. Remove cardboard.

Gloves

Materials and tension: as Beret.

RIGHT GLOVE

Using LN, cast on 38 sts, 12 sts on 1st needle and 13 sts on each of 2nd and 3rd needles.

Work in rounds of K I, P I rib for 2½ ins.

Next round: * K3, inc in next st, K2, inc in next st, rep from * to last 3 sts, K3, (48 sts).

K2 rounds.

Proceed in *Fair Isle patt* as follows:

1st–3rd rounds: As rounds 18–20 on beret.

4th and 5th rounds: Using LN, K.

6th–13th rounds: As 1st–8th rounds on beret.**

14th round: (3PY, I BG, I PY, I BG, 3PY, 3BG) twice, 2PY, sl next 7 sts on to a safety pin and leave, cast on 7, 3BG, 3PY, I BG, I PY, I BG, 3PY, 3BG.

15th–20th rounds: *** As rounds 6–1 on beret worked in backward rotation, i.e., 6, 5, 4, etc.

21st–27th rounds: As rounds 16–22 on beret.

Using LN, for remainder of glove work for fingers as follows, *noting* that sts should be divided on to three needles.

Little finger

Next round: K6, sl all but last 6 sts on to a length of wool and leave, K6.

K 18 rounds.

Shape top as follows:

Next round: (K2 tog) 6 times.

Thread wool through remaining sts and fasten off securely.

3rd finger

Sl 6 sts from each end of length of wool on to needles, with palm of glove facing.

K11, inc in next st (13 sts).

K25 rounds.

Shape top as follows:

Next round: K1, (K2 tog) 6 times.

Thread wool through remaining sts and fasten off securely.

Middle finger: As 3rd finger *noting* that 29 rounds in place of 25 rounds should be worked.

1st finger

Sl remaining 12 sts on to needles.

Complete as for 3rd finger.

Thumb

Sl 7 sts from safety pin on to needle, *knit up* 7 sts from 7 cast on sts.

K 23 rounds.

Shape top as follows:

Next round: (K2 tog) 7 times.

Thread wool through remaining sts and fasten off securely.

LEFT GLOVE

Work as right glove until ** is reached.

Next round: 3PY, 1BG, 1PY, 1BG, 3PY, 3BG, 3PY, sl next 7 sts on to a safety pin and leave.

98

Cast on 7 sts, 2BG, (3PY, 1BG, 1PY, 1BG, 3PY, 3BG) twice.
Complete as for right glove working from *** to end.

Ringing the Changes

The same instructions may be used for a plain glove, the Fair
Isle portion being worked in self-colour stocking stitch throughout.

To knit a glove for a larger child, use 4-ply fingering and
No 10 in place of No 11 needles.

LADY'S VEST WITH BUILT-UP TOP OR
SHOULDER STRAPS
Illustrated in Plate 13a

5 oz Vest Wool. Two No 12 and two No 10 needles.
To fit 33–35 inch bust. Length from top of shoulder, 30 ins.

This garment must be worked at a tension of 7½ sts and
9½ rows to one square inch on No 10 needles, measured over
stocking stitch.

FRONT

Using No 10 needles and *double* wool, cast on 112 sts.
Break off 1 ball of wool.
Proceed in rib as follows:
1st row: K1, * K5, P2, rep from * to last 6 sts, K6.
2nd row: K1, * P5, K2, rep from * to last 6 sts P5, K1.
Rep these 2 rows until work measures 13 ins from beg, finishing at end of a 2nd row.

Change to No 12 needles.
Next row: K2, * P1, K1, rep from * to end.
Work this row 31 times more.

Change to No 10 needles and proceed in *fancy rib* as follows:
1st row: K1, * K1, wf, sl 1, K2 tog, psso, wf, K1, P2, rep from
* to last 6 sts, K1, wf, sl 1, K2 tog, psso, wf, K2.
2nd, 4th, and 6th rows: K1, * P5, K2, rep from * to last 6 sts,
P5, K1.

3rd row: K1, * K2, wf, sl1, K1, psso, K1, P2, rep from * to last 6 sts, K2, wf, sl1, K1, psso, K2.

5th row: K1, * K5, P2, rep from * to last 6 sts, K6.

These 6 rows form the patt.

Continue in patt until work measures 22 ins from beg, finishing so that right side of work will be facing when working next row.

Special Note. If an evening vest is required, slip the stitches on to a length of wool and leave for present. Work back to match, slip the stitches from the front on to the same needle as the back and work picot edge as given for neckband on these stitches.

Make up as vest with built-up top, adding ribbon for shoulder straps.

Keeping patt correct, *shape armholes* by casting off 8 sts at beg of next 2 rows. Dec 1 st at both ends of every row until 80 sts remain, every alt row until 70 sts remain.**

Shape neck as follows:

Next row: Patt 22, cast off 26, patt to end.

Continue on *each* group of 22 sts, dec 1 st at neck edge on every row until 15 sts remain; every alt row until 13 sts remain.

Continue on these sts until work measures 8 ins from beg of armhole shaping.

Cast off.

BACK

Work as front until ** is reached.

Continue on these 69 sts until work measures 28 ins from beg.

Shape neck as follows:

Next row: Patt 21, cast off 28, patt to end.

Continue on *each* group of 21 sts, dec 1 st at neck edge on every row until 13 sts remain.

Continue on these sts until work measures 8 ins from beg of armhole shaping.

Cast off.

NECKBAND

Using a flat seam join right shoulder seam.

Using No 12 needles, with right side of work facing, *knit up* 165 sts round neck.

Work *picot edge* as follows:

1st row: P.

2nd row: K I, * wf, K2 tog, rep from * to end.

3rd row: P.

Cast off loosely.

Join left shoulder seam.

ARMBANDS

Using No 12 needles, with right side of work facing, *knit up* 133 sts round armhole.

Work picot edge as given for neckband.

Work second armband in same manner.

MAKE UP

With wrong side of work facing, block fabric by pinning out round edges. Press lightly using a warm iron and damp cloth. Using a flat seam join side seams. Fold over picot edges at row of holes and stitch down on wrong side of work.

Press all seams.

LADY'S KNICKERS
IN RIB AND LACE OR ALL-OVER PATTERN
Illustrated in Plate 13a

4 oz Vest Wool. Two No 12 and two No 10 needles. Length of elastic.

To fit 35–37 inch hips. Length at side, 18 ins.

This garment must be worked at a tension of 7½ sts and 9½ rows to one square inch on No 10 needles, measured over stocking stitch.

LEFT LEG

Using No 12 needles, cast on 126 sts.

1st row: K2, * P I, K I, rep from * to end.

Work this row 19 times more.

Change to No 10 needles and proceed in rib with *fancy rib panels* as follows:

1st row: K I, (K 5, P 2) 7 times, (K I, wf, sl I, K 2 tog, psso, wf, K I, P 2) 4 times, (K 5, P 2) 6 times, K 6.

2nd and 4th rows: K I, * P 5, K 2, rep from * to last 6 sts, P 5, K I.

3rd row: K I, (K 5, P 2) 7 times, (K 2, wf, sl I, K I, psso, K I, P 2) 4 times, (K 5, P 2) 6 times, K 6.

5th row: Inc in first st, * K 5, P 2, rep from * to last 6 sts, K 5, inc in last st (128 sts).

6th row: K 2, * P 5, K 2, rep from * to end.

Keeping patt and knit st edges correct throughout, inc I st at both ends of next and every alt row until there are 152 sts, working extra sts in rib.

Work I row.

Dec I st at both ends of next and every following 4th row until 102 sts remain.

Continue on these sts until work measures 11 ins from first dec row, finishing so that right side of work will be facing when working next row.**

Shape back as follows:

1st row: Patt to last 10 sts, turn.

2nd row: Patt to end.

3rd row: Patt to last 20 sts, turn.

Continue in this manner until the row 'Patt to last 90 sts, turn' has been worked.

Next row: Inc in first st, patt to last st, inc in last st (104 sts).

Change to No 12 needles and work 12 rows in rib as at commencement.

Next row: (on which holes for elastic are worked), K 2, * wf, K 2 tog, P I, K I, rep from * to last 2 sts, wf, K 2 tog.

Work 4 more rows in rib.

Cast off in rib.

RIGHT LEG

Work as left leg until ** is reached.

Work I row.

Shape Back and complete as for left leg, *noting* that 11 rows in place of 12 rows in rib should be worked before making holes for elastic.

Using No 10 needles, cast on 3 sts.

1st row: Inc in first 2 sts, K1.

2nd and alt rows: K1, P to last st, K1.

3rd row: Inc in first st, K to last 2 sts, inc in next st, K1.

Continue in this manner, inc 1 st at both ends of every alt row until there are 25 sts.

Work 1 row.

Dec 1 st at both ends of next and every alt row until 3 sts remain. Cast off.

MAKE UP

Omitting K1, P1 rib, block and press each piece. Using a flat seam join front and back seams from waist to first dec. Stitch gusset into position. Join remainder of leg seams. Thread elastic through holes at waist. Press seams.

For lace knickers, in place of rows 1–6, page 102, work rows 1–6 as follows:

1st row: K1, (K1, wf, sl1, K2 tog, psso, wf, K1, P2) 17 times, K1, wf, sl1, K2 tog, psso, wf, K2.

2nd and 4th rows: K1, * P5, K2, rep from * to last 6 sts, P5, K1.

3rd row: K1, (K2, wf, sl1, K1, psso, K1, P2) 17 times, K2, wf, sl1, K1, psso, K2.

5th row: Inc in first st, * K5, P2, rep from * to last 6 sts, K5, inc in last st (128 sts).

6th row: K2, * P5, K2, rep from * to end.

TWO-PLY JUMPER WITH SQUARE NECK
TWO NECKLINES — ONE FOR DAY — THE OTHER FOR COCKTAIL TIME

Illustrated in Plate 13b

4 oz 2-ply Fingering. Two No 13 and two No 11 needles.
Set of four No 13 needles with points at both ends.
Bust, 34 ins. Length, 20 ins. Sleeve, 3 ins.

This garment must be worked at a tension of $8\frac{1}{2}$ sts and

10½ rows to one square inch on No 11 needles measured over stocking stitch.

FRONT

Using No 11 needles, cast on 133 sts.

Proceed in rib as follows:

1st row: P2, * KB3, P3, rep from * to last 5 sts, KB3, P2.

2nd row: K2, * PB3, K3, rep from * to last 5 sts, PB3, K2.

Rep these 2 rows until work measures 3 ins from beg finishing at end of a 2nd row.

Next row: P2, (KB3, PI, P2 tog) 6 times, (KB3, P3) 9 times, KB3, (P2 tog, PI, KB3) 6 times, P2 (121 sts).

Next row: (K2, PB3) 7 times, (K3, PB3) 9 times, (K2, PB3) 6 times, K2.

Keeping rib correct, continue until work measures 4½ ins from beg.

Change to No 13 needles and continue until work measures 7½ ins from beg, finishing so that right side of work will be facing when working next row.

Change to No 11 needles and work 4 rows.

Keeping rib correct throughout, *shape* as follows:

1st row: (P2, KB3) 6 times, PI, MI, PI, (KB3, P3) 9 times, KB3, PI, MI, PI, (KB3, P2) 6 times.

2nd row: (K2, PB3) 6 times, (K3, PB3) 11 times, (K2, PB3) 5 times, K2.

3rd row: (P2, KB3) 6 times, (P3, KB3) 11 times, (P2, K3) 5 times, P2.

4th row: As 2nd row.

5th and 6th rows: As 3rd and 4th.

7th row: (P2, KB3) 5 times, PI, MI, PI, (KB3, P3) 11 times, KB3, PI, MI, PI, (KB3, P2) 5 times.

8th row: (K2, PB3) 5 times, (K3, PB3) 13 times, (K2, PB3) 4 times, K2.

Keeping rib correct, work 4 rows.

Next row: (P2, KB3) 4 times, PI, MI, PI, (KB3, P3) 13 times, KB3, PI, MI, PI, (KB3, P2) 4 times.

Next row: (K2, PB3) 4 times, (K3, PB3) 15 times, (K2, PB3) 3 times, K2.

Keeping rib correct, work 4 rows.

Continue inc in this manner on next and every following 6th row until the row 'P2, KB3, P1, M1, P1, (KB3, P3) 19 times, KB3, P1, M1, P1, KB3, P2' has been worked, and there are 133 sts.

Work 5 rows.

Working extra sts into rib patt throughout, inc 1 st at both ends of next and every following 6th row until there are 141 sts.

Continue on these sts until work measures 14½ ins from beg, finishing so that right side of work will be facing when working next row.

Shape front as follows:

Next row: Rib 45, turn, and keeping rib patt correct proceed on these 45 sts, casting off 9 sts at beg of next and every alt row until all 45 sts have been cast off.

Next row: With right side of work facing, rejoin wool to remaining sts, work to end.

Next row: Rib 45, turn, and working on these 45 sts shape to match other half of front.

Rejoin wool and proceed in rib patt on remaining group of 51 sts for 4 ins. (For cocktail neckline work for 2 in place of 4 ins).

Cast off.

BACK

Work as front, working on centre group of 51 sts after shaping on back has been worked for 6½ ins in place of 4 ins.

SLEEVES

Using No 13 needles and the through sts method, cast on 109 sts.

1st row: P.

2nd row: K.

3rd row: P.

4th row: P.

Proceed in patt as follows:

1st row: * P1, (P2 tog) 3 times, won, K1, (wf, K1) 4 times, wrn, (P2 tog) 3 times, rep from * to last st, P1.

2nd row: P.

3rd row: K.

4th row: P.

These 4 rows form the patt.

Continue in patt until work measures 2 ins from beg.

Change to No 11 needles and continue in patt until work measures
3 ins from beg. (Mark this point with a length of coloured
wool.) Still working in patt, continue until work measures
5¼ ins from point marked with coloured wool.

Cast off loosely.

NECKBAND

Fold in scalloped edge along top of sleeve. Press firmly to form
straight edge and neatly flat stitch scalloped edge down on
wrong side of work.

Using a back-stitch seam join edge of sleeve from point marked
with coloured wool to shaped edge of front and back.

Using a back-stitch seam join front and back pieces into position
along top of sleeves, thus leaving square neck opening.

Using set of No 13 needles, *knit up* 123 sts (163 sts for cocktail
neckline) round neck.

1st and 2nd rounds: K.

3rd round: K 1, * wf, K 2 tog, rep from * to end.

4th and 5th rounds: K.

Cast off *very* loosely.

MAKE UP

Block fabric and press lightly on wrong side using a warm iron
and damp cloth. Fold neckband at row of holes and neatly
stitch on wrong side of work, cast-off edge to knitted-up edge
to form picot. Using a back-stitch seam join side seams and
ends of sleeves. Press all seams.

CLASSIC TWIN SET WITH FULLY FASHIONED
SHOULDERS AND DART SHAPINGS

Illustrated in Plate 14a

Jumper

6/7/7 oz 3-ply Fingering. Two No 14 and two No 12 needles.
Four-inch zipp fastener.

Bust, 32/34/36 ins. Length, 18¾/19/19¼ ins. Sleeve, 5 ins.

This garment must be worked at a tension of 8½ sts and 10½
rows to one square inch on No 12 needles measured over stocking
stitch.

FRONT

Using No 14 needles, cast on 106/114/122 sts.

Work in rib for 3½ ins as follows:

1st and every row: * K I, P I, rep from * to end.

On the last row of the ribbing inc I st (107/115/123 sts).

Change to No 12 needles and work in stocking stitch with *dart
  shapings* as follows:

1st row: K.

2nd row: P.

3rd row: K 35/38/40, M I, K to last 35/38/40 sts, M I, K to end.

4th row: P.

Rep 1st–4th rows 14 times more (137/145/153 sts).

Continue on these sts until work measures 12 ins from beg,
finishing at end of a P row.

Shape armholes as follows:

1st and 2nd rows: Cast off 7/8/9 sts, work to end.

3rd row: K 3, K 2 tog tbl, K to last 5 sts, K 2 tog, K 3.

4th row: P.

Rep 3rd and 4th rows until 109/115/121 sts remain.

Continue on these sts until work measures 5/5¼/5½ ins from beg
of armhole shaping, finishing at end of a P row.

Shape neck as follows:

Next row: K 42/45/48, cast off 25, K to end.

Proceed on *each* group of 42/45/48 sts as follows:

Dec 1 st at neck edge on next and every alt row until 36/39/42 sts remain. Continue on these sts until work measures 6¾/7/7¼ ins from beg of armhole shaping, finishing at armhole edge.

Shape shoulder by casting off 12/13/14 sts at beg of next and every alt row until all sts are cast off.

BACK

Work as instructions for front until 3½/3¾/4 ins have been completed from beg of armhole shaping, finishing at end of a P row (109/115/121 sts).

Divide for back opening as follows:
Next row: K54/57/60 cast off 1, K to end.
Knitting stitch at inside edge on every row, proceed on *each* group of 54/57/60 sts until work measures same as front up to shoulder shaping.
Cast off all across.

SLEEVES

Using No 14 needles, cast on 86/90/94 sts.
Work in rib as on front for 1 inch.

Change to No 12 needles and proceed in stocking stitch, inc 1 st at both ends of 3rd and every following 3rd row until there are 106/110/114 sts on needle. Continue on these sts until work measures 5 ins from beg.

Shape top by casting off 3 sts at beg of next 6 rows. Dec 1 st at both ends of every row until 76/80/84 sts remain; every alt row until 64/68/72 sts remain; then every following 3rd row until 42/46/50 sts remain.
Cast off 6/6/7 sts at beg of next 6 rows.
Cast off.

Special Note. If long sleeves are required for the jumper, using No 14 needles cast on 52/56/60 sts and work as instructions for sleeves of cardigan on page 110, noting there will be 4 sts less throughout the knitting of the sleeve (106/110/114 when the increases are completed and 42/46/50 before the final 'cast off 6/6/7 sts at beginning of next 6 rows' is worked).

108

NECKBAND

Using a back-stitch seam join shoulders of back and front.

Using No 14 needles, with right side of work facing *knit up* 120/124/128 sts round neck. Work in K1, P1 rib for ¾ inch. Cast off in rib.

TO MAKE UP

Omitting ribbing, with wrong side of work facing, block and press each piece using a warm iron and damp cloth. Using a back-stitch seam join side and sleeve seams and stitch sleeves into position, placing sleeve seam ½ inch to front of side seam. Stitch zipp fastener into back opening. Press all seams.

V Neck Cardigan

8/9/9 oz 3-ply Fingering. Two No 14 and two No 12 needles. Nine buttons.

Bust, 32/34/36 ins. Length, 19¾/20/20¼ ins. Sleeve, 18 ins. Tension – as Jumper.

BACK

Using No 14 needles, cast on 106/114/122 sts.

Working 4¼ ins of rib in place of 3½ ins, and making work ¾ inch longer than back of jumper up to armhole shaping, work as back of jumper until the point 'Divide for back opening' is reached (109/115/121 sts).

Continue on these sts until work measures 7/7¼/7½ ins from beg of armhole shaping.

Cast off all across.

RIGHT FRONT

Using No 14 needles, cast on 52/56/60 sts.

Work in rib as on front of jumper for 4¼ ins.

Change to No 12 needles and work in stocking stitch with *dart shapings* as follows:

1st row: K.

2nd row: P.

3rd row: K to last 35/38/40 sts, M1, K to end.

4th row: P.

Rep 1st–4th rows 13 times more 66/70/74 sts **.

Shape front slope as follows:

Dec 1 st at beg of next and every following 8th row until work measures 12¾ ins from beg finishing at end of a K row. Still dec at front edge on every 8th row from previous dec as before, *shape armhole* by casting off 8/9/10 sts at beg of next row. Dec 1 st at armhole edge as on back, on next and every alt row until 9/10/11 dec have been worked at armhole edge.

Continue without further dec at armhole edge but still dec at front edge on every *6th/8th/10th* row from previous dec until 36/39/42 sts remain.

Continue on these sts until work measures 7/7½/7½ ins from beg of armhole shaping, finishing at armhole edge.

Shape shoulder by casting off 12/13/14 sts at beg of next and every alt row until all sts are cast off.

LEFT FRONT

Using No 14 needles, cast on 52/56/60 sts.
Work in ribbing to match right front for 4¼ ins.

Change to No 12 needles and proceed in stocking stitch with *dart shaping* as follows:

1st row: K.
2nd row: P.
3rd row: K35/38/40 M1, K to end.
4th row: P.

Rep 1st–4th rows 13 times more (66/70/74 sts).

Complete to match right front, reversing front slope, armhole and shoulder shapings.

SLEEVES

Using No 14 needles, cast on 56/60/64 sts.
Work in K1, P1 rib as on right front for 3 ins.

Change to No 12 needles and proceed in stocking stitch inc 1 st at both ends of 5th and every following 5th row until there are 110/114/118 sts on needle. Continue on these sts until work measures 18 ins from beg.

Shape top as on jumper sleeve, *noting* that there will be 4 more sts after each set of dec has been completed.

Cast off.

Work other sleeve in same manner.

FRONT BAND

Using No 14 needles, cast on 13 sts.

1st row: K2, * P1, K1, rep from * to last st, K1.

2nd row: K1, * P1, K1, rep from * to end.

3rd and 4th rows: As 1st and 2nd.

5th row: Rib 5, cast off 3, rib to end.

6th row: Rib 5, cast on 3, rib to end.

Continue in rib, working a buttonhole as on 5th and 6th rows on 15th and 16th rows from previous buttonhole, until 9 buttonholes in all have been completed.

Continue in rib without further buttonholes until work measures 44/44½/45 ins (not stretched) from beg.

Cast off in rib.

TO MAKE UP

Omitting ribbing, with wrong side of work facing, block and press each piece using a warm iron and damp cloth. Using a backstitch seam join shoulder, side and sleeve seams and stitch sleeves into position, placing sleeve seam ½ inch to front of side seam. Using a flat seam neatly stitch front band into position. Attach buttons. Press all seams.

Cardigan (high neck version)

8/9/9 oz 3-ply Fingering. Two No 14 and two No 12 needles. Twelve buttons.

Bust, 32/34/36 ins. Length, 19¾/20/20¼ ins. Sleeve, 18 ins.

Tension – as Jumper.

BACK AND SLEEVES

Work as instruction for V neck Cardigan, page 109 and page 110.

RIGHT FRONT

Work as instructions on page 109-110 to **.

111

Continue on these sts until work measures 12¾ ins from beg, finishing at end of a K row. *Shape armhole* by casting off 8/9/10 sts at beg of next row, then dec one st at armhole edge on next and every alt row until 49/51/53 sts remain.

Continue on these sts until work measures 5½/5½/5½ ins from beginning of armhole shaping, finishing at front edge.

Shape neck by casting off 7/6/5 sts at beg of next row, then dec one st at beg of next and every alt row until 36/39/42 sts remain.

Continue on these sts until work measures 7/7½/7½ ins from beg of armhole shaping, finishing at armhole edge.

Shape shoulder by casting off 12/13/14 sts at beg of next and every alt row until all sts are worked off.

LEFT FRONT

Work to match right front reversing all shapings, working dart shaping as left front, page 110.

RIGHT FRONT BAND

Work as front band on page 111 until 11th row after 11th buttonhole has been worked. Sl sts on to a safety pin and leave for present.

LEFT FRONT BAND

Omitting buttonholes, work as right front band.

NECKBAND

Using a back-stitch seam join shoulders of back and fronts.

Using No 13 needle, rib across 13 sts at top of right front band, using same needle, with right side of work facing *knit up* 119/123/127 sts round neck, rib across sts at top of left front band.

Next row: As 2nd row of right front band.

Work 1st and 2nd rows of right front band, twice.

On next 2 rows work buttonhole as on 5th and 6th rows on front band.

Work 4 more rows in rib.

Cast off in rib.

MAKE UP

See Cardigan on page III.

CLASSIC CARDIGAN WITH LOW V NECKLINE
Illustrated in Plate 14b

10/11/12 oz 4-ply Fingering. Two No 11 and two No 9 needles. Five buttons. Bust, 34/36/38 ins. Length, 22 ins. Sleeve, 17¼ ins.

This garment must be worked at a tension of 6½ sts and 8½ rows to one square inch on No 9 needles measured over stocking stitch.

RIGHT FRONT

Using No 9 needles, cast on 44/48/52 sts. Proceed in rib as follows:

1st row: K I, * P2, K2, rep from * to last 3 sts, P2, K I.

2nd row: P I, * K2, P2, rep from * to last 3 sts, K2, P I.

Rep these 2 rows until work measures 3½ ins from beg.

Change to No 11 needles and continue repeating rows I and 2 until work measures 6/5¾/5½ ins from beg, finishing at end of a 2nd row.

Change to No 9 needles and work in stocking stitch with cable panel as follows:

1st row: P I, K I0, P I, K I, K2 tog tbl, K to end.

2nd row: P.

3rd row: P I, C2F, K2, C2B, P I, K to end.

4th row: P.

These 4 rows form the patt used on the I2 st cable panel.

5th row: Patt I2, K to last st, inc in last st.

6th row: P to last I2 sts, patt I2.

7th row: Patt I2, K I, K2 tog tbl, K to end.

8th row: P to last I2 sts, patt I2.

9th row: As 5th row.

10th–12th rows: As 2nd–4th.

13th row: Patt I2, K I, K2 tog tbl, K to last st inc in last st.

14th–16th rows: As 2nd–4th.

17th row: As 5th.

18th row: As 2nd.

19th row: Patt 12, K1, K2 tog tbl, K to end.

20th row: As 2nd.

21st row: As 5th.

22nd–24th rows: As 2nd–4th.

Continue in this manner, dec 1 st at front edge as before on next and every following 16th row, *at the same time* working side shapings as before on next and every following 4th row until 8 inc *in all* have been worked at side edge. Continue without further inc at side edge but still dec at front edge as before on every 16th row from previous dec until work measures 15/14¾/14½ ins from beg, finishing at outside edge. Still dec at front edge on every 16th row as before, *shape armhole* by casting off 6/8/10 sts at beg of next row, then dec 1 st at armhole edge on next and every alt row until 8 dec have been worked at armhole edge. Continue without further dec at armhole edge but still dec at front edge on every 16th row from previous dec until 27/30/33 sts remain. Continue on these sts until work measures 7/7¼/7½ ins from beg of armhole shaping, finishing at armhole edge.

Shape shoulder by casting off 9/10/11 sts at beg of next and every alt row until all sts are cast off.

LEFT FRONT

Using No 9 needles cast on 44/48/52 sts and work ribbing to match right front.

Change to No 11 needles and work to match right front reading on rows 1–24, K for P and P for K throughout, thus reversing all shapings, the first 8 rows placing the cable panel and side shapings being as follows:

1st row: K1, P10, K1, P1, P2 tog tbl, P to end.

2nd row: K all across.

3rd row: K1, C2F purlwise, P2, C2B purlwise, K1, P to end.

4th row: As 2nd row.

5th row: Patt 12, P to last st, inc in last st.

6th row: K to last 12 sts, patt 12.

7th row: Patt 12, P1, P2 tog tbl, P to end.

8th row: K to last 12 sts, patt 12.

BACK

Using No 9 needles, cast on 88/92/96 sts. Work in rib as on front for 3½ ins.

Change to No 11 needles and continue in rib until work measures 6/5¾/5½ ins from beg finishing at end of a 2nd row.

Change to No 9 needles and proceed in stocking stitch with centre dart as follows:

1st row: K43/45/47, M1, K2, M1, K43/45/47.
2nd row: P.
3rd row: K.
4th row: P.
5th row: K44/46/48, M1, K2, M1, K44/46/48.
6th–8th rows: As 2nd–4th.

Continue shaping in this manner on next and every following 4th row, *noting* that there will be 1 st more before and after the inc st on each side of the 2 centre sts on every inc row, the next row being: 'K45/47/49, M1, K2, M1, K45/47/49' until there are 108/114/120 sts on needle. Continue on these sts until work matches fronts up to armhole shaping.

Shape armholes by casting off 6 sts at beg of next 2 rows. Dec 1 st at both ends of next and every alt row until 86/90/94 sts remain. Continue on these sts until work matches fronts up to shoulder shaping.

Cast off all across.

SLEEVES

Using No 11 needles, cast on 52/56/60 sts. Work in rib as on fronts for 2¾ ins.

Change to No 9 needles and proceed in stocking stitch inc 1 st at both ends of 5th and every following 6th row until there are 88/92/96 sts on needle. Continue on these sts until work measures 17¼ ins from beg.

Shape top by casting off 2 sts at beg of next 8 rows. Dec 1 st at both ends of every row until 60/64/68 sts remain; every alt row until 48/52/56 sts remain: then every following 3rd row until 36/40/44 sts remain. Cast off 7 sts at beg of next 4 rows.

Cast off.

FRONT BAND

Using No 11 needles, cast on 9 sts. Proceed as follows:
1st row: K2, (P1, K1) 3 times, K1.
2nd row: (K1, P1) 4 times, K1.
3rd and 4th rows: As 1st and 2nd.
5th row: Rib 3, cast off 3, rib to end.
6th row: Rib 3, cast on 3, rib to end.
Continue in this manner, working a buttonhole as on 5th and
6th rows on 13th and 14th rows from previous buttonhole
until 5 buttonholes *in all* have been completed. Continue in
rib without further buttonholes until work measures 47½ ins
(not stretched) from beg.
Cast off.

TO MAKE UP

Omitting ribbing, with wrong side facing block and press each
piece using a warm iron and damp cloth. Using a back-stitch
seam join shoulder, side, and sleeve seams and stitch sleeves into
position, placing sleeve seam ½ inch to front of side seam.
Using a flat seam, stitch on front band, attach buttons to correspond with buttonholes. Press all seams.

JACKET
Illustrated in Plate 15a

16/17/18 oz Double Knitting Wool. Two No 10 and two No 8
needles. Eight buttons.
Bust, 34/36/38 ins. Length, 22/22¼/22½ ins. Sleeve, 18 ins.
    This garment must be worked at a tension of 5½ sts and 7½
rows to one square inch on No 8 needles, measured over stocking
stitch.

RIGHT FRONT

Using No 8 needles, cast on 44/47/50 sts and work in K1, P1
rib for 1 inch.
Proceed in *embossed rib patt* as follows:
1st row: * KB1, P1, rep from * to last 2/3/2 sts, KB1, P1/KB1,
P1, KB1/KB1, P1.

116

2nd row: K I, PB I/PB I, K I, PB I/K I, PB I; * K I, PB I, rep from * to end.

3rd–6th rows: Rep 1st and 2nd rows twice.

7th row: * P I, KB I, rep from * to last 2/3/2 sts, P I, KB I/P I, KB I, P I/P I, KB I.

8th row: PB I, K I/K I, PB I, K I/PB I, K I; * PB I, K I, rep from * to end.

9th and 10th rows: As 1st and 2nd.

11th and 12th rows: As 7th and 8th.

These 12 rows form the patt.

Rep rows 1–12 once more, then rep 1st and 2nd rows.

Keeping patt correct, shape the side by dec 1 st at end of next and every following 4th row until 39/42/45 sts remain.

Work 1 row.

Change to No 10 needles and work 4 rows, thus completing 48 rows of the patt.

Work waistband as follows:

1st row: * KB I, PB I, rep from * to last 1/2/1 sts, KB I/KB I, PB I/KB I.

2nd row: KB I, PB I/PB I, KB I, PB I/KB I, PB I; * KB I, PB I, rep from * to end.

3rd–10th rows: Rep 1st and 2nd rows 4 times.

Now work rows 7 and 8 of the patt.

Change to No 8 needles and commencing with the 9th row of the patt continue in patt inc 1 st at outside edge on next and every following 6th row until there are 46/49/52 sts on needle.

Continue on these sts until work measures 16 ins from beg, finishing at front edge.

Shape V-neck and armhole as follows:

1st row: Work 2 tog, patt to end.

2nd row: Cast off 6/7/8, patt to end.

3rd row: Patt to last 2 sts, work 2 tog.

4th, 6th, 8th, 10th, and 12th rows: Patt all across.

5th row: As 3rd row.

7th row: Work 2 tog, work to last 2 sts, work 2 tog.

9th and 11th rows: As 3rd row.

13th row: As 7th row.

The armhole shaping is now completed and there are 31/33/35 sts on needle.

Keeping patt correct, continue without further dec at armhole edge but still dec at front edge on every 6th row from previous dec until 25/27/29 sts remain.

Continue on these sts until work measures $7/7\frac{1}{4}/7\frac{1}{2}$ ins from beg of armhole shaping, finishing at armhole edge.

Shape shoulder as follows:

1st row: Cast off 8/9/9, work to end.

2nd row: Work all across.

3rd row: Cast off 8/9/10, work to end.

4th row: Work all across.

5th row: Cast off 9/9/10.

LEFT FRONT

Work to match right front, reversing all shapings.

BACK

Using No 8 needles, cast on 93/99/105 sts.

Work in K1, P1, rib for 1 inch.

Proceed in *patt* as follows:

1st row: * KB1, P1, rep from * to last st, KB1.

2nd row: * PB1, K1, rep from * to last st, PB1.

3rd–6th rows: Rep 1st and 2nd rows twice.

7th row: * P1, KB1, rep from * to last st, P1.

8th row: * K1, PB1, rep from * to last st, K1.

9th and 10th rows: As 1st and 2nd.

11th and 12th rows: As 7th and 8th.

These 12 rows form the patt.

Rep 1st–12th rows once more.

Keeping patt correct, dec 1 st at both ends of next and every following 4th row until 83/89/95 sts remain.

Work 3 rows.

Change to No 10 needles and work 4 rows, thus completing 48 rows of patt.

Work waistband as follows:

1st row: * PB1, KB1, rep from * to last st, PB1.

2nd row: * KB1, PB1, rep from * to last st, KB1.

3rd–10th rows: Rep 1st and 2nd rows 4 times.

Now work rows 1 and 2 of the patt.

Change to No 8 needles and keeping patt correct, inc 1 st at both ends of 3rd and every following 6th row until there are 95/101/107 sts on needle.

Continue on these sts until work matches fronts up to armhole shaping.

Shape armholes by casting off 5/6/7 sts at beg of next 2 rows. Dec 1 st at both ends of next and every alt row until 73/77/81 sts remain.

Continue on these sts until work matches fronts up to shoulder shaping.

Shape shoulders as follows:

1st and 2nd rows: Cast off 8/9/9, work to end.

3rd and 4th rows: Cast off 8/9/10, work to end.

5th and 6th rows: Cast off 9/9/10, work to end (23 sts).

Cast off.

SLEEVES

Using No 10 needles, cast on 56/60/64 sts.

Proceed in rib for 3 ins as follows, inc 1 st at end of last row:

1st and every row: * KB1, PB1, rep from * to end.

Change to No 8 needles and proceed in patt as on back, inc 1 st at both ends of 3rd and every following 10th row until there are 77/81/85 sts on needle.

Continue on these sts until work measures 18 ins from beg.

Shape top by casting off 3 sts at beg of next 4 rows; 2 sts at beg of next 4 rows. Dec 1 st at both ends of every row until 49/53/57 sts remain; every alt row until 37/41/45 sts remain; every following 3rd row until 25/29/33 sts remain.

Cast off 4 sts at beg of next 6 rows.

Cast off.

FRONT BAND

Using No 10 needles, cast on 11 sts.

Proceed in rib as follows:

1st row: K1, (KB1, PB1) 4 times, KB1, K1.

2nd row: K1, (PB1, KB1) 4 times, PB1, K1.

3rd and 4th rows: As 1st and 2nd.

5th row: Rib 4, cast off 3, rib 4.

6th row: Rib 4, cast on 3, rib 4.

Continue in this manner, working a buttonhole on 15th and 16th rows from previous buttonhole until the 2nd row after the 8th buttonhole from beg has been worked.

Shape collar as follows, working extra sts into twisted rib throughout:

1st row: Rib 10, M1, K1.

2nd–4th rows: Rib all across.

5th row: Rib 11, M1, K1.

6th–8th rows: Rib all across.

9th row: Rib 12, M1, K1.

10th–12th rows: Rib all across.

Continue inc in this manner until there are 26 sts on needle. Work 39/41/43 rows, thus finishing at front edge.

Shape second half of collar working dec in rib patt as follows:

1st row: Rib to last 3 sts, work 2 tog, K1.

2nd–4th rows: Rib all across.

Rep these 4 rows until 11 sts remain.

Complete to match right front band omitting buttonholes.

Cast off in rib.

MAKE UP

With wrong side of work facing, block and press each piece using a warm iron and damp cloth. Using a back-stitch seam join side and sleeve seams and stitch sleeves into position, placing sleeve seam $\frac{1}{2}$ inch to front of side seam. Turn under K1, P1 rib at lower edge of jacket and stitch into position on wrong side of work. Using a flat seam, stitch on front band and collar, placing shaped edge of collar to neck. Attach buttons to correspond with buttonholes. Press all seams.

5 oz Ground Shade, 7 oz Contrast, 4-ply Fingering. Two No 11, two No 10, and two No 9 needles. Thirteen buttons.

Bust, 34 ins. Length, 20½ ins. Sleeve seam, 18 ins.

This garment must be worked at a tension of 7 sts and 7 rows to one square inch on No 9 needles, measured over Shetland patt.

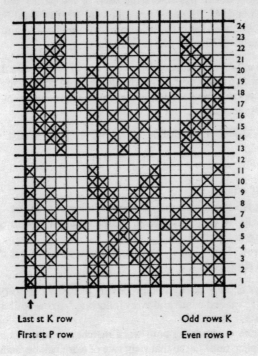

Last st K row   Odd rows K

First st P row   Even rows P

Key
☐ Ground Shade
☒ Contrast

BACK

Using No 11 needles and ground shade, cast on 108 sts.

1st row: P1, * K2, P2, rep from * to last 3 sts, K2, P1.

121

2nd row: K1, * P2, K2, rep from * to last 3 sts, P3, K1.
3rd row: P1, * TW2, P2, rep from * to last 3 sts, TW2, P1.
4th row: As 2nd row.

Rep these 4 rows until work measures 4 ins from beg, inc 1 st at end of last row (4th row of patt) (109 sts).

Change to No 9 needles and proceed in Shetland patt from chart (stranding colours at back of work throughout by carrying the colours not in use across the back of the work), inc 1 st at both ends of 5th and every following 6th row until there are 121 sts, working extra sts into patt throughout. Continue on these sts until work measures 13 ins from beg.

Shape armholes by casting off 5 sts at beg of next 2 rows. Dec 1 st at both ends of next and every alt row until 99 sts remain.

Continue on these sts until work measures 7 ins from beg of armhole shaping.

Shape shoulders by casting off 11 sts at beg of next 6 rows (33 sts).

Cast off.

RIGHT FRONT

Using No 11 needles and ground shade, cast on 52 sts.

Work in rib patt as on back, finishing at 3rd row in place of 4th row of rib patt.

Next row: Inc in first st, rib 25, inc in next st, rib to last st, inc in last st (55 sts).

Change to No 9 needles and proceed in Shetland patt as on back, inc 1 st at end of 7th and every following 8th row until there are 58 sts.

Continue on these sts until work matches back up to armhole shaping, finishing so that right side of work will be facing when working next row.

Shape armhole by casting off 5 sts at beg of next row then dec 1 st at armhole edge on next and every alt row until 47 sts remain.

Continue on these sts until work measures 5½ ins from beg of armhole shaping, finishing at front edge.

Shape neck by casting off 4 sts at beg of next row.

Dec 1 st at neck edge on every row until 33 sts remain. Continue on these sts until work matches back up to shoulder shaping, finishing at armhole edge.

Shape shoulder by casting off 11 sts at beg of next and every alt row until all sts are cast off.

LEFT FRONT

Work to match right front, reversing all shapings.

SLEEVES

Using No 11 needles and ground shade, cast on 56 sts.

Work in rib as on back for 3 ins, finishing at end of a 3rd row.

Next row: Rib 2, (inc in next st, rib 4) 10 times, inc in next st, rib to end (67 sts).

Break off ground shade.

Change to No 10 needles and using contrast throughout proceed in stocking stitch, inc 1 st at both ends of 9th and every following 10th row until there are 91 sts.

Continue on these sts until work measures 18 ins from beg. (Mark this point with length of coloured wool.)

Work 6 rows.

Shape top by dec 1 st at both ends of next and every alt row until 69 sts remain.

Cast off 6 sts at beg of next 10 rows.

Cast off.

RIGHT FRONT BAND

Using No 11 needles and contrast, cast on 15 sts.

1st row: K2, (P1, K1) 6 times, K1.

2nd row: (K1, P1) 7 times, K1.

3rd and 4th rows: As 1st and 2nd.

5th row: Rib 7, won, K2 tog, rib to end.

6th row: As 2nd row.

Continue working buttonholes as on 5th row on every 16th row from previous buttonhole until 11th row after 12th buttonhole from beg has been worked.

Slip sts on to a safety pin and leave.

LEFT FRONT BAND

Omitting buttonholes, work as right front band.

NECKBAND

Using a back-stitch seam join shoulders of back and fronts. With
right side of work facing, using No 11 needles and contrast
rib across 15 sts at top of right front band, *knit up* 83 sts
round neck, rib across 15 sts from left front band (113 sts).
Work 5 rows in K1, P1 rib as on front bands.
On next row make buttonhole as on 5th row.
Work 3 rows in rib.
Cast off in rib.

MAKE UP

Omitting ribbing, block and press on wrong side using a warm
iron and damp cloth. Using a back-stitch seam join side and
sleeve seams and stitch sleeves into position. Using a flat seam,
stitch front bands into position. Attach buttons to correspond
with buttonholes. Press seams.

LADY'S OUTSIZE TWIN SET
Illustrated in Plate 16a

Jumper

8/9/9 oz 3-ply Fingering. Two No 13 and two No 11 needles. A
cable needle. One stitch-holder.
Bust 40/42/44 ins. Length, 22/22¼/22½ ins. Sleeve, 5 ins.
    This garment must be worked at a tension of 8 sts and 10 rows to
one square inch on No 11 needles measured over stocking stitch

FRONT

Using No 11 needles, cast on 121/129/137 sts. Proceed in K1,
P1 rib as follows:
1st row: * P1, K1, rep from * to last st, P1.
2nd row: * K1, P1, rep from * to last st. K1.
Rep these 2 rows until work measures 2 ins from beg.

Change to No 13 needles and continue in rib until work measures
3½ ins from beg, finishing at end of a 2nd row of rib.

Change to No 11 needles and proceed in stocking stitch with *dart shapings* and *centre panel* as follows:

1st row: K32/36/40, * P1, K6, wf, K2 tog tbl, K2, wf, K2 tog tbl, K6, P1, * P2, K13, P2, rep from * to * K32/36/40.

2nd and every alt row: P.

3rd row: (first row of dart shaping) K31/35/39, M1, K1, * P1, K4, K2 tog, wf, K1, wf, K2 tog tbl, K2, wf, K2 tog tbl, K5, P1, * P2, C3F, K1, C3B, P2, rep from * to * K1, M1, K31/35/39.

5th row: K33/37/41, * P1, K3, K2 tog, wf, K3, wf, K2 tog tbl, K2, wf, K2 tog tbl, K4, P1, * P2, K13, P2, rep from * to * K33/37/41.

7th row: (2nd row of dart shaping) K32/36/40, M1, K1, * P1, K2, K2 tog, wf, K2, K2 tog, wf, K1, wf, K2 tog tbl, K2, wf, K2 tog tbl, K3, P1, * P2, C3F, K1, C3B, P2, rep from * to * K1, M1, K32/36/40.

9th row: K34/38/42, * P1, K1, K2 tog, wf, K2, K2 tog, wf, K3, wf, K2 tog tbl, K2, wf, K2 tog tbl, K2, P1, * P2, K13, P2, rep from * to * K34/38/42.

11th row: (3rd row of dart shaping) K33/37/41, M1, K1, * P1, K3, wf, K2 tog tbl, K2, wf, K2 tog tbl, wf, K2 tog, wf, K2, K2 tog, wf, K2 tog, K1, P1, * P2, C3F, K1, C3B, P2, rep from * to * K1, M1, K33/37/41.

13th row: K35/39/43, * P1, K4, wf, K2 tog tbl, K2, wf, K3 tog, wf, K2, K2 tog, wf, K3, P1, * P2, K13, P2, rep from * to * K35/39/43.

15th row: (4th row of dart shaping) K34/38/42, M1, K1, * P1 K5, wf, K2 tog tbl, K2, wf, K2 tog tbl, K1, K2 tog, wf, K4, P1, * P2, C3F, K1, C3B, P2, rep from * to * K1, M1, K34/38/42.

16th row: P.

These 16 rows form the patt used in centre panel, dart incs having been worked on 3rd, 7th, 11th, and 15th rows.

Keeping centre panel correct, and working dart inc as before on every 4th row from previous set of inc, continue in this manner until there are 159/167/175 sts on needle. Continue on these sts until work measures 14½ ins from beg, finishing so that right side of work will be facing when working next row.

Shape top darts as follows:

1st and 2nd rows: Work to last 7 sts, turn.

3rd and 4th rows: Work to last 13 sts, turn.
5th and 6th rows: Work to last 19 sts, turn.
7th and 8th rows: Work to last 25 sts, turn.
9th row: Work to end, *noting* that when turns have been worked you pick up loop lying between sts just worked and following st, K into back of this loop, place it on to left-hand needle then K tog st you have just made from loop and following st, thus closing up gaps where turns have been made.
10th row: Work all across, *noting* that you will P into back of loops you pick up before slipping on to left-hand needle and P tog made st and following st.

Shape fully fashioned armholes as follows:
1st row: K2, K2 tog tbl, work to last 4 sts, K2 tog, K2.
2nd row: P.
Rep rows 1 and 2, 11 times more (135/143/151 sts).

Divide for front opening as follows:
Next row: K2, K2 tog tbl, patt 63/67/71, cast off 1, patt to last 4 sts, K2 tog, K2.
Next row: Patt 66/70/74, slip remaining group of 66/70/74 sts on to stitch-holder and leave for present.
Keeping patt correct, continue dec at armhole edge as before on next and every alt row until 13/14/15 more dec have been worked at armhole edge (53/56/59 sts).
Continue on these sts until work measures $5\frac{3}{4}/6/6\frac{1}{4}$ ins from beg of armhole shaping, finishing at inside (neck) edge.

Shape neck by casting off 8/9/10 sts at beg of next row, then dec 1 st at neck edge on next and every alt row until 37/39/41 sts remain.
Continue on these sts until work measures $7\frac{1}{2}/7\frac{3}{4}/8$ ins from beg of armhole shaping, finishing at armhole edge.

Shape shoulder as follows:
1st row: Cast off 12/13/13, work to end.
2nd row: Work all across.
3rd row: Cast off 12/13/14, work to end.
4th row: Work all across.
Cast off.

126

Slip sts on stitch-holder on to a No 11 needle, point to inside (neck) edge.

Complete to match other half of Front, reversing all shapings and *noting* that you will work K2 tog tbl in place of K2 tog throughout armhole shaping.

BACK

Work ribbing as on Front.

Change to No 11 needles and proceed in stocking stitch with centre panel and dart shapings as follows:

1st row: K 51/55/59, P3, K 13, P3, K 51/55/59.

2nd and every alt row: P.

3rd row: K 50/54/58, M1, K1, P3, C3F, K1, C3B, P3, K1, M1, K 50/54/58.

5th row: K 52/56/60, P3, K 13, P3, K 52/56/60.

7th row: K 51/55/59, M1, K1, P3, C3F, K1, C3B, P3, K1, M1, K 51/55/59.

8th row: P.

Two reps of patt have been worked in these 8 rows, dart shapings having been worked on 3rd and 7th rows.

Continue in this manner working dart shapings as before on every 4th row from previous shaping until there are 159/167/175 sts on needle.

Continue on these sts until work matches Front up to armhole shaping.

Shape armholes by working 1st and 2nd rows of armhole shaping as on Front 25/26/27 times, thus giving you 109/115/121 sts on needle.

Continue on these sts until work matches Front up to shoulder shaping.

Shape shoulders as follows:

1st and 2nd rows: Cast off 12/13/13, work to end.

3rd and 4th rows: Cast off 12/13/14, work to end.

5th and 6th rows: Cast off 13/13/14, work to end.

Cast off remaining sts.

SLEEVES

Using No 13 needles, cast on 84/88/92 sts.

Work in K1, P1 rib for ¾ inch, inc 1 st at end of last row (85/89/93 sts).

Change to No 11 needles and proceed in stocking stitch, inc 1 st at both ends of 3rd and every following 3rd row until there are 111/115/119 sts on needle.
Work 3 rows in stocking stitch.

Shape top by working 1st and 2nd rows of armhole shaping as on Front 25/26/27 times (61/63/65 sts).
Cast off.
Work another sleeve in same manner.

TIE AND NECKBAND

Using No 13 needles, cast on 7 sts.
Proceed in rib as follows:
1st row: K2, (P1, K1) twice, K1.
2nd row: (K1, P1) 3 times, K1.
Rep these 2 rows until work measures 25 ins from beg.
Cast off in rib.

MAKE UP

Omitting ribbing, block and press each piece of work on wrong side using a warm iron and damp cloth. Using a back-stitch seam join shoulder, side, and sleeve seams up to ribbing and stitch sleeves into position. Use a flat seam to join ribbing and stitch neck-band round neck, leaving ends at centre front of neck to tie into a bow. Press all seams.

Cardigan

10/11/11 oz 3-ply Fingering. Two No 13 and two No 11 needles. 4 buttons.
Bust, 40/42/44 ins. Length, 22/22½/22½ ins. Sleeve, 17½ ins.

This garment must be worked at a tension of 8 sts and 10 rows to one square inch on No 11 needles measured over stocking stitch.

RIGHT FRONT

Using No 11 needles, cast on 58/62/66 sts.

Proceed in rib as follows:

1st and every row: * K I, P I, rep from * to end.

Continue in rib until work measures 3 ins from beg.

Change to No 13 needles and continue in rib until work measures 4½ ins from beg.

Change to No 11 needles and proceed in stocking stitch with fancy panel as follows:

1st row: P2, K6, wf, K2 tog tbl, K2, wf, K2 tog tbl, K6, P2, K to last st, inc in last st.

2nd and every alt row: P.

3rd row: P2, K4, K2 tog, wf, K I, wf, K2 tog tbl, K2, wf, K2 tog tbl, K5, P2, K to end.

5th row: P2, K3, K2 tog, wf, K3, wf, K2 tog tbl, K2, wf, K2 tog tbl, K4, P2, K I, K2 tog, K to last st, inc in last st.

7th row: P2, K2, K2 tog, wf, K2, K2 tog, wf, K I, wf, K2 tog tbl, K2, wf, K2 tog tbl, K3, P2, K to end.

9th row: P2, K I, K2 tog, wf, K2, K2 tog, wf, K3, wf, K2 tog tbl, K2, wf, K2 tog tbl, K2, P2, K to last st, inc in last st.

11th row: P2, K3, wf, K2 tog tbl, K2, wf, K2 tog tbl, wf, K2 tog, wf, K2, K2 tog, wf, K2 tog, K I, P2, K to end.

13th row: P2, K4, wf, K2 tog tbl, K2, wf, K3 tog, wf, K2, K2 tog, wf, K3, P2, K I, K2 tog, K to last st, inc in last st.

15th row: P2, K5, wf, K2 tog tbl, K2, wf, K2 tog tbl, K I, K2 tog, wf, K4, P2, K to end.

16th row: P.

These 16 rows form the patt, side shapings having been worked on 1st, 5th, 9th, and 13th rows, shapings inside front panel for the front slope having been worked on 5th and 13th rows.

Continue working in this manner, dec inside front panel as before on every 8th row from previous dec, *at the same time* inc at outside edges as before on next and every following 4th row until 15 more inc (*19 in all*) have been worked at side edge (68/72/76 sts).

Continue without further inc at side edge, but still dec inside front panel on 8th row following (*12th row* from previous dec) and every following 12th row until 25 more rows *in all* have been worked, thus finishing at front edge (66/70/74 sts).

Shape top dart as follows:

1st row: Patt to last 7 sts, turn.

2nd and every alt row: P.

3rd row: Patt to last 13 sts, turn.

5th row: Patt 22, K to last 19 sts, turn.

7th row: Patt 22, K 1, K2 tog, K to last 25 sts, turn.

9th row: Patt all across, *noting* that where the turns have been worked you pick up the loop between the st just worked and the following st, K into back of loop, slip it on to left-hand needle then K tog the st you have just made from the loop and the following st, thus preventing gaps in the work where the turns have been made.

10th row: P.

Shape armhole as follows:

1st row: Patt to last 5 sts, K2 tog, K 3.

2nd row: P.

Still dec at front edge as before on 7th row following and every 12th row, continue to dec at armhole edge as on last 2 rows until 46/50/54 sts remain.

The front edge dec have now been completed on 40 and 42 inch sizes.

Still dec *on 44 inch size only* at front edge as before, continue dec as before at armhole edge *on all 3 sizes* until 25/26/27 dec *in all* have been worked at armhole edge (37/39/42 sts).

The armhole dec are now completed on all sizes.

Work 1 more dec *on 44 inch size only* inside the front panel on the 2nd row following, thus giving you 37/39/41 sts on the needle.

Continue on these sts until work measures 7½/7¾/8 ins from beg of armhole shaping, finishing at armhole edge.

Shape shoulder as follows:

1st row: Cast off 12/13/13, work to end.

2nd row: Work all across.

3rd row: Cast off 12/13/14, work to end.

4th row: Work all across.

Cast off remaining sts.

LEFT FRONT

Work to match Right Front reversing all shapings, the first 16 rows after the ribbing being as follows:

1st row: Inc in first st, K to last 22 sts, P2, K6, wf, K2 tog tbl, K2, wf, K2 tog tbl, K6, P2.

2nd and every alt row: P.

3rd row: K to last 22 sts, P2, K4, K2 tog, wf, K1, wf, K2 tog tbl, K2, wf, K2 tog tbl, K5, P2.

5th row: Inc in first st, K to last 25 sts, K2 tog, K1, P2, K3, K2 tog, wf, K3, wf, K2 tog tbl, K2, wf, K2 tog tbl, K4, P2.

7th row: K to last 22 sts, P2, K2, K2 tog, wf, K2, K2 tog, wf, K1, wf, K2 tog tbl, K2, wf, K2 tog tbl, K3, P2.

9th row: Inc in first st, K to last 22 sts, P2, K1, K2 tog, wf, K2, K2 tog, wf, K3, wf, K2 tog tbl, K2, wf, K2 tog tbl, K2, P2.

11th row: K to last 22 sts, P2, K3, wf, K2 tog tbl, K2, wf, K2 tog tbl, wf, K2 tog, wf, K2, K2 tog, wf, K2 tog, K1, P2.

13th row: Inc in first st, K to last 25 sts, K2 tog, K1, P2, K4, wf, K2 tog tbl, K2, wf, K3 tog, wf, K2, K2 tog, wf, K3, P2.

15th row: K to last 22 sts, P2, K5, wf, K2 tog tbl, K2, wf, K2 tog tbl, K1, K2 tog, wf, K4, P2.

16th row: P.

Special Note: The *top dart* turns will be worked on the P rows in place of the K rows, (24 rows being worked before commencing top dart), the action of purling up the loop and working it tog with the following st being worked purlwise.

The first row of the armhole shaping will read:

'K3, K2 tog tbl, work to end.'

BACK

Using No 11 needles, cast on 120/128/136 sts.

Work in ribbing as on Right Front until 4½ ins have been completed, inc 1 st at end of last row (121/129/137 sts).

Change to No 11 needles and proceed in stocking stitch with *dart shapings* as follows:

1st row: K.

2nd row: P.

3rd row: K59/63/67, M1, K3, M1, K59/63/67.

4th row: P.

131

5th and 6th rows: As 1st and 2nd.

7th row: K60/64/68, M1, K3, M1, K60/64/68.

8th row: P.

9th and 10th rows: As 1st and 2nd.

11th row: K61/65/69, M1, K3, M1, K61/65/69.

12th row: P.

13th and 14th rows: As 1st and 2nd.

Continue inc in this manner on next and every following 4th row until there are 159/167/175 sts on needle.

Work 25 rows in stocking stitch on these sts.

Shape armholes as follows:

1st row: K3, K2 tog tbl, K to last 5 sts, K2 tog, K3.

2nd row: P.

Rep these 2 rows 24/25/26 times (109/115/121 sts).

Continue on these sts until work matches Fronts up to shoulder shaping.

Shape shoulders as follows:

1st and 2nd rows: Cast off 12/13/13, work to end.

3rd and 4th rows: Cast off 12/13/14, work to end.

5th and 6th rows: Cast off 13/13/14, work to end.

Cast off.

SLEEVES

Using No 13 needles, cast on 64/68/72 sts.

Work in K1, P1 rib for 3 ins.

Next row: Rib 2/4/6, (inc in next st, rib 5) 10 times, inc in next st, rib to end (75/79/83 sts).

Change to No 11 needles and proceed in stocking stitch, inc 1 st at both ends of 5th and every following 7th row until there are 111/115/119 sts on needle. Continue on these sts until work measures 17½ ins from beg (or length required), finishing at end of a P row.

Shape top as on sleeve of Jumper.

Work another sleeve in same manner.

FRONT BAND

Using No 13 needles, cast on 11 sts.

132

Proceed as follows:

1st row: K I, (K I, P I) 4 times, K 2.

2nd row: (K I, P I) 5 times, K I.

3rd and 4th rows: As Ist and 2nd.

5th row: K I, K I, P I, K I, cast off 3, rib to end.

6th row: Rib 4, cast on 3, (P I, K I) twice.

Continue in rib as on Ist and 2nd rows working buttonhole as on 5th and 6th rows on 15th and 16th rows from previous button-hole until 4 buttonholes *in all* have been worked.

Continue in rib without further buttonholes until work measures 48/48½/49 ins (not stretched) from beg.

Cast off in rib.

MAKE UP

Omitting ribbing, block and press each piece on wrong side. Using a back-stitch seam join shoulder, side, and sleeve seams and stitch sleeves into position. Using a flat seam join ribbing, stitch on front band. Attach buttons to correspond with buttonholes. Press all seams.

BASIC SUIT IN THREE SIZES
Illustrated in Plate 16b

Coat

13/14/15 oz Bouclet. Two No 13, two No 12, two No 11, and two No 10 needles. 11 Buttons.

Bust, 34/36/38 ins. Length, 23/23¼/23½ ins. Sleeve, 18 ins.

This garment must be worked at a tension of 7½ sts and 9½ rows to one square inch on No 10 needles measured over stocking stitch.

RIGHT FRONT

Using No 11 needles, cast on 62/66/70 sts.

Work 4 rows in K I, P I rib.

Proceed in rib as follows:

1st row: * P 2, K 8, rep from * to last 2/6/0 sts, P 2/P 2, K 4/0.

2nd row: K 2/P 4, K 2/0, * P 8, K 2, rep from * to last 2 sts, K 2.

Rep these 2 rows until work measures 2½ ins from beg.

Change to No 12 needles and continue until work measures $4\frac{1}{2}$ ins from beg, finishing at end of a 2nd row.

Next row: * P2, K2 tog, K6, rep from * to last 2/6/0 sts, P2/P2, K4/0 (56/60/63 sts).

Keeping rib correct, continue until work measures 5 ins from beg.

Change to No 13 needles and continue until work measures $5\frac{1}{4}$ ins from beg, finishing so that right side of work will be facing when working next row.

Next row: * P2, K5, K2 tog, rep from * to last 2/6/0 sts, P2/P2, K4/0 (50/54/57 sts).

Keeping rib correct, continue until work measures 7 ins from beg, finishing so that right side of work will be facing when working next row.

Change to No 10 needles and working extra sts in 2 and 6 rib throughout, inc 1 st at side edge of 3rd and every following 6th row until there are 64/68/72 sts on needle.

Continue on these sts until work measures 16 ins from beg, finishing at side edge.

Shape armhole by casting off 7/8/9 sts at beg of next row. Dec 1 st at armhole edge on next and every alt row until 7/8/9 dec *in all* have been worked at armhole edge; *at same time* dec 1 st at front edge on 3rd and every following 4th row until armhole shaping is completed.

Continue without further dec at armhole edge, but still dec at front edge on every following 3rd row from previous dec until 33/36/39 sts remain.

Continue on these sts until work measures $7\frac{1}{4}/7\frac{1}{2}/7\frac{3}{4}$ ins from beg of armhole shaping, finishing at armhole edge.

Shape shoulder by casting off 11/12/13 sts at beg of next and every alt row until all sts are cast off.

LEFT FRONT

Work as for Right Front, reading K for P and P for K throughout, thus reversing all shapings.

BACK

Using No 11 needles, cast on 122/126/130 sts.

134

Work 4 rows in K I, P I rib.

Proceed in rib as follows:

1st row: K0/2/4, * P2, K8, rep from * to last 2/4/6 sts, P2/P2. K2/P2, K4.

2nd row: K2/P2, K2/P4, K2, * P8, K2, rep from * to last 0/2/4 sts, P0/2/4.

Rep these 2 rows until work measures 2½ ins from beg.

Change to No 12 needles and continue until work measures 4½ ins from beg, finishing at end of a 2nd row.

Next row: K0/2/4, * P2, K2 tog, K6, rep from * to last 2/4/6 sts, P2/P2, K2/P2, K4 (110/114/118 sts).

Keeping rib patt correct, continue until work measures 5 ins from beg.

Change to No 13 needles and continue until work measures 5¼ ins from beg, finishing so that right side of work will be facing when working next row.

Next row: K0/2/4, * P2, K5, K2 tog, rep from * to last 2/4/6 sts, P2/P2, K2/P2, K4 (98/102/106 sts).

Continue in rib until work measures 7 ins from beg, finishing so that right side of work will be facing when working next row.

Change to No 10 needles and keeping 2 and 6 rib correct, inc I st at both ends of next and every following 5th row until there are 130/134/138 sts on needle. Continue on these sts until work measures same as Fronts up to armhole shapings.

Shape armholes by casting off 5/6/7 sts at beg of next 2 rows. Dec I st at both ends of every row until 98/102/104 sts remain.

Continue on these sts until work matches Fronts up to shoulder shaping.

Cast off.

SLEEVES

Using No 13 needles, cast on 58 sts.

Work 4 rows in K I, P I rib.

Proceed as follows:

1st row: * P2, K6, rep from * to last 2 sts, P2.

2nd row: * K2, P6, rep from * to last 2 sts, K2.

135

Continue in rib as on these 2 rows until work measures 2 ins from beg.

Change to No 11 needles and continue until work measures 3 ins from beg.

Change to No 10 needles and continue in rib, inc 1 st at both ends of next and every following 7th/6th/6th row until there are 96/100/104 sts on needle.
Continue on these sts until work measures 18 ins from beg.

Shape top by casting off 2 sts at beg of next 8 rows; dec 1 st at both ends of every row until 64/68/72 sts remain; every alt row until 56/60/64 sts remain, then every following 3rd row until 36/40/44 sts remain.
Cast off 5/5/6 sts at beg of next 6 rows.
Cast off.
Work another sleeve in same manner.

FRONT BAND

Using No 13 needles, cast on 18 sts.
Work in double knitting as follows:
1st row: * K 1, wft, sl 1 purlwise, wb, rep from * to end.
2nd to 6th rows: As 1st row.
7th row: (K 1, wft, sl 1 purlwise, wb) 3 times, K 1, * K 2 tog, cast off 1 st, rep from * twice more, patt to end (6 sts each side of buttonhole).
8th row: Patt 6, cast on 6, patt to end.
Continue in this manner, working a buttonhole on every 25th and 26th row from previous buttonhole until 11 buttonholes in all have been worked.
Continue without further buttonholes until work measures 47 ins (not stretched) from beg.
Cast off, knitting 2 tog all across.

TO MAKE UP

Omitting K 1, P 1 rib, block and press each piece using a warm iron and damp cloth. Using a back-stitch seam join shoulder, side, and sleeve seams, and stitch sleeves into position. Using a flat seam stitch on Front Band, attach buttons to correspond with buttonholes. Press seams.

17/18/19 oz Bouclet. Two No 13, two No 11, and two No 10 needles. One length of petersham to fit waist. Two hooks and eyes. One 6 inch zipp fastener.

Length, 29 ins. Waist, 27/29/31 ins. Hips, 38/40/42 ins.

FRONT

Using No 10 needles, cast on 270 sts for all 3 sizes.

Work 4 rows in K 1, P 1 rib.

1st row: K23, * P14, K21, rep from * to last 2 sts, K2.

2nd row: P23, * K14, P21, rep from * to last 2 sts, P2.

Rep these 2 rows until work measures 9 ins from beg, finishing at end of a 2nd row.

Proceed as follows:

1st row: K22, * K2 tog tbl, P12, K2 tog, K19, rep from * to last 3 sts, K3 (256 sts).

2nd row: P23, * K12, P21, rep from * to last 2 sts, P2.

3rd row: K23, * P12, K21, rep from * to last 2 sts, K2.

Continue as on last 2 rows until work measures 11 ins from beg, finishing at end of a 2nd row.

Next row: K22, * K2 tog tbl, P10, K2 tog, K19, rep from * to last 3 sts, K3 (242 sts).

Next row: P23, * K10, P21, rep from * to last 2 sts, P2.

Keeping rib correct, continue dec in P panels on every 12th row from previous dec until 2 P sts remain (186 sts).

Work in rib for 19 rows.

Next row: K21, * K2 tog tbl, P2, K2 tog, K17, rep from * to last 4 sts, K4 (172 sts).

Work in rib for 19 rows.

Next row: K20, * K2 tog tbl, P2, K2 tog, K15, rep from * to last 5 sts, K5 (158 sts).

Keeping rib correct, continue dec at each side of K panels on every 20th row from previous dec until 116/130/144 sts remain.

Proceed in stocking stitch until work measures 23½ ins from beg.

Change to No 11 needles and continue in stocking stitch until work measures 26½ ins from beg.

Change to No 13 needles and continue in stocking stitch until work measures 27½ ins from beg.

Proceed in K I, P I rib until work measures 29 ins from beg. Cast off in rib.

BACK

Work as for Front.

TO MAKE UP

With wrong side facing, block and press each piece using a warm iron and damp cloth. Using a back-stitch seam, join side seams leaving 6 inch opening at left side. Stitch zipp into side opening. Neatly attach petersham band to top of skirt. Attach hooks and eyes. Press seams.

THREE-PLY DRESS
Illustrated in Plate 17a

21 oz 3-ply Fingering. Two No 13 and two No 11 needles. Four inch zipp. A Belt. ¾yd 1 inch wide elastic.
Bust, 34–36 ins. Length, 44 ins. Sleeve seam, 5 ins.

This garment must be worked at a tension of 8 sts and 10 rows to one square inch on No 11 needles measured over stocking stitch.

FRONT

Using No 11 needles, cast on 322 sts.
Work in K I, P I rib for 2 ins.
Proceed in *rib patt* as follows:
1st row: * K B I, P 2, rep from * to last st, K B I.
2nd row: * P B I, K 2, rep from * to last st, P B I.
Continue in rib patt until work measures 24 ins from *top of* K I, P I *rib*, finishing at end of a 2nd row.
Next row: * K 2, K 2 tog, rep from * to last 2 sts, K 2 tog (241 sts).
Next row: P 12, (P 2 tog, P 22) 9 times, P 2 tog, P to end (231 sts).
Proceed in lace patt as follows:
1st row: * K 5, wf, K 2 tog tbl, K 3, rep from * to last st, K I.
2nd and every alt row: P.
3rd row: * K 3, K 2 tog, wf, K I, wf, K 2 tog tbl, K 2, rep from * to last st, K I.

138

5th row: * K2, K2 tog, wf, K3, wf, K2 tog tbl, K1, rep from * to last st, K1.

7th row: * K1, K2 tog, wf, K5, wf, K2 tog tbl, rep from * to last st, K1.

9th row: K2 tog, wf, K7, * wf, K3 tog, wf, K7, rep from * to last 12 sts, wf, K3 tog, wf, K7, wf, K2 tog tbl.

10th row: P.

Rep 1st to 10th rows 4 times more.

Next row: * K2 tog, P2 tog, rep from * to last 3 sts, K2 tog, P1 (116 sts).

Change to No 13 needles and work in K1, P1 rib for 1 in. finishing so that wrong side of work will be facing when working next row.

Next row: Rib 11, (inc in next st, rib 21) 4 times, inc in next st, rib to end (121 sts).

Change to No 11 needles and proceed in fabric patt as follows:

1st row: * P1, KB1, rep from * to last st, P1.

2nd row: * K1, PB1, rep from * to last st, K1.

3rd and 4th rows: As 1st and 2nd.

5th row: * KB1, P1, rep from * to last st, KB1.

6th row: * PB1, K1, rep from * to last st, PB1.

These 6 rows form the patt.

Keeping patt correct, inc 1 st at both ends of next and every following 5th row until there are 139 sts.

Continue on these sts until work measures 6½ ins from top of K1, P1 rib.**

Shape raglan armholes as follows:

1st and 2nd rows: Cast off 8 sts, patt to end.

3rd and 4th rows: Work 2 tog, work to last 2 sts, work 2 tog.

5th row: Work in patt.

Rep 3rd–5th rows 21 times more.

Shape neck as follows:.

Next row: Work 6, cast off 23, work to end.

Proceed on *each* group of 6 sts as follows:

Dec 1 st at neck edge on next and every alt row until all sts are worked off.

BACK

Work as Front to ** (139 sts).

Work 1st to 5th rows of armhole shaping as on Front (119 sts).
then rep 3rd to 5th rows 9 times (83 sts).

Divide for back opening as follows:

Next row: Work 2 tog, patt 39, cast off 1, patt 39, work 2 tog.

Proceed on *each* group of 40 sts as follows:

Knitting st at inside edge on every row continue dec on raglan
armhole as before until 17 sts remain.

Continue on these sts for 10 rows.

Cast off.

SLEEVES

Using No 13 needles and the through stitches method, cast on 82 sts.

Work in K1, P1 rib for 1 in.

Proceed in rib patt as on skirt until work measures 2 ins from
beg, finishing at end of a 2nd row.

Next row: *Make hem* by knitting tog 1 st from needle and 1 loop
from cast-on edge all across row.

Next row: P6, (inc in next st, P3) 16 times, inc in next st, P to
end (99 sts).

Change to No 11 needles and proceed in fabric patt as on bodice
inc 1 st at both ends of 5th and every following 3rd row until
there are 125 sts.

Continue on these sts until work measures 5 ins from beg.

Shape top by working 1st to 5th rows of armhole shaping as on
Front, then rep 3rd to 5th rows 21 times.

Cast off.

COLLAR (TWO PIECES ALIKE)

Using No 13 needles, cast on 111 sts.

1st row: K2, * P1, K1, rep from * to last st, K1.

2nd row: * K1, P1, rep from * to last st, K1.

3rd and 4th rows: As 1st and 2nd.

5th row: Cast off 20 (1 st on needle after cast-off), P1, KB1,
(P2, KB1) 22 times, P2, cast off 20.

Rejoin wool and continue in *rib patt* on remaining 70 sts, dec

140

I st at both ends of 3rd and every following 4th row for 23
rows (59 sts).
Cast off.

MAKE UP

Block and very lightly press on wrong side, using a warm iron
and damp cloth. Using a back-stitch seam join side and sleeve
seams. Stitch sleeves into position. Turn up K I, P I rib at lower
edge of skirt and stitch down to form hem. Stitch ribbed ends
of collar along side and stitch collar into position. Stitch
broad elastic to wrong side of K I, P I waistband. Stitch zipp
into back opening. Press all seams.

LADY'S BEDJACKET
Illustrated in plate 17b

8/9/9 oz 3-ply Fingering. Two No 12 and two No 10 needles.
10/10/11 buttons.
Bust, 34/38/42 ins. Length, 19/19¾/20½ ins. Sleeve 4½ ins.

This garment must be worked at a tension of 7½ sts and 9½ rows
to one square inch on No 10 needles, measured over stocking
stitch.

BACK

Using No 12 needles, cast on 114/128/142 sts.
Work in K I, P I rib for 2½ ins.

Small size only:
Next row: Rib 5, (inc in next st, rib 7) 13 times, inc in next st, rib
to end (128 sts).

Middle size only:
Next row: Rib 5, (inc in next st, rib 8) 13 times, inc in next st,
rib to end (142 sts).

Large size only:
Next row: Rib 5, (inc in next st, rib 9) 13 times, inc in next st,
rib to end (156 sts).

All sizes:

Change to No 10 needles and proceed in *lace rib patt* as follows:

1st row: * P2, K2 tog, wf, K1, wf, K2 tog tbl, rep from * to last 2 sts, P2.

2nd row: * K2, P5, rep from * to last 2 sts, K2.

3rd row: * P2, K5, rep from * to last 2 sts, P2.

4th row: * K2, P5, rep from * to last 2 sts, K2.

These 4 rows form the patt.

Continue in patt until work measures 12/12½/12½ ins from beg, finishing so that right side of work will be facing when working next row.

Keeping patt correct, cast on 28 sts at beg of next 2 rows for sleeves (184/198/212 sts). Continue on these sts until work measures 6¾/7¼/7¾ ins from cast-on sts for sleeves.

Shape top edges as follows:

Next 2 rows: Cast off 13/14/15 sts, work to end.

Next 2 rows: Cast off 13/14/14 sts, work to end.

Next 2 rows: Cast off 13/13/14 sts, work to end.

Next 6 rows: Cast off 12/13/14 sts, work to end (34/38/42 sts).

Cast off.

RIGHT FRONT

Using No 12 needles, cast on 54/60/66 sts.

Work in K1, P1 rib for 2½ ins.

Small size only:

Next row: Rib 4, (inc in next st, rib 8) 5 times, inc in next st, rib to end (60 sts).

Middle size only:

Next row: Rib 5, (inc in next st, rib 7) 6 times, inc in next st, rib to end (67 sts).

Large size only:

Next row: Rib 5, (inc in next st, rib 7) 7 times, inc in next st, rib to end (74 sts).

All sizes:

Change to No 10 needles and proceed in *lace rib patt* as follows:

1st row: K2, P2, * K2 tog, wf, K1, wf, K2 tog tbl, P2, rep from * to end.

2nd row: * K2, P5, rep from * to last 4 sts, K2, P2.

3rd row: K2, P2, * K5, P2, rep from * to end.

4th row: * K2, P5, rep from * to last 4 sts, K2, P2.

These 4 rows form the patt.

Continue in patt until work measures 12/12¼/12½ ins from beg, finishing at side edge.

Keeping patt correct, cast on 28 sts at beg of next row for sleeve (88/95/102 sts).

Continue in patt on these sts until work measures 5/5½/6 ins from cast-on sts for sleeve, finishing at front edge.

Shape neck by casting off 8/10/12 sts at beg of next row. Dec 1 st at neck edge on every alt row until 75/80/85 sts remain.

Continue on these sts until work measures 6¾/7¼/7¾ ins from beg of sleeve, finishing at sleeve edge.

Shape top edge as follows:

1st row: Cast off 13/14/15 sts, work to end.

2nd and every alt row: Work all across.

3rd row: Cast off 13/14/14 sts, work to end.

5th row: Cast off 13/13/14 sts, work to end.

7th row: Cast off 12/13/14 sts, work to end.

8th row: Work all across.

Rep last 2 rows twice. Cast off.

LEFT FRONT

Work to match Right Front reversing all shapings, *noting* that the first 4 rows of patt will read as follows:

1st row: * P2, K2 tog, wf, K1, wf, K2 tog tbl, rep from * to last 4 sts, P2, K2.

2nd row: P2, K2, * P5, K2, rep from * to end.

3rd row: * P2, K5, rep from * to last 4 sts, P2, K2.

4th row: P2, K2, * P5, K2, rep from * to end.

SLEEVE EDGINGS

Using a back-stitch seam, join top edges. Using No 12 needles, with right side of work facing *knit up* 127/133/141 sts along sleeve edge.

Work picot edge as follows:

1st row: P.

143

2nd row: K.
3rd row: P1, * wrn, P2 tog, rep from * to end.
4th row: K.
5th row: P.
Cast off.

RIGHT FRONT BAND

Using No 12 needles, cast on 11 sts.
1st row: K2, (P1, K1) 4 times, K1.
2nd row: (K1, P1) 5 times, K1.
3rd and 4th rows: As 1st and 2nd.
5th row: Rib 4, cast off 3, rib to end.
6th row: Rib 4, cast on 3, rib to end.
Continue in rib, working a buttonhole as on 5th and 6th rows on
   every following 21st and 22nd/21st and 22nd/19th and 20th
   rows from previous buttonhole, until 9/9/10 buttonholes *in all*
   have been worked.
Work 6/14/6 rows.
Slip sts on to a length of wool and leave.

LEFT FRONT BAND

Omitting buttonholes, work to match Right Front Band, finishing
   at end of a 2nd row of rib.

NECKBAND

Slip 11 sts of Right Front Band on to a No 12 needle, using same
   needle, with right side of work facing *knit up* 101/105/109 sts
   round neck, rib across sts of Left Front Band (123/127/131 sts).
Work 7 rows in K1, P1 rib, working a buttonhole as before on
   4th and 5th rows.
Work rows 2–5 incl of picot edge as on sleeve.
Cast off.

MAKE UP

Omitting ribbing, block and press on wrong side using a warm
   iron and damp cloth. Fold over picot edging at row of holes
   and stitch into position on wrong side. Using a back-stitch
   seam join side and sleeve seams. Using a flat seam, stitch Front
   Bands into position. Attach buttons to correspond with buttonholes. Press all seams.

LADY'S BEDJACKET
Illustrated in Plate 17b

2 oz Contrast, 12 oz Ground Shade, Double Knitting Wool. Two No 7 and two No 5 needles. Cable needle. Five buttons.

Bust 34–36 ins. Length, 17 ins. Sleeves seam, 13½ ins.

This garment must be worked at a tension of 4¾ sts and 6 rows to one square inch on No 5 needles, measured over stocking stitch.

Worked in one piece up to armhole shaping.

Using No 5 needles and Contrast and the through stitches method, cast on 181 sts.

Proceed in shell patt as follows:

1st and 2nd rows: Using Contrast, K.

3rd row: Using Contrast, P.

4th row: Using Contrast, K.

5th row: Using Ground Shade, * K1, (K2 tog) 3 times, (wf, K1) 5 times, wf, (K2 tog tbl) 3 times, rep from * to last st, K1.

6th row: Using Ground Shade, P.

7th row: Using Ground Shade, K.

8th row: Using Ground Shade, P.

9th to 20th rows: Rep 5th to 8th rows 3 times.

These 20 rows form the patt.

Rep 1st to 20th rows twice more.

Divide for Back and Fronts as follows, *noting* that remainder of Back and Fronts is worked in Ground Shade throughout.

Next row: K42, cast off 6, K84 (there now being 85 sts on needle after cast-off), cast off 6, K to end.

Proceed on first group of 42 sts for *Left Front* as follows:

Next row: P.

Next row: P2 tog, P6, (K9, P2) 3 times, K1.

Proceed in cable patt for *Yoke* as follows:

1st row: K3, (P9, K2) 3 times, K5.

2nd row: P2 tog, P3, (P2, C2F, K1, C2B) 3 times, P3.

3rd row: K3, (P9, K2) 3 times, K4.

4th row: P2 tog, P2, (P2, K9) 3 times, P3.

These 4 rows form the patt, armhole shapings having been worked on 2nd and 4th rows.

Keeping patt correct, continue to dec at armhole edge on every alt row as before until 2 more dec have been worked (37 sts).

Continue in patt until work measures 4 ins from beg of armhole shaping, finishing at front edge.

Dec 1 st at neck edge on next and every alt row until 28 sts remain, thus finishing at armhole edge.

Shape shoulder by casting off 14 sts at beg of next and following alt row.

Proceed on 2nd group of 85 sts for *Back* as follows:

Next row: P.

Next row: P3 tog, P8, (K9, P2) 6 times, P6, P2 tog (82 sts).

Proceed in cable patt as on Left Front, dec 1 st at *both ends* of every alt row until 72 sts remain.

Continue on these sts until work matches Front up to shoulder shaping.

Cast off 14 sts at beg of next 4 rows.

Cast off.

RIGHT FRONT

Rejoin wool to remaining group of 42 sts and complete to match Left Front, reversing all shapings.

SLEEVES

Using No 7 needles and Contrast, cast on 54 sts.

K 11 rows.

Next row: K7, (inc in next st, K2) 13 times, inc in next st, K to end (68 sts).

Break off Contrast.

Change to No 5 needles and using Ground Shade, proceed as follows:

1st row: (P2, K4, sl1, K4) 6 times, P2.

2nd row: (K2, P9) 6 times, K2.

3rd row: (P2, C2F, sl1, C2B) 6 times, P2.

4th row: As 2nd row.

These 4 rows form the patt.

Continue in patt until work measures 13½ ins from beg.

Keeping patt correct, *shape top* by casting off 3 sts at beg of next 4 rows; 2 sts at beg of next 4 rows. Dec 1 st at both ends of

146

every row until 40 sts remain, every alt row until 30 sts remain; every following 3rd row until 22 sts remain.

Cast off.

RIGHT FRONT BAND

Using No 7 needles and Ground Shade, cast on 7 sts.

Work in garter stitch (every row K) until piece fits along front edge to beg of yoke patt when slightly stretched.

Next row: Make buttonhole as follows: K3, wf, K2 tog, K2.

Continue in garter stitch, making buttonholes 1 in from previous buttonhole until 5 buttonholes have been worked.

Work 2 rows.

Cast off.

LEFT FRONT BAND

Omitting buttonholes, work as Right Front Band.

COLLAR

Using No 7 needles and Ground Shade, cast on 18 sts.

Work in garter stitch for 10 ins.

Cast off.

MAKE UP

Very lightly press on wrong side. Using a back-stitch seam join shoulder and sleeve seams and stitch sleeves into position. Using a flat seam stitch on front bands and collar. Attach buttons to correspond with buttonholes. Press all seams.

SHAWL

Illustrated in Plate 18

10 oz 2-ply Fingering. Two No 11 needles.

42 ins by 42 ins (when pressed).

This shawl must be worked at a tension of 8½ sts and 10½ rows to one square inch on No 11 needles.

Using No 11 needles, cast on 341 sts.

K 2 rows.

Proceed in Shetland patt for centre with 2 st border as follows:

1st row: K2, (K5, K2 tog, wf, K1, wf, K2 tog, K9, K2 tog, wf, K1, wf, K2 tog, K4) 12 times, K3.

2nd row: K3, (K3, K2 tog, wf, K3, wf, K2 tog, K7, K2 tog, wf, K3, wf, K2 tog, K4) 12 times, K2.

3rd row: K2, [K3, (K2 tog, wf) twice, K1, (wf, K2 tog) twice, K5, (K2 tog, wf) twice, K1, (wf, K2 tog) twice, K2] 12 times, K3.

4th row: K3, [K1, K2 tog, wf, K7, wf, K2 tog, K3, (K2 tog, wf) twice, K3, (wf, K2 tog) twice, K2] 12 times, K2.

5th row: K2, [K1, K2 tog, wf, K2, wf, K2 tog, K1, K2 tog, wf, K2, wf, K2 tog, K1, (K2 tog, wf) twice, K1, wf, sl1, K2 tog, psso, wf, K1, (wf, K2 tog) twice] 12 times, K3.

6th row: K3, (wf, K2 tog, K9, K2 tog, wf, K1, wf, K2 tog, K3, wf, sl1, K2 tog, psso, wf, K3, K2 tog, wf, K1) 12 times, K2.

7th row: K2, (K1, wf, K2 tog, K2, K2 tog, wf, K1, wf, K2 tog, K2, K2 tog, wf, K1, wf, K2 tog, K1, wf, sl1, K2 tog, psso, wf, K1, wf, sl1, K2 tog, psso, wf, K1, K2 tog, wf) 12 times, K3.

8th row: K3, (wf, K2 tog, K9, K2 tog, wf, K1, wf, K2 tog, K1, K2 tog, wf, K3, wf, K2 tog, K1, K2 tog, wf, K1) 12 times, K2.

9th row: K2, [K1, wf, K2 tog, K2, wf, K2 tog, K1, K2 tog, wf, K2, K2 tog, wf, K1, wf, (K2 tog) twice, wf, K1, wf, sl1, K2 tog, psso, wf, K1, wf, (K2 tog) twice, wf] 12 times, K3.

10th row: K3, (wf, K2 tog, K9, K2 tog, wf, K1, wf, K2 tog, K3, wf, sl1, K2 tog, psso, wf, K3, K2 tog, wf, K1) 12 times, K2.

11th row: As 7th row.

12th row: As 8th row.

13th row: K2, [K2, (wf, K2 tog, K1) twice, K2 tog, wf, K1, K2 tog, wf, K3, wf, K2 tog, K2, wf, sl1, K2 tog, psso, wf, K2, K2 tog, wf, K1] 12 times, K3.

14th row: K3, (K2, wf, K2 tog, K5, K2 tog, wf, K5, wf, K2 tog, K1, wf, sl1, K2 tog, psso, wf, K1, K2 tog, wf, K3) 12 times, K2.

15th row: K2, (K4, wf, K2 tog, K3, K2 tog, wf, K7, wf, K2 tog, K3, K2 tog, wf, K3) 12 times, K3.

16th row: K3, [wf, K2 tog, K2, wf, K2 tog, K1, K2 tog, wf, K3, K2 tog, (wf) twice, K2 tog, K2, wf, K2 tog, K1, K2 tog, wf, K3, K2 tog, wf] 12 times, K2.

17th row: K2, [K6, wf, sl1, K2 tog, psso, wf, K11, (knitting into front and back of '(wf) twice' of previous row throughout) wf, sl1, K2 tog, psso, wf, K5] 12 times, K3.

148

18th row: K3, [K2 tog, (wf) twice, K2 tog, K6, K2 tog, (wf) twice, (K2 tog) twice, (wf) twice, K2 tog, K6, K2 tog, (wf) twice, K2 tog] 12 times, K2.

19th row: K.

20th row: K3, [wf, (K2 tog) twice, (wf) twice, K2 tog, K2, K2 tog, (wf) twice, (K2 tog) twice, (wf) twice, (K2 tog) twice, (wf) twice, K2 tog, K2, K2 tog, (wf) twice, (K2 tog) twice, wf] 12 times, K2.

21st row: K.

22nd row: As 18th row:

23rd row: K.

24th row: K3, [wf, K2 tog, K2, K2 tog, wf, K1, wf, K2 tog, K3, K2 tog, (wf) twice, K2 tog, K2, K2 tog, wf, K1, wf, K2 tog, K3, K2 tog, wf], 12 times, K2.

25th row: K2, (K4, K2 tog, wf, K3, wf, K2 tog, K7, K2 tog, wf, K3, wf, K2 tog, K3) 12 times, K3.

26th row: K3, [K2, (K2 tog, wf) twice, K1, (wf, K2 tog) twice, K5, (K2 tog, wf) twice, K1, (wf, K2 tog) twice, K3] 12 times, K2.

27th row: K2, [K2, K2 tog, wf, K7, wf, K2 tog, K3, (K2 tog, wf) twice, K3, (wf, K2 tog) twice, K1] 12 times, K3.

28th row: K3, [K2 tog, wf, K2, wf, K2 tog, K1, K2 tog, wf, K2, wf, K2 tog, K1, (K2 tog, wf) twice, K1, wf, sl1, K2 tog, psso, wf, K1, (wf, K2 tog,) twice, K1] 12 times, K2.

29th row: K2, (K1, wf, K2 tog, K9, K2 tog, wf, K1, wf, K2 tog, K3, wf, sl1, K2 tog, psso, wf, K3, K2 tog, wf) 12 times, K3.

30th row: K3, (wf, K2 tog, K2, K2 tog, wf, K1, wf, K2 tog, K2, K2 tog, wf, K1, wf, K2 tog, K1, wf, sl1, K2 tog, psso, wf, K1, wf, sl1, K2 tog, psso, wf, K1, K2 tog, wf, K1) 12 times, K2.

31st row: K2, (K1, wf, K2 tog, K9, K2 tog, wf, K1, wf, K2 tog, K1, K2 tog, wf, K3, wf, K2 tog, K1, K2 tog, wf) 12 times, K3.

32nd row: K3, [wf, K2 tog, K2, wf, K2 tog, K1, K2 tog, wf, K2, K2 tog, wf, K1, wf, (K2 tog) twice, wf, K1, wf, sl1, K2 tog, psso, wf, K1, wf, (K2 tog) twice, wf, K1] 12 times, K2.

33rd row: As 29th.

34th row: As 30th.

35th row: K2, (K1, wf, K2 tog, K9, K2 tog, wf, K1, wf, K2

149

tog, K1, K2 tog, wf, K3, wf, K2 tog, K1, K2 tog, wf) 12 times, K3.

36th row: K3, [K1, (wf, K2 tog, K1) twice, K2 tog, wf, K1, K2 tog, wf, K3, wf, K2 tog, K2, wf, sl1, K2 tog, psso, wf, K2, K2 tog, wf, K2] 12 times, K2.

37th row: K2, (K3, wf, K2 tog, K5, K2 tog, wf, K5, wf, K2 tog, K1, wf, sl1, K2 tog, psso, wf, K1, K2 tog, wf, K2) 12 times, K3.

38th row: K3, (K3, wf, K2 tog, K3, K2 tog, wf, K7, wf, K2 tog, K3, K2 tog, wf, K4) 12 times, K2.

39th row: K2, (K5, wf, K2 tog, K1, K2 tog, wf, K9, wf, K2 tog, K1, K2 tog, wf, K4) 12 times, K3.

40th row: K3, (K5, wf, sl1, K2 tog, psso, wf, K11, wf, sl1, K2 tog, psso, wf, K6) 12 times, K2.

Rep 1st–40th rows 9 times more then rep 1st–20th rows.
Cast off.

BORDER

Cast on 17 sts.

1st row: Sl1 knitwise, P2, K1, K2 tog, wf, K1, wf, K2 tog tbl, P6, K2.

2nd row: Sl1 knitwise, K6, P2 tog tbl, wrn, P3, wrn, P2 tog, P2, inc in last st purlwise.

3rd row: Inc in first st purlwise, P2, K2 tog, wf, K5, wf, K2 tog tbl, P4, K2.

4th row: Sl1, K4, P2 tog tbl, wrn, P1, P2 tog tbl, wrn, (P1, wrn, P2 tog) twice, P2, inc in last st.

5th row: Inc in first st purlwise, P2, K2 tog, wf, K1, K2 tog, wf, K3, wf, K2 tog tbl, K1, wf, K2 tog tbl, P2, K2.

6th row: Sl1, K2, P2 tog tbl, wrn, P1, P2 tog tbl, wrn, P5, wrn, P2 tog, P1, wrn, P2 tog, P3.

7th row: Sl1, P2 (K1, wf, K2 tog tbl) twice, K3, (K2 tog, wf, K1) twice, P1, K2.

8th row: Sl1, K1, inc in next st knitwise, P2 tog, (wrn, P2 tog, P1) twice, P2 tog tbl, (wrn, P1, P2 tog tbl) twice, P2.

9th row: Sl1, P1, (K2 tog tbl, K1, wf) twice, sl1, K2 tog, psso, wf, K1, K2 tog, wf, K2 tog, inc in next st purlwise, P1, K2.

10th row: Sl1, K3, inc in next st knitwise, P2 tog, wrn, P2 tog, P3, P2 tog tbl, wrn, P1, P2 tog tbl, P2.

11th row: Sl I, P I, K2 tog tbl, K I, wf, K2 tog tbl, K I, K2 tog, wf, K2 tog, inc in next st purlwise, P3, K2.

12th row: Sl I, K5, inc in next st knitwise, P2 tog, wrn, sl I, P2 tog, psso, wrn, P I, P2 tog tbl, P I, inc in last st purlwise.

These 12 rows form the patt.

Rep these 12 rows until 4¾ yards have been worked.

Cast off.

MAKE UP

Using a flat seam, stitch on border, allowing 2 ins for easing at each corner. Press seams.

MATCHING SCARF AND GLOVES
Illustrated in Plate 19a

Scarf

2 oz 3-ply Fingering. Two No 10 needles.

Length, 30 ins. Width, 5½ ins.

This garment must be worked at a tension of 7½ sts and 9½ rows to one square inch on No 10 needles, measured over stocking stitch.

Using the through stitches method, cast on 41 sts.

Work 6 rows in stocking stitch.

Next row: K I, * wf, K2 tog, rep from * to end.

Commencing with a P row, work 7 rows in stocking stitch.

Next row: *Make hem* by knitting tog one st from needle and one loop from cast-on edge all across row.

K3 rows.

Next row: K I, * wf, K2 tog, rep from * to end of row.

Continue in garter stitch (every row K) slipping first st on every row until work measures 29 ins from beg, finishing so that right side of work will be facing when working next row.

Next row: K I, * wf, K2 tog, rep from * to end.

K 3 rows.

Work 6 rows in stocking stitch.

Next row: K I, * wf, K2 tog, rep from * to end.

Commencing with a P row work 5 rows in stocking stitch.
Cast off.

MAKE UP

Block and press on wrong side using a warm iron and damp
cloth. Join side of picot. Fold picot in half at row of holes
and st into position on wrong side.

Gloves

2 oz 3-ply Fingering. Set of four No 14 needles, with points at
both ends.
To fit an average hand.

These gloves must be worked at a tension of 9½ sts and 11½
rows to one square inch on No 14 needles, measured over
stocking stitch.

RIGHT GLOVE

Using the through stitches method, cast on 60 sts *loosely* (20 sts
on each of 3 needles).
K 6 rounds.
Next round: * wf, K2 tog, rep from * to end of round.
K 7 rounds.
Next round: *Make hem* by knitting tog one st from needle and
one st from cast-on edge all round.
Proceed as follows:
1st round: P.
2nd round: K.
3rd round: P.
4th round: * wf, K2 tog, rep from * to end of round.
Rep 1st–3rd rounds once.
K 6 rounds.

Make *thumb gusset* as follows:
1st round: P1, (inc in next st, K1) twice, P1, K to end of round.
2nd–4th rounds: Keeping purl ribs correct, work 3 rounds.
5th round: P1, inc in next st, K3, inc in next st, K1, P1, K to
end of round.
6th–8th rounds: Keeping P ribs correct, work 3 rounds.

9th round: P1, inc in next st, K5, inc in next st, K1, P1, K to end of round.

Continue in this manner until there are 20 sts between the 2 P sts.

Keeping rib correct, work 2 rounds.

Next round: K1, sl next 20 sts on to length of wool and leave for thumb, cast on 4 sts, K to end of round.

K 20 rounds. **

1st finger: K first 6 sts of round, sl all but last 11 sts of round on to a length of wool and leave, cast on 3 sts.

Divide the 20 sts on to 3 needles.

Work in stocking stitch for 2¼ ins.

Shape top as follows:

Next round: (K2 tog) 10 times.

Thread wool through remaining sts and fasten off securely.

2nd finger: K next 8 sts of round, cast on 2 sts, K last 7 sts of round, *knit up* 3 sts at base of 1st finger. Divide these 20 sts on to 3 needles.

Work in stocking stitch for 3 ins.

Shape top as on 1st finger.

3rd finger: K next 7 sts of round, cast on 3 sts, K last 8 sts of round, *knit up* 2 sts at base of 2nd finger.

Divide these 20 sts on to 3 needles.

Work in stocking stitch for 2½ ins.

Shape top as on 1st finger.

4th finger: K remaining 13 sts of round, K 4 sts at base of 3rd finger.

Divide these 17 sts on to 3 needles.

Work in stocking stitch for 2¼ ins.

Shape top as follows:

Next round: (K2 tog) 8 times, K1.

Thread wool through remaining sts and fasten off securely.

Thumb: Sl 20 sts left on length of wool on to needle, *knit up* 3 sts at base of thumb.

Divide these 23 sts on to 3 needles.

Next round: K, dec twice over the 3 sts which were knitted up (21 sts).

Work in stocking stitch for 2¼ ins.

Shape top as follows:

Next round: (K2 tog) 10 times, K1.

Thread wool through remaining sts and fasten off securely.

LEFT GLOVE

Work as right glove until ** is reached.

1st finger: K first 17 sts of round, sl remaining sts on to a length of wool and leave, cast on 3 sts. *Divide* these 20 sts on to 3 needles.

Complete finger and work remainder of glove as given for right glove, beginning at *back* of glove to K up sts for remaining fingers.

Press gloves on wrong side using a warm iron and damp cloth.

MAN'S CARDIGAN
Illustrated in Plate 19b

11/12/13 oz 3-ply Fingering. Two No 11 and two No 9 needles. Ten buttons.

Chest, 36/38/40 ins. Length, 23¾/24/24¼ ins. Sleeve, 19 ins.

This garment must be worked at a tension of 7 sts and 9 rows to one square inch on No 9 needles measured over stocking stitch.

RIGHT FRONT

Using No 11 needles, cast on 76/79/82 sts and work in K1, P1 rib for 2 ins.

Change to No 9 needles and proceed in twist st rib as follows:

1st row: * P1, TW2, rep from * to last st, P1.

2nd row: P.

3rd row: * P1, K2, rep from * to last st, P1.

4th row: P.

These 4 rows form the patt.

Continue in patt until work measures 15½ ins from beg, finishing so that the wrong side of work will be facing when working next row.

Shape armhole and front slope as follows:

Cast off 9/10/11 sts at beg of next row, then dec 1 st at armhole edge on next and every alt row until 9 dec *in all* have been worked at armhole edge, *at the same time* dec 1 st at front edge on first row of armhole shaping and on every following 3rd row until armhole shaping has been completed. Continue without further dec at armhole edge but still dec on every 3rd row from previous dec at front edge as before until 36/39/42 sts remain.

Continue on these sts until work measures 8¼/8½/8¾ ins from beg of armhole shaping, finishing at armhole edge.

Shape shoulder by casting off 12/13/14 sts at beg of next and every alt row until all sts are cast off.

LEFT FRONT

Work to match right front reversing all shapings, *noting* that right side of work instead of wrong side will be facing at the beg of armhole shaping.

BACK

Using No 11 needles, cast on 136/139/142 sts.
Work in K 1, P 1 rib for 2 ins.

Change to No 9 needles and proceed in patt as on right front until work matches fronts up to armhole shaping.

Shape armholes by casting off 7/8/9 sts at beg of next 2 rows, then dec 1 st at both ends of next and every alt row until 108/111/114 sts remain.

Continue on these sts until work matches fronts up to shoulder shaping.

Shape shoulders by casting off 12/13/14 sts at beg of next 6 rows.
Cast off.

SLEEVES

Using No 11 needles, cast on 61/64/67 sts.
Work in K 1, P 1 rib for 3 ins.

Change to No 9 needles and proceed in patt as on right front inc 1 st at both ends of 3rd and every following 5th/4th/4th row until there are 109/112/115 sts on needle, then on every following 3rd row until there are 119/122/125 sts on needle.
Continue on these sts until work measures 19 ins from beg.

Shape top by casting off 8 sts at beg of next 2 rows, then dec 1 st at both ends of next and every alt row until 47/50/53 sts remain.
Cast off 7 sts at beg of next 6 rows.
Cast off.

POCKETS

Using No 9 needles, cast on 46 sts.
Work in patt as on right front for 4½ ins, finishing so that right side of work will be facing when working next row and inc 1 st at end of last row (47 sts).

Change to No 11 needles and proceed in K1, P1 rib as follows:
1st row: K2, * P1, K1, rep from * to last st, K1.
2nd row: * K1, P1, rep from * to last st, K1.
Rep these 2 rows for 1 inch.
Cast off in rib.
Work a second pocket in the same manner.

FRONT BAND

Using No 11 needles, cast on 13 sts.
1st row: K2, * P1, K1, rep from * to last st, K1.
2nd row: * K1, P1, rep from * to last st, K1.
3rd and 4th rows: As 1st and 2nd.
5th row: Rib 5, cast off 3, rib to end.
6th row: Rib 5, cast on 3, rib to end.
Continue in this manner, working a buttonhole as on 5th and 6th rows on 13th and 14th rows from previous buttonhole until 10 buttonholes *in all* have been worked.
Continue in rib without further buttonholes until 49 ins (not stretched) from beg has been completed. Cast off in rib.

MAKE UP

Block and press fabric. Stitch pockets into position as shown on photograph. Using a back-stitch seam throughout, join shoulder, side, and sleeve seams, and stitch sleeves into position; on 38- and 40-inch chest sizes, stitch sleeve seams ½ inch to front of side seams. Neatly stitch on front band. Attach buttons to correspond with buttonholes. Press all seams.

MAN'S SLEEVELESS PULLOVER
Illustrated in Plate 19b

7/8/8 oz 3-ply Fingering. Two No 12 and two No 9 needles. Set of four No 11 needles, with points at both ends. A cable needle. Chest, 36/38/40 ins. Length 21¾/22/22¼ ins.

This garment must be worked at a tension of 7 sts and 9 rows to one square inch on No 9 needles measured over stocking stitch.

FRONT

Using No 12 needles, cast on 134/140/146 sts.

Work in K1, P1 rib for 3½ ins, inc 1 st at end of last row (135/141/147 sts).

Change to No 9 needles and proceed in stocking stitch with cable stitch panels as follows:

1st row: K15/18/21, (P1, TW3, P2, K6, sl1, K6, P2, TW3, P1, K15) twice, P1, TW3, P2, K6, sl1, K6, P2, TW3, P1, K15/18/21.

2nd row: P15/18/21, (P4, K2, P13, K2, P19) twice, P4, K2, P13, K2, P19/22/25.

3rd row: K15/18/21, (P1, K3, P2, C3F, sl1, C3B, P2, K3, P1, K15) twice, P1, K3, P2, C3F, sl1, C3B, P2, K3, P1, K15/18/21.

4th row: As 2nd row.

These 4 rows form the patt used in the cable panel throughout the front.

Continue in patt until work measures 12¼ ins from beg, finishing so that right side of work will be facing when working next row.

Divide for V neck as follows:

Next row: Patt across 67/70/73 sts, cast off 1, patt to end.

157

Proceed on first group of 67/70/73 sts as follows:

1st row: Work across 67/70/73 sts, thus finishing at neck edge.

2nd row: K2 tog, work to end.

3rd to 5th rows: Work all across.

6th row: As 2nd row.

7th to 9th rows: Work all across.

Continue dec in this manner on next and every following 4th row from previous dec until work measures 13¼ ins from beg, finishing at outside edge.

Still decreasing on every 4th row at the neck edge as before, *shape armhole* by casting off 8 sts at beg of next row, then dec 1 st at armhole edge on next and every alt row until 9/10/11 dec *in all* have been completed at armhole edge.

When armhole shaping is completed, continue dec on front edge *only* on every 4th row from previous dec as before until 33/36/39 sts remain.

Continue on these sts until work measures 8½/8¾/9 ins from beg of armhole shaping, finishing at armhole edge.

Shape shoulder by casting off 11/12/13 sts at beg of next and every alt row until all sts are cast off.

Rejoin wool to remaining group of 67/70/73 sts and complete to match other half of front.

BACK

Using No 12 needles, cast on 134/140/146 sts.

Work in K1, P1 rib for 3½ ins, inc 1 st at end of last row (135/141/147 sts).

Change to No 9 needles and proceed in stocking stitch (1 row K, 1 row P) until work measures same as Front up to armhole shaping.

Shape armholes by casting off 8 sts at beg of next 2 rows. Dec 1 st at both ends of next and every alt row until 101/105/109 sts remain.

Continue on these sts until work measures same as Front up to shoulder shaping.

Shape shoulders by casting off 11/12/13 sts at beg of next 6 rows. Cast off.

ARMBANDS

Using a back-stitch seam join shoulders of back and front.

Using No 12 needles, with right side of work facing *knit up* 154/158/162 sts round armhole.

Work in K 1, P 1 rib for 1 in.

Cast off in rib.

Complete second armband to match.

NECKBAND

Using set of four No 12 needles, with right side of work facing *knit up* 170/174/178 sts round neck, including 1 st knitted up through cast-off st at centre front of V. (Mark this st with a length of coloured wool).

Proceed in rounds of K 1, P 1 rib, dec 1 st on every round at each side of marked st knitted up through cast-off st at centre front for 1 inch.

Cast off loosely in rib.

MAKE UP

Block and press fabric. Using a back-stitch seam, join side seams. Join armbands. Press seams.

MAN'S ROUND NECKED SLEEVELESS PULLOVER

9/10/10 oz 4-ply Fingering. Two No 12 and two No 10 needles. Set of four No 12 needles with points at both ends.

Chest, 38/40/42 ins. Length, 22/22½/22½ ins.

This garment must be worked at a tension of 7 sts and 9 rows to one square inch on No 10 needles measured over stocking stitch.

FRONT

Using No 12 needles, cast on 135/139/144 sts.

Work in K 1, P 1 rib for 3½ ins, inc 1 st at end of last row *on 2nd and 3rd sizes only* (135/140/145 sts).

Change to No 10 needles and proceed in embossed patt as follows:

1st row: * P 1, KB 4, rep from * to end.

2nd row: * PB3, K2, rep from * to end.

3rd row: * P3, KB2, rep from * to end.

4th row: * PB1, K4, rep from * to end.

5th row: * KB1, P4, rep from * to end.

6th row: * K3, PB2, rep from * to end.

7th row: * KB3, P2, rep from * to end.

8th row: * K1, PB4, rep from * to end.

These 8 rows form the patt.

Continue in patt until work measures 13½ ins from beg.

Shape armholes as follows:

Keeping patt correct, cast off 7/8/9 sts at beg of next 2 rows. Dec 1 st at both ends of next and every alt row until 105/108/111 sts remain.

Continue on these sts until work measures 6/6¼/6½ ins from beg of armhole shaping.

Shape neck as follows:

Next row: Patt 43/44/45, cast off 19/20/21, patt to end.

Proceed on *each* group of 43/44/45 sts as follows:

Dec 1 st at neck edge on next and every alt row until 33/34/35 sts remain.

Continue on these sts until work measures 8½/8¾/9 ins from beg of armhole shaping, finishing at armhole edge.

Shape shoulder by casting off 11 sts at beg of next and every alt row until 11/12/13 sts remain.

Work 1 row.

Cast off.

BACK

Work as front until neck shaping is reached.

Continue on 105/108/111 sts until work matches front up to shoulder shaping.

Shape shoulders by casting off 11 sts at beg of next 4 rows; 11/12/13 sts at beg of next 2 rows.

Cast off.

ARMBANDS

Using a back-stitch seam, join shoulders of back and front.

17a. Three-ply dress (p. 138)

17b. Two bedjackets (p. 141, 145)

18. Shawl (p. 147)

19a. Matching scarf and gloves (p. 151), Pom-pom trimmed hat (p. 192)

19b. Man's cardigan (p. 154), Man's sleeveless pullover (p. 157)

20a. Polo neck sweater in three sizes (p. 161)

20b. Man's waistcoat in three sizes (p. 163)

21a. Evening blouse with draped *décolletage* (p. 193)

21b. Man's continental slipover (p. 200)

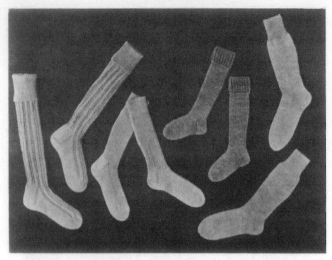

22a. Golf stockings (p. 175), Fancy rib socks (p. 172),
Boy's stockings (p. 173), Man's plain socks (p. 171)

22b. Child's socks (p. 177)

23a. Small lace doily (p. 185)

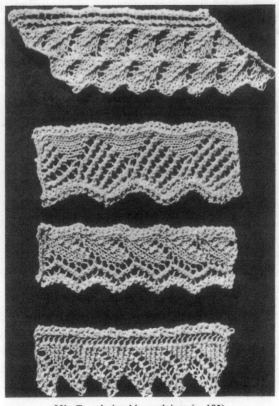

23b. Four knitted lace edgings (p. 183)

24. Tea cosy (p. 179)

25. Lady's evening jumper (p. 204), Evening stole (p. 211)

26. Evening shawl (p. 212), Evening stoles (p. 211, 213)

27b. Brushed wool coat (p. 214)

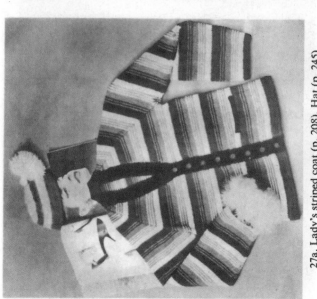

27a. Lady's striped coat (p. 208). Hat (p. 245)

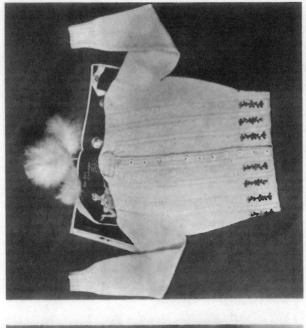

28b. Four-ply Tyrolean coat (p. 223)

28a. Two-ply separates (p. 217)

29b. Man's continental sweater (p. 233)

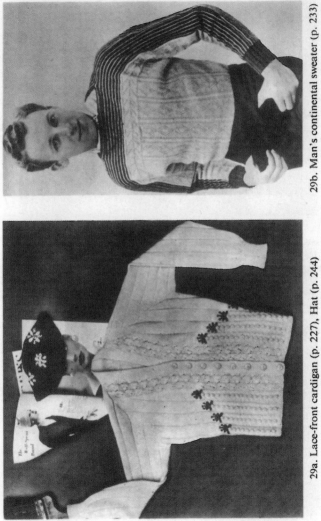

29a. Lace-front cardigan (p. 227), Hat (p. 244)

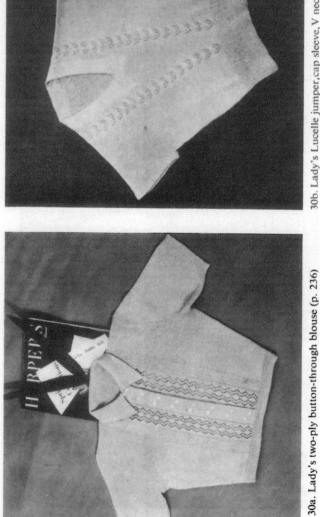

30a. Lady's two-ply button-through blouse (p. 236)

30b. Lady's Lucelle jumper, cap sleeve, V neck (p. 240)

31. Three lady's hats (p. 244, 245, 246)

32. Lady's jumper with V-shaped panel and yoke (p. 248)

With right side of work facing, using No 12 needles rejoin wool and *knit up* 132/136/140 sts round armhole.
Work in K I, P I rib for I inch.
Cast off in rib.

NECKBAND

Using a set of No 12 needles *knit up* 114/118/122 sts round neck.
Work in rounds of K I, P I rib for I inch.
Cast off loosely in rib.

MAKE UP

Omitting ribbing, block and press on wrong side using a warm iron and damp cloth. Using a flat seam, join ends of armbands and ribbing at lower edge. Using a back-stitch seam, join side seams. Press seams.

POLO NECK SWEATER IN THREE SIZES
Illustrated in Plate 20a

18/18/19 oz Double Knitting. Two No 10 and two No 7 needles. Set of four No 11 needles with points at both ends. Two stitch-holders. One cable needle.
Chest, 38/40/42 ins. Length, 24 ins. Sleeve, 18 ins.

This garment must be worked at a tension of $5\frac{1}{4}$ sts and 7 rows to one square inch on No 7 needles measured over stocking stitch.

FRONT

Using No 10 needles, cast on 108/112/116 sts.
Work in K2, P2 rib for $3\frac{1}{2}$ ins, inc I st at end of last row (109/113/117 sts).

Change to No 7 needles and proceed in patt as follows:
1st row: K I/3/5, (P2, K B I, P I, K3, P I, K B I, P2, K6, keeping wool at back of needle sl I purlwise, K6) 4 times, P2, K B I, P I, K3, P I, K B I, P2, K I/3/5.
2nd row: P I/3/5, (K2, P B I, P5, P B I, K2, P I3) 4 times, K2, P B I, P5, P B I, K2, P I/3/5.

161

3rd row: K1/3/5, (P2, KB1, P1, TW3, P1, KB1, P2, C3F, sl1, C3B) 4 times, P2, KB1, P1, TW3, P1, KB1, P2, K1/3/5.

4th row: As 2nd row.

5th and 6th rows: As 1st and 2nd.

7th row: K1/3/5, (P2, KB1, P1, TW3, P1, KB1, P2, K6, sl1, K6) 4 times, P2, KB1, P1, TW3, P1, KB1, P2, K1/3/5.

8th row: P1/3/5, (K2, PB1, P5, PB1, K2, P13) 4 times, K2, PB1, P5, PB1, K2, P1/3/5.

These 8 rows form the patt.

Continue in patt until work measures 15½ ins from beg.

Keeping patt correct, *shape armholes* by casting off 6/7/8 sts at beg of next 2 rows. Dec 1 st at both ends of next and every alt row until 87/89/91 sts remain.

Continue on these sts until work measures 6 ins from beg of armhole shaping, finishing so that right side of work will be facing when working next row.

Shape neck as follows:

Patt 34/35/36, work next 19 sts on to a stitch-holder, patt to end.

Proceed on *each* group of 34/35/36 sts as follows:

Dec 1 st at neck edge on next and every alt row until 29/30/31 sts remain.

Continue on these sts until work measures 8½ ins from beg of armhole shaping, finishing at armhole edge.

Shape shoulder as follows:

1st row: Cast off 10 sts, work to end.

2nd row: Work all across.

Rep 1st and 2nd rows once.

Cast off.

BACK

Work as front until work measures 7 ins in place of 6 ins from beg of armhole shaping, finishing so that right side of work will be facing when working next row.

Shape neck and shoulders as on front, noting that neck shaping will be worked on every row in place of every alt row.

SLEEVES

Using No 10 needles, cast on 48 sts.

Work in K2, P2 rib for 3½ ins.

Change to No 7 needles and proceed in stocking stitch, inc 1 st at both ends of 3rd and every following 7th row until there are 72 sts on needle.

Continue on these sts until work measures 18 ins from beg.

Shape top by casting off 6 sts at beg of next 2 rows.

Dec 1 st at both ends of next and every alt row until 26 sts remain. Cast off 5 sts at beg of next 4 rows.

Cast off.

Work another sleeve in same manner.

POLO NECK

Using a back-stitch seam join shoulders of back and front.

Using set of No 11 needles, with right side of work facing *knit up* 108 sts round neck including sts from stitch-holders.

Work in rounds of K2, P2 rib for 5 ins.

Cast off loosely in rib.

MAKE UP

Omitting ribbing, block and press on wrong side using a warm iron and damp cloth. Using a back-stitch seam join side and sleeve seams and stitch sleeves into position. Press seams.

MAN'S WAISTCOAT IN THREE SIZES
Illustrated in Plate 20b

11/12/12 oz Double Knitting. Two No 9 needles. Eight buttons. Two stitch-holders.

38/40/42 inch chest. Length at centre back (excluding band) 20½/20¾/21 ins.

This garment must be worked at a tension of 5¾ sts and 7¾ rows to one square inch on No 9 needles measured over stocking stitch.

POCKETS (*both alike*)

Cast on 23 sts.

Work in stocking stitch for 3 ins, finishing at end of a K row. Break off wool. Slip sts on to stitch-holder and leave.

RIGHT FRONT

Cast on 2 sts.

1st row: Inc in first st, K 1, cast on 4.

2nd row: P.

3rd row: Inc in first st, P 2, K 2, P 2, cast on 4.

4th row: * P 2, K 2, rep from * to end.

These 4 rows form the ridge patt.

Keeping ridge patt correct, continue inc and casting on as on 3rd row on next and every alt row until there are 52 sts.

Next row: Work all across (38 inch size).

For the *40 inch size* work the next row as follows:

Work all across casting on 3 sts at end of row (55 sts), and for *42 inch size* on the next row work to the end and cast on 6 sts (58 sts).

Continue in patt on these 52/55/58 sts until work measures 3 ins at short (side) edge, finishing so that right side of work will be facing when working next row.

Place pocket as follows:

Next row: Work across 12 sts, *knit* next 23 sts on to stitch-holder and leave, work to end.

Next row: Work across 17/20/23 sts, sl 23 sts from top of pocket on to left-hand needle, work across these sts, work to end.

Continue in patt until work measures $10\frac{1}{4}/10\frac{1}{2}/10\frac{3}{4}$ ins at short (side) edge, finishing at side edge.

Shape armhole by casting off 7/8/9 sts at beg of next row. Dec 1 st at armhole edge on every row until 40 sts remain, every alt row until 37/38/39 sts remain.

Work 5/3/1 rows, thus finishing at front edge.

Commence front slope by dec 1 st at front edge on next and every following 4th row until 27/29/31 sts remain, every following 6th row until 25/26/27 sts remain.

Continue on these sts until work measures $9\frac{1}{2}$ ins from beg of armhole shaping, finishing at armhole edge.

Shape shoulder as follows:
1st row: Cast off 8/8/9, patt to end.
2nd row: Patt all across.
Rep 1st and 2nd rows once. Cast off.

POCKET TOP

Sl 23 sts from stitch-holder on to needle, rejoin wool and with right side of work facing, proceed in rib as follows:
1st row: K2, * P1, K1, rep from * to last st, K1.
2nd row: * K1, P1, rep from * to last st, K1.
Rep these 2 rows until work measures ¾ inch from beg.
Cast off in rib.

Special Note: You can vary the patterning on the waistcoat by applying any of the sts from pages 32 to 34 to the basic patt for the fronts.

LEFT FRONT

Work to match right front reversing all shapings.

BACK

Cast on 93/99/105 sts.
1st row: * K1, P1, rep from * to last st, K1.
2nd row: * P1, K1, rep from * to last st, P1.
Rep these 2 rows until work measures 2 ins from beg.
Continue in rib, inc 1 st at both ends of next and every following 10th row until there are 105/111/117 sts on needle.
Continue on these sts until work measures 11/11¼/11½ ins from beg.

Shape armholes by casting off 5/6/7 sts at beg of next 2 rows. Dec 1 st at both ends of every row until 81/85/89 sts remain.
Continue on these sts until work measures 9½ ins from beg of armhole shaping.
Cast off all across.

FRONT BAND

Cast on 7 sts.
1st row: K1, * K into back of next st, P1, rep from * to last 2 sts, K into back of st, K1.

2nd row: * K I, P into back of next st, rep from * to last st, K I.

Continue in rib as on these 2 rows until work measures 7/7¼/7½ ins from beg, finishing at end of a 1st row of rib.

Keeping rib correct, work mitred corner as follows:

1st row: Rib 2, turn.

2nd row: Sl I, K I.

3rd row: Rib 3, turn.

4th row: Sl I, rib to end.

5th row: Rib 4, turn.

6th row: As 4th row.

7th row: Rib 5, turn.

8th row: As 4th row.

9th row: Rib all across row.

Continue in rib until work measures 4 ins from mitred corner measured at inside (short) edge, finishing at inside edge.

Work buttonhole as follows:

1st row: Rib 3, cast off 1, rib to end.

2nd row: Rib 3, cast on 1, rib to end.

Continue in rib, working a buttonhole on 11th and 12th rows from previous buttonhole until 8 buttonholes *in all* have been worked.

Continue in rib until work measures 37/37½/38 ins from last buttonhole, finishing at end of a 1st row of rib.

Work mitred corner as before. Continue in rib until 7/7¼/7½ ins from mitred corner (measured at inside edge) have been worked.

Cast off in rib.

ARMBANDS

Using a back-stitch seam join shoulders of back and fronts, leaving 31 sts free at back of neck.

With right side of work facing *knit up* 119 sts round armhole.

Commencing with a 2nd row proceed in rib as on front band for ¾ inch.

Cast off in rib.

Work second armband in same manner.

MAKE UP

Omitting ribbing, with wrong side of work facing, block fabric by pinning out round edges. Omitting ribbing, press fabric using a warm iron and damp cloth. Using a back-stitch seam, join side seams, leaving ¾ inch of back free at lower edge. Using a flat seam, stitch on front band, joining ends to ¾-inch overlaps at lower edge of back. Stitch pockets into position on wrong side of work and pocket tops on right side of work. Attach buttons. Press all seams.

MAN'S FAIR ISLE SCARF AND GLOVES
Illustrated in Plate 12b

Gloves

2 oz Ground Shade, small quantity Contrast 4-ply Fingering. Set of four No 13 and set of four No 12 needles with points at both ends.

Length, 7¾–8¼/8½–9 ins.

For the larger size use No 12 needles in place of No 13s and No 11 needles in place of No 12s and work from same instructions.

These gloves must be worked at a tension of 8½ sts and 10½ rows on No 13 needles and 8 sts and 10 rows on No 12 needles to one square inch measured over stocking stitch.

RIGHT GLOVE

Using two No 13 needles and Ground Shade, cast on 64 sts.

1st row: K2, * P1, K1, rep from * to end.

CHART FOR GLOVES

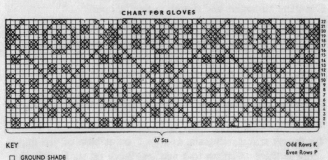

67 Sts

KEY

☐ GROUND SHADE

☒ CONTRAST

Odd Rows K
Even Rows P

Rep 1st row until work measures $3\frac{1}{2}$ ins from beg.

Next row: K1, P4, sl these 5 sts on to a safety pin and leave for thumb gusset. The thumb gusset and thumb are worked separately and stitched into position when glove is completed.

Work across remaining 59 sts as follows:

* P6, inc in next st purlwise, rep from * to last 3 sts, P2, K1 (67 sts).

** *Change to No 12 needles* and work rows 1–22 incl, then rows 1–3 incl from chart, reading K rows from *right* to left and P rows from *left* to right.

Using Ground Shade, cast on 5 sts at end of last row (72 sts). Keeping the 5 cast-on sts in stocking stitch and Ground Shade, continue working from chart as before to end of 15th row.

Break off Contrast.

Divide sts equally on to 3 needles and proceed as follows:

With right side of work facing, join into round and K1 round.

Change to No 13 needles

Next round: K7, * K2 tog, K6, rep from * to last st, K1 (64 sts). **

Divide for fingers as follows:

1st finger: K1, sl all but last 17 sts of round on to a thread, cast on 2 sts, divide these 20 sts on to 3 needles. Join into round, and work in stocking stitch (every row K) for 3 ins.

Next round: (K2 tog) 10 times.

Break off wool, thread through remaining sts and fasten off securely.

Complete all fingers and thumb in this manner.

2nd finger: K next 8 sts of round, cast on 2 sts, K last 8 sts in round, *knit up* 2 sts from 2 cast-on sts at base of previous finger, divide these 20 sts on to 3 needles.

Work in stocking stitch on these 20 sts for $3\frac{1}{2}$ ins. Complete as 1st finger.

3rd finger: Work as 2nd finger but working 3 ins in place of $3\frac{1}{2}$ ins.

4th finger: K remaining sts, *knit up* 2 sts at base of 3rd finger, divide these 16 sts on to 3 needles. Work on sts for $2\frac{1}{2}$ ins.

Next round: (K2 tog) 8 times.

Thumb gusset and thumb: Sl 5 sts for thumb gusset on to a No 13 needle.

With right side of work facing, join in ground shade and proceed as follows:

1st row: K.

2nd row: K I, P to last st, K I.

3rd row: Inc in first st, K to last 2 sts, inc in next st, K I.

Continue in stocking stitch, inc 1 st at both ends of every 4th row until there are 19 sts.

Work 4 rows, casting on 5 sts at end of last row (24 sts).

Divide these 24 sts on to 3 needles. Join into round.

Next 2 rounds: K, dec 2 sts in each round over the 5 cast-on sts (20 sts).

Continue on these 20 sts until work measures 2½ ins from cast-on sts.

Next round: (K 2 tog) 10 times.

LEFT GLOVE

Work rib as on right glove.

Next row: K I, P 2, * inc in next st purlwise, P 6, rep from * to last 5 sts, sl these 5 sts on to a safety pin and leave for thumb gusset.

Work from ** to ** as on right glove.

Divide for fingers as follows:

1st finger: K first 17 sts, sl all but last st of round on to a thread, cast on 2 sts, divide these 20 sts on to 3 needles.

Join into round.

Finish finger and work remainder of glove as given for right glove, beg at *back* of glove to pick up sts for remaining fingers.

MAKE UP

Sew in ends. Stitch thumb gusset into position. Join side seam. Press on wrong side.

SELF-COLOURED OR LADY'S GLOVES

For a self-coloured glove, work to the same instructions, the Fair Isle portion of the glove being worked in self colour throughout.

Use a size 11 needle in place of size 12 needle and 3-ply Fingering in place of 4-ply Fingering, adjusting the finger lengths to suit individual needs.

Man's Fair Isle Scarf

6 oz Ground Shade, 4 oz Contrast, 3-ply Fingering. Set of four No 12 needles with points at both ends. Crochet hook.
Width, 6¾ ins. Length (without fringe) 44 ins.

This scarf must be worked at a tension of 8½ sts and 10½ rows to one square inch on No 12 needles, measured over stocking stitch.

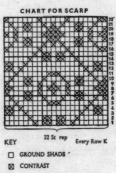

CHART FOR SCARF

KEY   22 St rep   Every Row K

☐ GROUND SHADE
☒ CONTRAST

Using Ground Shade, cast on 132 sts, 44 sts on each of 3 needles.
K 1 round.
Join in Contrast and work 22 st rep from chart, reading *all* rows from right to left.
Continue in patt until work measures 44 ins from beg, finishing at end of a 2nd or 13th row of chart.
Break off Contrast.
K 1 round.
Cast off.

MAKE UP

Fasten off ends. Press carefully. Using Ground Shade, make fringe as follows:
Wind wool over a piece of cardboard 2½ ins wide and cut through one end. Taking 4 strands together, double them and

170

using crochet hook draw a loop through the end of the scarf, pass the ends through the loop and knot firmly. Rep at even intervals along both ends of scarf. Trim evenly.

MAN'S PLAIN SOCKS
Illustrated in Plate 22a

3 oz 3-ply Fingering. Set of four No 13 needles with points at both ends.

To fit $10\frac{1}{2}/11/11\frac{1}{2}$ inch foot.

These socks must be worked to a tension of 9 sts and 11 rows to one square inch measured over stocking stitch.

Cast on 76 sts, 22 on each of 1st and 3rd needles, 32 on 2nd needle.

Work in rounds of K1, P1 rib for $3\frac{1}{2}$ ins.

Next round: Inc in first st, rib to last 2 sts, inc in next st, P1 (78 sts).**

Proceed in stocking stitch (every round K) for $3\frac{1}{2}$ ins.

Shape as follows:

1st round: K1, K2 tog, K to last 3 sts, K2 tog tbl, K1.

K5 rounds.

Rep these 6 rounds until 66 sts remain.

Continue in stocking stitch until work measures $11\frac{1}{2}$ ins from beg.

Divide for heel as follows:

K17, sl the last 17 sts of round on to other end of same needle (these 34 sts are for heel).

Divide remaining sts on to two needles and leave for instep.

1st row: Sl1 purlwise, P to end.

2nd row: Sl1 knitwise * K1, keeping wool at back of work, sl1 purlwise, rep from * to last st, K1.

Work these 2 rows 16 times more, then 1st row once.

Turn heel as follows:

K24, sl1, K1, psso, turn, * P15, P2 tog, turn, K15, sl1, K1, psso, turn, rep from * until all sts are worked on to one needle again.

Next row: K8, thus completing heel (8 sts remain on left-hand needle).

Sl all instep sts on to one needle again.

Using spare needle, κ remaining 8 heel sts, *knit up* 18 sts from side of heel; with 2nd needle κ across instep sts; with 3rd needle *knit up* 18 sts from other side of heel, κ8 heel sts (84 sts).

Shape instep as follows:

1st round: κ.

2nd round: *1st needle:* κ to last 3 sts, κ2 tog, κ1. *2nd needle:* κ. *3rd needle:* κ1, κ2 tog tbl, κ to end.

Rep these 2 rounds until 66 sts remain.

Continue without shaping until work, from where stitches were knitted up at heel, measures:

6¾ ins for 10½-inch foot.

7¼ ins for 11-inch foot.

7¾ ins for 11½-inch foot.

Shape toe as follows:

1st round: *1st needle:* κ to last 3 sts, κ2 tog, κ1. *2nd needle:* κ. *3rd needle:* κ1, κ2 tog tbl, κ to end.

2nd round: κ.

3rd round: *1st needle:* κ to last 3 sts, κ2 tog, κ1. *2nd needle:* κ1, κ2 tog tbl, κ to last 3 sts, κ2 tog, κ1. *3rd needle:* κ1, κ2 tog tbl, κ to end.

Rep last 2 rounds until 24 sts remain.

κ sts from 1st needle on to end of 3rd needle.

Cast off sts from two needles tog or graft sts.

Work a second sock in the same manner.

MAKE UP

Press on wrong side using a warm iron and damp cloth.

FANCY RIB SOCKS

Illustrated in Plate 22a

Materials, measurements: As Plain Socks.

Work as Plain Socks (page 171) until ** is reached.

Proceed in fancy rib as follows:

172

1st round: * P I, K I, P I, K 2, P I, rep from * to end of round.
2nd round: * P I, K 2, P I, K I, P I, rep from * to end of round.
Working fancy rib in place of stocking stitch, work as instructions for Plain Socks (page 171) until heel is reached.
Work heel as in Plain Socks (page 171).
Continue as for Plain Socks, (page 172) but *noting* that the instep sts should be worked in rib until toe shaping is reached.
Complete as for Plain Socks (page 172).

BOY'S STOCKINGS WITH RIBBED OR FANCY TOPS
Illustrated in Plate 22a

3 oz Ground Shade (oddment of Contrast for Fancy Top). 4-ply Fingering. Set of four No 12 needles with points at both ends.
Length from top to lower edge of heel (with top turned over) 13½ ins (or length required).
Length of foot 7½ ins (or length required).

These stockings must be worked at a tension of 8 sts and 10 rows to one square inch on No 12 needles measured over stocking stitch.

Using Ground Shade, cast on 68 sts (20 on 1st needle, and 24 on each of 2nd and 3rd needles).
Work in rounds of K I, P I rib for 3 rounds.

For ribbed top continue in rib until work measures 6 ins from beg then work from ** to end.

For Fancy Top proceed as follows:
1st round: Using Contrast, *K 3, keeping wool at back of needle sl I purlwise, rep from * to end.
2nd round: As 1st round.
3rd round: Using Ground Shade, K.
4th and 5th rounds: Using Ground Shade, * P 3, K I, rep from * to end.
Rep these 5 rounds 6 times, then 1st, 2nd, and 3rd rounds once.
Break off Contrast.
Proceed in K I, P I rib until work measures 6 ins from beg.
Turn work inside out to reverse fabric.

Work ribbed leg as follows:
** **1st round:** * K3, P1, rep from * to end of round.
Rep this round for 3 ins.

Shape leg as follows:
Next round: K2 tog, K1, P1, * K3, P1, rep from * to last 8 sts
of round, K1, K2 tog tbl, P1, K3, P1.
Work 6 rounds without shaping.
Continue dec once at beg and end of round (outside centre
panel of P1, K3, P1) on next and every following 7th round
until 60 sts remain. Continue without shaping until work
measures 14 ins (or length required) from beg. *To commence
heel* (K3, P1) 3 times, sl last 17 sts of round on to other end
of same needle (these 29 sts are for the heel). Divide remaining
sts on to two needles and leave for instep.
Work 21 rows on heel sts in stocking stitch (1 row K, 1 row P),
always slipping first and knitting last st on every row.

Turn heel as follows:
1st row: K18, sl1, K1, psso, turn.
2nd row: P8, P2 tog, turn.
3rd row: K8, sl1, K1, psso, turn.
4th row: P8, P2 tog, turn.
Rep 3rd and 4th rows until all sts are worked on to one needle
again.
K back 5 sts (thus completing heel).
Sl all instep sts on to one needle again. Taking another needle
K remaining 4 heel sts, *knit up* 15 sts from side of heel, with
2nd needle work in rib across instep sts, with 3rd needle
knit up 15 sts from side of heel and remaining 5 sts.

Shape instep as follows:
1st round: K on 1st and 3rd needles and work in rib on 2nd
needle.
2nd round: K to last 3 sts of 1st needle, K2 tog, K1; on 2nd
needle work in rib all across; on 3rd needle, K1, K2 tog tbl,
K to end.
Rep these 2 rounds 4 times more.
Continue without further shaping until foot measures 4½ ins
(or length required) from where sts were knitted up at heel.
Next round: K, dec 1 st at each end of 2nd needle.

174

Shape toe as follows:

1st round: K to last 3 sts of 1st needle, K2 tog, K1; on 2nd needle K1, K2 tog tbl, K to last 3 sts, K2 tog, K1; on 3rd needle K1, K2 tog tbl, K to end.

2nd round: K.

Rep these 2 rounds until 26 sts remain in round.

K sts from 1st needle on to end of 3rd needle.

Cast off sts from two needles together or graft sts.

Work a second sock in the same manner.

MAKE UP

Press on wrong side using a warm iron and damp cloth.

GOLF STOCKINGS
Illustrated in Plate 22a

6 oz 4-ply Fingering. Set of four No 11 needles with points at both ends.

Length of foot, 10/10½/11 ins.

These stockings must be worked at a tension of 7½ sts and 9½ rows to one square inch on No 11 needles measured over stocking stitch.

Cast on 76 sts, 26 on each of 1st and 2nd needles, 24 on 3rd needle.

Proceed in rounds of K1, P1 rib until work measures 8 ins from beg.

Next round: * Rib 14, inc in next st, rep from * to last st, P1 (81 sts).

Divide sts equally on needles, i.e., 27 sts on each needle.

Work in rib patt as follows:

1st round: * P2, won, K4, pass won over the 4 K sts, P2, wb, sl1 purlwise, wft, rep from * to end of round.

2nd round: * P2, K4, P2, KB1, rep from * to end of round.

3rd round: * P2, K4, P2, wb, sl1 purlwise, wft, rep from * to end of round.

4th round: As 2nd round.

These 4 rounds form the patt.

Continue in patt until work measures 13½ ins from beg.

Shape leg as follows:

1st round: Patt 2, work 2 tog, patt to last 5 sts of round, work 2 tog, patt 3.

2nd–6th rounds: Work in patt without shaping.

Rep these 6 rounds 5 times (69 sts).

Work 32 rounds without shaping.

Commence heel as follows:

K17, sl last 18 sts of round on to same needle.

Divide remaining sts on to two needles and leave for instep.

   Work on 35 heel sts as follows:

1st row: K1, P3, (P2 tog, P10) twice, P2 tog, P4, K1 (32 sts).

Work 28 rows in stocking stitch on these 32 sts, always slipping first and knitting last st.

Turn heel as follows:

1st row: K20, K2 tog, turn.

2nd row: P9, P2 tog, turn.

3rd row: K10, K2 tog, turn.

4th row: P11, P2 tog, turn.

5th row: K12, K2 tog, turn.

Continue in this manner until all sts are worked on to one needle (20 sts).

Next row: K10, thus finishing in centre of heel sts.

Slip all instep sts on to one needle.

Using another needle, K remaining 10 heel sts and *knit up* 15 sts from side of heel, with 2nd needle work in patt across instep sts; with 3rd needle *knit up* 15 sts from other side of heel, K remaining 10 sts.

Shape instep as follows:

1st round: 1st and 3rd needles: K; 2nd needle: work in patt.

2nd round: 1st needle: K to last 3 sts, K2 tog, K1; 2nd needle: work in patt; 3rd needle: K1, K2 tog tbl, K to end.

Rep these 2 rounds until 16 sts remain on *each* of 1st and 3rd needles.

Continue without further shaping until foot measures (from where sts were knitted up at heel):

6 ins for 10-inch foot.

6½ ins for 10½-inch foot.

7 ins for 11-inch foot.

Next round: 1st needle: K; 2nd needle: K1, K2 tog tbl, K to last 3 sts, K2 tog, K1; 3rd needle: K.

Shape toe as follows:

1st round: 1st needle: K to last 3 sts, K2 tog, K1; 2nd needle: K1, K2 tog tbl, K to last 3 sts, K2 tog, K1; 3rd needle: K1, K2 tog tbl, K to end.

2nd round: K.

Rep these 2 rounds until 28 sts remain.

K sts of 1st needle on to end of 3rd needle.

Cast off sts from two needles together or graft sts.

Work a second sock in the same manner.

MAKE UP

Using a warm iron and damp cloth press on wrong side.

CHILD'S SOCKS
Illustrated in Plate 22b

1/2/2 oz 3-ply Fingering. Set of four No 13 needles with points at both ends.

Length from top to base of heel, 6/7½/8½ ins. Foot, 5/6/7 ins.

This design must be worked at a tension of 9 sts and 11 rows to one square inch on No 13 needles measured over stocking stitch.

Rib Patt:

1st round: * P1, K3, P1, K1, rep from * to end of round.

2nd round: * P1, K3, P2, rep from * to end of round.

These 2 rounds form the rib patt.

Lace Rib:

1st round * K1, wf, sl1, K2 tog, psso, wf, K2, rep from * to end of round.

2nd round: K.

These 2 rounds form the lace rib patt.

Cast on 42/48/54 sts, 14/16/18 sts on each of 3 needles.

Work in rounds of K1, P1 rib for 1½/2/2½ ins.

Proceed in stocking stitch (every round κ) or in Rib Patt or Lace Rib (given above) until work measures 4½/5½/6½ ins from cast on edge.

Divide sts for heel as follows: .

κ 10/11/13, slip last 11/12/14 sts of round on to other end of same needle (these 21/23/27 sts are for heel).

Divide remaining sts on to two needles and leave for instep.

Work heel as follows:

1st row: Sl I purlwise, P to end.

2nd row: Sl I knitwise, κ to end.

Work these 2 rows 7/9/11 times more, then 1st row once.

Turn heel as follows:

1st row: κ 13/15/17, sl I, κ I, psso, turn.

2nd row: P6/8/8, P2 tog, turn.

3rd row: κ7/9/9, sl I, κ I, psso, turn.

4th row: P8/10/10, P2 tog, turn.

Continue in this manner until all sts are worked on to one needle again.

Next row: κ 7/8/9, thus completing heel.

Slip all instep sts on to one needle.

Using spare needle, κ 6/7/8 heel sts, *knit up* 9/11/13 sts along side of heel; using 2nd needle κ or work in patt across instep sts; using 3rd needle *knit up* 9/11/13 sts along other side of heel, κ7/8/9 heel sts (52/62/70 sts).

Shape instep as follows:

1st round: *1st needle*, κ; *2nd needle*, κ or work in patt; *3rd needle*, κ.

2nd round: *1st needle*, κ to last 3 sts, κ2 tog, κ I; *2nd needle*, κ or work in patt; *3rd needle*, κ I, κ2 tog tbl, κ to end.

Rep these 2 rounds until 42/50/54 sts remain in round.

Continue on these sts until work measures 3/3½/4¼ ins from where sts were knitted up at heel.

Shape toe as follows:

1st round: *1st needle*, κ to last 3 sts, κ2 tog, κ I; *2nd needle*, κ I, κ2 tog tbl, κ to last 3 sts, κ2 tog, κ I; *3rd needle*, κ I, κ2 tog tbl, κ to end.

2nd round: κ.

Rep these 2 rounds until 22/26/26 sts remain in round.

178

K sts from 1st needle on to end of 3rd needle.

Graft sts or cast off sts from 2 needles tog.

Work a second sock in same manner.

MAKE UP

Press, using a warm iron and damp cloth.

TEA COSY

Illustrated in Plate 24

4 oz Double Knitting, oddments of wool for embroidery and door. One button. Two No 8 needles.

Height, 8 ins.

This tea cosy must be knitted to a tension of 5½ sts and 7½ rows to one square inch on No 8 needles, measured over stocking stitch.

FIRST HALF

Cast on 56 sts. Work 8 rows in stocking stitch (1 row K, 1 row P).

9th row: * Using right-hand needle pick up and *knit* top loop of P st from 7th row below on wrong side of work and place st just made on left-hand needle, K2 tog (st picked up and st on needle), rep from * to end.

10th row: P.

Work in ridge patt as follows:

1st row: K.

2nd row: P.

Rep these 2 rows twice more.

7th row: As 9th row of hem.

8th row: P.

These 8 rows form the ridge patt.

Work rows 1–8 incl 7 times more, then rows 1–7 incl once.

Next row: * P2 tog, P4, P2 tog, rep from * to end (42 sts).

Work rows 1–8 incl once then rows 1–7 incl once.

Next row: * P2, P2 tog, rep from * to end (32 sts).

Work rows 1–8 incl once, then rows 1–7 incl once.

Next row: * P1, P2 tog, rep from * to last st, P1 (22 sts).

179

Work rows 1–8 incl once, then rows 1–7 incl.
Next row: P2 tog all across (11 sts).
Next row: * K 1, P 1, rep from * to end.
Rep last row twice more.
Cast off in rib.

SECOND HALF

Work to match first half.

DOOR

Using Contrast, cast on 7 sts.
Proceed in moss stitch as follows:
1st–4th rows: * K 1, P 1, rep from * to last st, K 1.
Keeping moss stitch correct dec 1 st at both ends of next and
    every 4th row until 3 sts remain. Work 1 row.
Cast off.

BUTTON COVER

Cast on 9 sts. Work in moss stitch for 10 rows.
Cast off.

MAKE UP

Press work very lightly on wrong side, using a warm iron and
    damp cloth. Using a flat seam join sides neatly, joining ridges
    together and leaving space at each side for handle and spout.
    Run thread round top, draw up and fasten off securely. Flat
    stitch door into position, work border round door in chain

stitch in Contrast. Embroider Bees on door of cosy and top of
button cover (as in diagram). Cover button with button cover
and firmly stitch to top of cosy.

Knitted blankets are very easy to make, using up oddments of wool from your work basket. Oddments of 4-ply wool, worked on a No 10 needle can be used for a lightweight blanket. If you select delicate pastel shades with a self-coloured border, these are ideal for pram blankets or cot covers.

Oddments of double knitting can be used to produce a heavier weight of blanket. If you use gay colours you can use up these oddments to make a delightful pram cover.

The blankets are worked in squares, which are stitched together with a flat seam to make the centre of the blanket itself. To finish off the blanket add borders in garter stitch, mitred at each corner.

You can use any fabric stitch you like on the squares. This blanket design is worked in stocking stitch and elongated embossed check pattern.

Using No 10 needles for 4-ply wool, or No 8 needles for Double Knitting, cast on 27 sts. This will give you a 4 inch square when completed in 4-ply wool, a 5 inch square when completed in Double Knitting.

For the stocking-stitch square work 35 rows in 4-ply and 37 rows in Double Knitting. Cast off.

For the elongated embossed check square, cast on 27 sts and proceed as follows:

1st row: * P I, K B I, rep from * to last st, P I.

2nd row: * K I, P B I, rep from * to last st, K I.

3rd row: * K B I, P I, rep from * to last st, K B I.

4th row: * P B I, K I, rep from * to last st, P B I.

Rep these 4 rows until 35 rows have been worked if you are using 4-ply, 37 rows if you are using Double Knitting.
Cast off.

When you have completed the squares (35 *in all* will be required for the above blanket), join them together, 5 squares across in width, 7 squares down in length.

To complete the blanket, work the border first of all across the 21 inch width of the oblong centre as follows:

With right side of the work facing, using No 10 needles, *knit up* 135 sts. Work in garter stitch (every row K) for 2½ ins, inc 1 st at beg of every row. Cast off.

Complete the other end to match.

With right side of the work facing *knit up* 189 sts along the side of the centre. Work in garter stitch, inc 1 st at beg of every row as before.

Complete the other side to match.

TO MAKE UP

Using a flat seam join mitred corners of borders. Block the blanket with wrong side facing. Press lightly on wrong side using a warm iron and damp cloth.

DOG'S COAT IN FIVE SIZES
Illustrated in Plate 16b

3/3/3/4/4 oz Double Knitting. Two No 6 needles.
Width all round, 13/13¾/14/14½/14¾ ins. Length (with polo neck turned back), 10/12/14/16/18 ins.

This garment must be worked at a tension of 5 sts and 6½ rows to one square inch on No 6 needles measured over stocking stitch.

Cast on 55/57/59/61/63 sts.
1st row: (Right side of work) K.
2nd row: * K 1, P 1, rep from * to last st, K 1.
These 2 rows form the patt.
Rep these 2 rows twice more.
Keeping patt and knit st edge correct, inc 1 st at both ends of next and every following 3rd/4th/5th/6th/7th row until there are 71/73/77/79/81 sts on needle.
Continue on these sts until work measures 5¾/7/8½/10¼/12 ins from beg, finishing at end of a 2nd row.
Keeping patt correct, divide for *forelegs* as follows:
** **1st row:** K 13/13/14/14/15, turn.
Work 13/15/17/17/19 rows on these sts. **
Next row: K 7/7/9/9/10, K 3 tog, K 3/3/2/2/2.
Break off wool.
Rejoin wool to remaining sts, K 45/47/49/51/51, turn.
Next row: K 2, * P 1, K 1, rep from * to last st, K 1.

Next row: K.

Rep these 2 rows 5/6/7/7/8 times more, then 1st row once.

Next row: K4/4/5/5/5, K3 tog tbl, K31/33/33/35/35, K3 tog, K4/4/5/5/5.

Break off wool.

Rejoin wool to last group of 13/13/14/14/15 sts.

Rep from ** to ** once.

Next row: K3/3/2/2/2, K3 tog tbl, K7/7/9/9/10.

Next row: Patt all across (63/65/69/71/73 sts).

Next row: K5/5/7/7/8, K3 tog, K7, K3 tog tbl, K27/29/29/31/31, K3 tog, K7, K3 tog tbl, K5/5/7/7/8 (55/57/61/63/65 sts).

Next row: Patt all across.

Next row: K3/3/5/5/6, K3 tog, K7, K3 tog tbl, K23/25/25/27/27, K3 tog, K7, K3 tog tbl, K3/3/5/5/6 (47/49/53/55/57 sts).

Next row: Patt all across.

Commence K1, P1 *rib* as follows:

1st row: K1, * K1, P1, rep from * to last 2 sts, K2.

2nd row: * K1, P1, rep from * to last st, K1.

Rep these 2 rows until work measures 2/2½/3/3½/3½ ins from beg of K1, P1 rib.

Cast off.

MAKE UP

Omitting K1, P1 rib, with wrong side of work facing, block and press fabric using a warm iron and damp cloth. Using a flat seam join edges leaving 3½/4/4½/5/5½ ins at lower edge.

FOUR KNITTED LACE EDGINGS
Illustrated in Plate 23b

Knitted laces can be made in crochet cotton ranging from size 10 to size 40. For size 10 cotton, use a No 13 needle; for size 20, a No 14 needle; for size 30, a No 15 needle; for size 40, a No 16 needle. Naturally the finer the cotton and needle, the finer the completed lace edging will be.

First Edging

Cast on 13 sts.

1st row: K7, yf, K2 tog, yf, K4.

2nd and every alt row: K2, P to last 2 sts, K2.

3rd row: K6, (yf, K2 tog) twice, yf, K4.

5th row: K5, (yf, K2 tog) 3 times, yf, K4.

7th row: K4, (yf, K2 tog) 4 times, yf, K4.

9th row: K3, (yf, K2 tog) 5 times, yf, K4 (18 sts).

11th row: K4, (yf, K2 tog) 5 times, K2 tog, K2 (17 sts).

13th row: K5, (yf, K2 tog) 4 times, K2 tog, K2.

15th row: K6, (yf, K2 tog) 3 times, K2 tog, K2.

17th row: K7, (yf, K2 tog) twice, K2 tog, K2.

19th row: K8, yf, (K2 tog) twice, K2 (13 sts).

20th row: K2, P to last 2 sts, K2.

These 20 rows form the patt.

Second Edging

Cast on 23 sts.

1st row: [yf, K1, yf, K2, (K2 tog) twice, K2] twice, (yf, K2 tog) twice, K1.

2nd and every alt row: P.

3rd row: [yf, K3, yf, K1, (K2 tog) twice, K1] twice, (yf, K2 tog) twice, K1.

5th row: [yf, K5, yf, (K2 tog) twice] twice, (yf, K2 tog) twice, K1.

7th row: [yf, K3, K2 tog, K2, yf, K2 tog] twice, (yf, K2 tog) twice, K1.

8th row: P.

These 8 rows form the patt.

Third Edging

Cast on 9 sts.

1st row: K2, yf, K2 tog, yf, K2, yf, K2 tog, K1.

2nd and every alt row: K2, yf, K2 tog, K to end.

3rd row: K2, yf, K2 tog, yf, K3, yf, K2 tog, K1.

5th row: K2, yf, K2 tog, yf, K4, yf, K2 tog, K1.

7th row: K2, yf, K2 tog, yf, K5, yf, K2 tog, K1.

9th row: K2, yf, K2 tog, yf, K6, yf, K2 tog, K1 (14 sts).

11th row: Cast off 5 sts, K 5 (6 sts on right-hand needle after cast-off), yf, K 2 tog, K 1 (9 sts).

12th row: K 2, yf, K 2 tog, K to end.

These 12 rows form the patt.

Fourth Edging

Cast on 13 sts.

1st row: Sl 1, K 3, yf, K 5, yf, K 2 tog, yf, K 2 (15 sts).

2nd and every alt row: K 2, P to last 2 sts, K 2.

3rd row: Sl 1, K 4, sl 1, K 2 tog, psso, K 2, (yf, K 2 tog) twice, K 1.

5th row: Sl 1, K 3, sl 1, K 1, psso, K 2, (yf, K 2 tog) twice, K 1.

7th row: Sl 1, K 2, sl 1, K 1, psso, K 2, (yf, K 2 tog) twice, K 1.

9th row: Sl 1, K 1, sl 1, K 1, psso, K 2, (yf, K 2 tog) twice, K 1 (10 sts).

11th row: K 1, sl 1, K 1, psso, K 2, yf, K 1, yf, K 2 tog, yf, K 2.

13th row: Sl 1, (K 3, yf) twice, K 2 tog, yf, K 2 (13 sts).

14th row: K 2, P to last 2 sts, K 2.

These 14 rows form the patt.

SMALL LACE DOILY
Illustrated in Plate 23a

One Ball Coats Mercer Crochet No 20. Set of four No 12 needles with points at both ends. A No 12 Crochet Hook.

Diameter, 7¼ ins.

This design must be worked at a tension of 10 sts and 13 rows to one square inch on No 12 needles measured over stocking stitch.

Note: Where 2 or more 'yf's' (yarn forward) occur together, knit into the front of the first 'yf' and then into the back of every following 'yf'.

On rounds 6, 8, and 10 the first stitch on every needle will be slipped on to the end of the previous needle.

On rounds 30 and 34 slip the last stitch of every needle on to the following needle.

Cast on 16 sts, 6 sts on 1st and 2nd needles, 4 sts on 3rd needle.

1st round: K.

2nd and every alt round: K.

3rd round: * yf, K 2 tog t bl, rep from * to end.

185

5th round: * (yf) twice, K 1, rep from * to end.

7th round: * (yf) twice, sl 1, K 2 tog, psso, rep from * to end.

9th round: As 7th round.

11th round: * (yf) 4 times, sl 1, K 2 tog, psso, rep from * to end.

13th round: K.

15th round: * K 9, yf, K 1, yf, rep from * to end.

17th round: * K 2 tog tbl, K 5, K 2 tog, yf, K 3, yf, rep from * to end.

19th round: * K 2 tog tbl, K 3, K 2 tog, yf, K 2, yf, K 1, yf, K 2, yf, rep from * to end.

21st round: * K 2 tog tbl, K 1, K 2 tog, yf, K 1, K 2 tog, yf, K 3, yf, K 2 tog tbl, K 1, yf, rep from * to end.

23rd round: * Sl 1, K 2 tog, psso, yf, K 1, K 2 tog, yf, K 5, yf, K 2 tog tbl, K 1, yf, rep from * to end.

25th round: * K 2, K 2 tog, yf, K 3, (yf) 5 times, K 2 tog tbl, K 2, yf, K 2 tog, K 1, rep from * to end.

27th round: * K 1, K 2 tog, yf, K 3, yf, K 2 tog tbl, rep from * to end.

29th round: * Sl 1, K 2 tog, psso, yf, K 4, yf, K 7, yf, K 4, yf, rep from * to end.

31st round: * K 4, K 2 tog, yf, K 1, yf, K 2 tog tbl, K 3, K 2 tog, yf, K 1, yf, K 2 tog tbl, K 3, rep from * to end.

33rd round: * K 5, yf, K 3, yf, sl 4, K 1, ps sts o, yf, K 3, yf, K 4, rep from * to end.

35th round: * yf, sl 1, K 2 tog, psso, yf, K 17, rep from * to end.

37th round: * yf, K 3, yf, K 2 tog tbl, K 3, K 2 tog, yf, K 3, yf, K 2 tog tbl, K 3, K 2 tog, rep from * to end.

38th round: K.

Cast off loosely.

MAKE UP

With wrong side of work facing, block and press fabric using a hot iron and damp cloth. Crochet round edge as follows:

* 5 chain, slip st into 5th chain from hook, thus forming picot, 1 dc into next st of edge, rep from * to end.

One of the most delightful accessories is a knitted lace stole. These can be knitted in 4, 3, or 2-ply wool.

The basic principle is to use a comparatively large needle, giving a delightful cobweb effect to the fabric, finishing the stoles off with edges in garter stitch which are knitted in with the stole itself.

The following needles are ideal for stoles of this type:

> 4-ply wool – Size No 7 needle
>
> 3-ply wool – Size No 6 needle
>
> 2-ply wool – Size No 5 needle

To design the stole, cast on a multiple of the number of stitches used for the lace pattern plus 12 extra stitches for border stitches along each side of the finished stole.

K 10 rows, then proceed in lace pattern, knitting 6 sts at each end of every row for the length required, less one inch. K 9 rows, cast off loosely.

To finish off the stole, pin it out on an ironing sheet, the wrong side facing, stretching the fabric slightly during the pinning process to emphasize the lacy texture of the fabric itself. Using a hot iron and wet cloth, press the stole well and leave pinned out on the ironing sheet until dry.

Let us now apply this principle for a stole knitted in 4-ply wool. The tension of 4-ply on a No 7 needle is 5½ stitches to the inch. This means that for a stole approximately 16 inches wide we shall need about 88 stitches.

Here is a simple lace pattern using a multiple of 7 stitches and 4 over. Take away 12 stitches from 88 and this gives you 76 stitches. For the lace portion of the stole we only need 74 stitches, therefore, instead of casting on 88 stitches we cast on 86 stitches and knit 10 rows.

Now proceed in lace pattern with garter stitch borders as follows:

1st row: K6, (K2, wf, K2 tog tbl, wf, K3 tog, wf) 10 times, K2, wf, K2 tog tbl, K6.

2nd row: K6, (K2, wf, K2 tog, P3) 10 times, K2, wf, K2 tog, K6.

3rd row: K6, (K2, wf, K2 tog tbl, K3) 10 times, K2, wf, K2 tog tbl, K6.

4th row: As 2nd row.

Rep these 4 rows until the stole measures 1 inch less than length required, finishing at end of a 1st row of patt.

K 9 rows, cast off.

For a lighter weight stole the same size, using 3-ply and No 6 needles, you will need approximately the same number of stitches.

The lace pattern I suggest for this stole needs a multiple of 18 stitches plus 2. First of all we subtract the 12 border stitches from the total number (88), giving 76 stitches, but again we only need 74 stitches for the pattern, thus 86 is the number of stitches we cast on for this stole.

Using No 6 needles, cast on 86 sts and K 10 rows.

Now proceed in fern lace patt with garter stitch border as follows:

1st row: K6, (P2, K9, wf, K1, wf, K3, K3 tog) 4 times, P2, K6.

2nd and every alt row: K6, P to last 6 sts, K6.

3rd row: K6, (P2, K10, wf, K1, wf, K2, K3 tog) 4 times, P2, K6.

5th row: K6, (P2, K3 tog, K4, wf, K1, wf, K3, wf, K1, wf, K1, K3 tog) 4 times, P2, K6.

7th row: K6, (P2, K3 tog, K3, wf, K1, wf, K9) 4 times, P2, K6.

9th row: K6, (P2, K3 tog, K2, wf, K1, wf, K10) 4 times, P2, K6.

11th row: K6, (P2, K3 tog, K1, wf, K1, wf, K3, wf, K1, wf, K4, K3 tog) 4 times, P2, K6.

12th row: K6, P to last 6 sts, K6.

Rep these 12 rows until stole is length required less 1 inch, finishing at end of 11th row of patt.

K 9 rows, cast off.

If you want a really cobwebby stole, use 2-ply wool and No 5 needles, again giving you approximately 88 stitches for a stole 16 inches wide. This time our lace pattern is a multiple of 11.

If we take our 12 border stitches from 88, this gives us 76 stitches. We shall need 77 stitches for 7 repeats of the lace pattern, 1 stitch more, therefore this time we cast on 89 stitches and knit 10 rows.

Proceed in lace fan patt with garter stitch border as follows:

1st row: K6, (K2 tog tbl, KB3, wf, K1, wf, KB3, K2 tog) 7 times, K6.

2nd row: K6, (PB4, P3, PB4) 7 times, K6.

3rd row: K6, (K2 tog tbl, KB2, wf, K1, wf, K2 tog tbl, wf, KB2, K2 tog) 7 times, K6.

4th row: K6, (PB3, P5, PB3) 7 times, K6.

5th row: K6, (K2 tog tbl, KB1, wf, K1, wf, K2 tog tbl, wf, K2 tog tbl, wf, KB1, K2 tog) 7 times, K6.

6th row: K6, (PB2, P7, PB2) 7 times, K6.

7th row: K6, (K2 tog tbl, wf, K1, wf, K2 tog tbl, wf, K2 tog tbl, wf, K2 tog tbl, wf, K2 tog) 7 times, K6.

8th row: K6, (PB5, P1, PB5) 7 times, K6

Rep these 8 rows until stole is 1 inch shorter than length required, finishing at end of a 7th row of patt.

K 9 rows, cast off.

Once you have mastered this simple principle for designing stoles you can apply it to any lace stitch, creating lovely designs to suit your own taste.

MAN'S SPORTS SWEATER WITH CONTRASTING YOKE

19 oz Main Shade, 4 oz Contrast, Double Knitting. Two No 10 and two pairs No 8 needles. Set of four No 10 needles with points at both ends.

Chest, 40–42 ins. Length, 24 ins.

This garment must be worked at a tension of 5½ sts and 7½ rows to one square inch on No 8 needles measured over stocking stitch.

Note: This garment is knitted in one piece.

FRONT

Using Main Shade and No 10 needles, cast on 100 sts.

1st row: K3, * P2, K2, rep from * to last st, K1.

2nd row: K1, * P2, K2, rep from * to last 3 sts, P2, K1.

Rep these 2 rows until work measures 4 ins from beg.

Change to No 8 needles and commence sleeve shaping as follows:

1st row: Inc in 1st st, K to last 2 sts, inc in next st, K1.

2nd row: P.

Work these 2 rows 24 times more (150 sts).

Divide for yoke as follows:

1st row: Inc in 1st st, K72, K2 tog, turn, slip remaining 75 sts on to a length of wool and leave.

2nd row: P to last st, inc in last st.

3rd row: Inc in 1st st, K to last 2 sts, K2 tog.

Rep these 2 rows until there are 104 sts.

Next row: P.

Next row: K to last 2 sts, K2 tog.

Work last 2 rows 19 times more (84 sts).

Join in wool to remaining group of 75 sts and work to match other half.

YOKE

Using Contrast and No 8 needles, with right side of work facing, *knit up* 2 sts at centre front, turn, P2, *pick up* and P1 st from yoke edge, taking care to insert the needle through the 2 loops between the knots formed by the dec sts, turn, K3, *knit up* 1 st from other side, turn, P4, *pick up* and P1 st from other side.

Continue in this manner until there are 81 sts.

Shape neck as follows:

Next row: K30, cast off 22 loosely, K28, (29 sts on needle after cast-off), *knit up* 1 st, turn.

Next row: P30.

Next row: K2 tog, K28, *knit up* 1 st, turn.

Rep these 2 rows until rows are even with those of side portion, ending with a P row, being careful *not* to pick up a st through the last 2 loops.

Next row: Inc in 1st st, K27, K2 tog.

Next row: P.

Work these 2 rows 3 times more.

Break off wool.

With wrong side of work facing, join in Contrast to remaining group of 30 sts at neck edge, P30, *pick up* and P1 st, turn.

Next row: K29, K2 tog.

Next row: P30, *pick up* and P1 st, turn.

Rep these 2 rows until rows are even with those of side portion, ending with a K row.

Next row: P30.

Next row: K2 tog, K26, inc in next st, K1.

Next row: P.

Work these 2 rows 3 times more.

Next row: K2 tog, K28, cast on 30, K28, K2 tog across remaining group of 30 sts (88 sts).

Commencing with a P row continue in stocking stitch, dec 1 st at both ends of every alt row until 2 sts remain, P2 tog.

Fasten off.

With wrong side of work facing and working on the 84 sts on right-hand side *pick up* and P 1 st in the adjacent portion, turn.

Proceed as follows:

1st row: K to end (cuff edge).

2nd row: P, *pick up* and P 1 st, turn.

Rep these 2 rows until there are 104 sts, finishing with a P row.

Continue picking up sts at yoke edge as before, *at the same time* dec 1 st at sleeve edge on every row until 75 sts remain, finishing with a P row.

Break off wool.

With right side of work facing, working across 84 sts of other side, work to match other half (75 sts).

Next row: K2 tog, K73, working across remaining group of 75 sts K to last 2 sts, K2 tog (148 sts).

Continue in stocking stitch, dec 1 st at both ends of every alt row until 100 sts remain.

Work 1 row.

Change to No 10 needles and proceed in rib as on Front.

Cast off in rib.

CUFFS

Using Main Shade and No 10 needles, with right side of work facing, *knit up* 44 sts along sleeve edge.

1st row: K1, * P2, K2, rep from * to last 3 sts, P2, K1.

2nd row: K3, * P2, K2, rep from * to last st, K1.

Rep these 2 rows for 4 ins.

Cast off loosely.

COLLAR

Using Contrast and set of four No 10 needles, with right side of work facing, *knit up* 92 sts round neck.

Work in rounds of K2, P2 rib as on Front for 5 ins.
Cast off loosely in rib.

MAKE UP

Omitting ribbing, block and press on wrong side using a warm
iron and damp cloth. Darn in ends. Using a back-stitch seam
join side and sleeve seams. Press all seams.

POM-POM TRIMMED HAT
Illustrated in Plate 19a

2 oz Double Knitting. Two No 4 needles. Crochet hook.
To fit an average head.

This hat must be worked at a tension of $4\frac{1}{2}$ sts and $5\frac{1}{2}$ rows
to one square inch on No 4 needles measured over stocking
stitch.

Cast on 81 sts *loosely*.

Proceed for *tuck* as follows:

1st row: (Wrong side of work) K.

2nd row: P.

3rd–9th rows: Rep these 2 rows 3 times, then 1st row once.

10th row: * K2 tog, K7, rep from * to end (72 sts).

11th–16th rows: Commencing with a P row work in stocking
stitch.

17th row: P to last 11 sts, turn.

18th row: K to last 11 sts, turn.

19th row: P to last 21 sts, turn.

20th row: K to last 21 sts, turn.

21st row: P to end.

Proceed for *2nd tuck* as follows:

22nd row: P all across.

23rd row: K.

Rep 22nd and 23rd rows 4 times.

Shape top as follows:

1st row: K.

2nd row: P.

3rd row: * K2 tog, K6, rep from * to end.

4th–6th rows: Work in stocking stitch.

7th row: * K2 tog, K5, rep from * to end.

8th–10th rows: Work in stocking stitch.

11th row: * K2 tog, K4, rep from * to end.

12th–14th rows: Work in stocking stitch.

15th row: * K2 tog, K3, rep from * to end.

16th–18th rows: Work in stocking stitch.

19th row: * K2 tog, K2, rep from * to end.

20th and 22nd rows: P.

21st row: * K2 tog, K1, rep from * to end.

23rd row: * K2 tog, rep from * to end.

24th row: P.

Break off wool, thread through remaining sts and fasten off securely.

MAKE UP

Press, using a warm iron and damp cloth. Using a back-stitch seam, join seam. Stitch together the K row before and after the 10 rows of the 2nd tuck, on wrong side of hat. Stitch the cast-on edge to the K row after the 1st tuck. Make 3 pom-poms. Using a crochet hook make 3 varying lengths of chain and attach pom-poms. Stitch on to Hat. Press seam.

LUCELLE EVENING BLOUSE WITH DRAPED DÉCOLLETAGE
Illustrated in Plate 21a

Ten ½-oz balls Patons Lucelle Fine Ply. Two No 14 needles. Beads for embroidery.

Bust, 40 ins. Length, 18¼ ins.

This garment must be worked at a tension of 11½ sts and 14¼ rows to one square inch on No 14 needles measured over stocking stitch.

LOWER PART OF RIGHT SLEEVE

Cast on 9 sts.

1st row: K.

2nd row: P, cast on 8 sts.

3rd row: K to last st, inc in last st.

4th row: P, cast on 8 sts.

5th row: K.
6th row: P, cast on 8 sts.
Rep rows 1–6 incl 3 times (109 sts).
Break off wool, slip sts on to a length of wool.

LOWER PART OF LEFT SLEEVE

Cast on 9 sts.
1st row: K, cast on 8 sts.
2nd row: P.
3rd row: Inc in 1st st, K to end, cast on 8 sts.
4th row: P.
5th row: K, cast on 8 sts.
6th row: P.
Rep rows 1–6 incl 3 times (109 sts).
Break off wool, slip sts on to a length of wool.

FRONT

Cast on 152 sts.
Work in K1, P1 rib for 3½ ins.
Next row: Rib 4, (inc in next st, rib 12) 11 times, inc in next st, rib to end (164 sts).**

Proceed in stocking stitch with *dart shapings* as follows:
1st row: K.
2nd row: P.
3rd row: K60, M1 knitwise, K to last 60 sts, M1 knitwise, K to end.
4th row: P.
5th row: K.
6th row: P60, M1 purlwise, P to last 60 sts, M1 purlwise, P60.
Rep rows 1–6 incl 11 times (212 sts).
Continue in stocking stitch, inc 1 st at both ends of every row until there are 236 sts.
Break off wool.

Place Lower part of Left and Right Sleeves as follows:
Next row: With right side of work facing, slip 109 sts from Lower part of Left Sleeve on to needle already holding sts, rejoin wool and K all across; with right side of work facing, slip 109 sts from Lower part of Right Sleeve on to other needle, point of needle to 8 cast-on sts, K to end (454 sts).

Next row: P.

Increasing I st at both ends of Ist and 7th rows, work I2 rows in stocking stitch (458 sts).

Still shaping sleeve end, *divide for draped décolletage* as follows:

Next row: Inc in Ist st, K 190, cast off 76 sts, K to last st, inc in last st.

Proceed on *last* group of 192 sts as follows:

1st row: P.

2nd row: Cast off 5 sts, K to end.

3rd row: P.

4th and 5th rows: As 2nd and 3rd.

6th row: Working a length of coloured wool into Ist st, cast off 5 sts, K to last st, inc in last st.

7th row: P to last 2 sts, P2 tog.

8th row: K2 tog, K to end.

9th and 10th rows: As 7th and 8th.

11th row: P.

12th row: K2 tog, K to last st, inc in last st.

13th row: P (174 sts).

Continue in stocking stitch, dec I st at neck edge on next and every following 6th row, *at the same time* inc I st at sleeve edge on 5th row following and every following 6th row until 12 increases *in all* have been worked at sleeve edge.

Still dec at neck edge on every 6th row from previous dec as before work 8 rows, thus finishing at sleeve edge.

*** Still dec at neck edge as before, *shape sleeve* by casting off 4 sts at beg of next and every alt row until 16 sts remain.

Continue without further shaping at neck edge but still shaping sleeve by casting off 4 sts at sleeve edge on every alt row until all sts are cast off.***

Rejoin wool to remaining 192 sts and proceed as follows:

1st row: Cast off 5 sts, P to end.

2nd row: K.

3rd and 4th rows: As Ist and 2nd.

5th row: Working a length of coloured wool into Ist st, work as Ist row.

6th row: Inc in Ist st, K to end.

7th row: P2 tog, P to end.

8th row: K to last 2 sts, K2 tog.

9th and 10th rows: As 7th and 8th.

11th row: As 7th row.

12th row: Inc in 1st st, K to last 2 sts, K2 tog.

13th row: P.

Continue in stocking stitch, dec 1 st at neck edge on next and every following 6th row, *at the same time* inc 1 st at sleeve edge on 5th row following and every following 6th row until 12 increases *in all* have been worked at sleeve edge.

Still dec at neck edge on every 6th row from previous dec, work 7 rows, thus finishing at sleeve edge.

Complete as for other half of Front, working from *** to ***.

LOWER PART OF RIGHT AND LEFT SLEEVES

Work as before.

BACK

Work as Front until ** is reached.

Next row: K82, cast on 1 st.

Leaving remaining sts on a length of wool, proceed on these 83 sts as follows:

1st row: P.

2nd row: K60, M1, K23.

3rd row: P.

4th row: K.

5th row: P24, M1 purlwise, P60.

6th row: K.

Continue in this manner inc 1 st on 2nd row and every following 3rd row until there are 107 sts.

Shape dolman by inc 1 st at side edge on every row until there are 119 sts, thus finishing at end of a P row.

Break off wool.

Place sleeve as follows:

With right side of work facing, slip 109 sts from Lower part of Left Sleeve on to needle already holding sts.

Rejoin wool and K all across (228 sts).

Next row: P.

Continue in stocking stitch, inc 1 st at sleeve edge on next and every following 6th row until there are 236 sts.

Work 7 rows in stocking stitch, thus finishing at sleeve edge.

Shape sleeve by casting off 4 sts at beg of next and every alt row until 76 sts remain.

Next row: P.

Cast off 16 sts at sleeve edge on next and every alt row until 28 sts remain.

Cast off.

Slip sts from length of wool on to needle, right side of work facing, rejoin wool and proceed as follows:

1st row: Cast on 1 st, K to end.

2nd row: P.

3rd row: K 23, M 1 knitwise, K 60.

4th row: P.

5th row: K.

6th row: P 60, M 1 purlwise, P 24.

Continue in this manner, inc 1 st on every following 3rd row until there are 107 sts.

Shape dolman by inc 1 st at side edge on every row until there are 119 sts.

Place sleeve as follows:

Next row: K to end, slip 109 sts from length of wool on to needle, right side of work facing, K across these sts (228 sts).

Complete to match other half of Back, reversing all shapings.

RIGHT HALF OF DRAPED DÉCOLLETAGE

Commencing at lower corner of centre front, cast on 14 sts.

1st row: K 10, working in length of coloured wool to mark centre front K 1, inc in next st, K 1, inc in last st.

2nd row: Inc in 1st st, P 3, inc in next st, P 11.

3rd row: K 11, inc in next st, K 5, inc in last st.

4th row: Inc in 1st st, P 7, inc in next st, P 11.

5th row: K 11, inc in next st, K 9, inc in last st.

6th row: Inc in 1st st, P 11, inc in next st, P 11.

Continue in this manner keeping 11 sts for front facing correct, inc 2 sts on every row as before until there are 76 sts on needle.

Next row: P.

Next row: K 11, inc in next st, K to last st, inc in last st.

Next row: P.

Rep these last 2 rows 27 times (132 sts).

Next row: K11, inc in next st, K to end.

Next row: P.

Rep these 2 rows 3 times (136 sts).

Next row: K11, inc in next st, K123, inc in last st.

Work 9 rows in stocking stitch.

Next row: K11, inc in next st, K125, inc in last st.

Work 9 rows in stocking stitch.

Next row: K11, inc in next st, K127, inc in last st.

Work 9 rows in stocking stitch.

Next row: K22, slip these sts on to a length of wool and leave for neck band, working a length of coloured wool into 1st st to mark neck edge of shoulder, K to end of row.

Next row: P to last 2 sts, P2 tog.

Next row: K2 tog, K to end.

Continue dec at neck edge on every row until 101 sts remain.

Work 16 rows in stocking stitch, working in a length of coloured wool at *beg* of last row to mark lower edge.

Continue without further shaping at shoulder edge but dec 1 st at lower edge on every row until 87 sts remain.

Cast off, working a length of coloured wool into last st to mark sleeve end of shoulder.

Slip 22 sts from length of wool on to needle.

Rejoin wool and work in stocking stitch for 2½ ins.

Cast off.

LEFT HALF OF DRAPED DÉCOLLETAGE

Commencing at lower corner of centre front, cast on 14 sts.

1st row: Inc in 1st st, K1, inc in next st, K1 working in a length of coloured wool to mark centre front, K10.

2nd row: P11, inc in next st, P3, inc in last st.

3rd row: Inc in 1st st, K5, inc in next st, K11.

4th row: P11, inc in next st, P7, inc in last st.

Continue in this manner keeping 11 sts for front facing correct, inc 2 sts on every row until there are 76 sts.

Next row: P.

Next row: Inc in 1st st, K to last 12 sts, inc in next st, K11.

Next row: P.

Rep these last 2 rows 27 times (132 sts).

Next row: K to last 12 sts, inc in next st, K11.

Next row: P.

Rep these 2 rows 3 times (136 sts).

Next row: Inc in 1st st, K123, inc in next st, K11.

Work 9 rows in stocking stitch.

Next row: Inc in 1st st, K125, inc in next st, K11.

Work 9 rows in stocking stitch.

Next row: Inc in 1st st, K127, inc in next st, K11.

Work 10 rows in stocking stitch.

Next row: P22, slip these sts on to a length of wool for neck band, P to end working a short length of coloured wool into 1st st to mark neck edge of shoulder.

Next row: K to last 2 sts, K2 tog.

Next row: P2 tog, P to end.

Continue dec 1 st at neck edge on every row until 101 sts remain.

Work 15 rows in stocking stitch, working in a length of coloured wool at end of last row to mark lower edge.

Continue without further shaping at shoulder edge but dec 1 st at lower edge on every row until 87 sts remain.

Cast off, working a length of coloured wool into 1st st to mark sleeve end of shoulder.

Slip 22 sts from length of wool on to needle.

Rejoin wool and work in stocking stitch for 2½ ins.

Cast off.

MAKE UP

Omitting ribbing, with wrong side of work facing, block each piece by pinning out round edges.

Omitting ribbing, press each piece using a warm iron and damp cloth. Using a back-stitch seam, join seam at centre back. Join neck band at centre back. Press seams.

Fold 11 sts of neckband and facing to wrong side and stitch into position.

Commencing 3 ins in from coloured wool at centre front run a gathering thread to one at lower edge on both neck pieces. Fold over 2 ins at front edge to form a knife pleat from lower edge to shoulder as on photograph. Press lightly on wrong side.

Pin *décolletage* into position on Front, and with wrong side of

work facing, using a back-stitch seam, stitch all round neck
opening.

Using a back-stitch seam, join shoulders and sleeve tops.

Using a back-stitch seam, join side and sleeve seams.

Stitch neckband to back of neck. Fold over end of sleeve for
¾ inch and stitch into position on wrong side of work.

Work embroidery on Front and Sleeves as shown in photograph.
Press seams.

MAN'S CONTINENTAL SLIPOVER
Illustrated in Plate 21b

13 oz Ground Shade, 1 oz First Contrast, 1 oz Second Contrast, 4-ply Fingering. Two No 12 and two No 10 needles. Set of
four No 12 needles with points at both ends.

Chest, 38–40 ins. Length, 24½ ins. Sleeve, 18 ins.

This garment must be worked at a tension of 7 sts and 9 rows
to one square inch on No 10 needles measured over stocking
stitch.

FRONT

Using No 12 needles, Ground Shade, and the through sts method,
cast on 156 sts.

Work 6 rows in K 1, P 1 rib.

Work 6 rows in stocking stitch.

Next row: *Make hem* by knitting tog 1 st from needle and 1 loop
from cast-on edge all across row.

Next row: P.

Work rows 1–11 incl from Chart A (odd rows K, even rows P)
repeating from A to B on odd rows and B to A on even rows

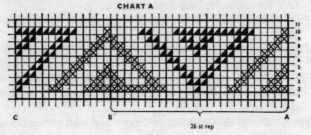

CHART A

26 st rep

throughout, stranding colours by carrying the colours not in use across back of work.

Next row: P5, (P2 tog, P9) 13 times, P2 tog, P to end (142 sts).

Change to No 10 needles and continue in stocking stitch until work measures 14½ ins from beg, finishing at end of a P row.

Cast off 5 sts at beg of next 2 rows (132 sts).**

Shape neck and raglan armhole as follows:

Next row: K 66, turn and proceed on this group of 66 sts as follows:

Next row: Work to last 2 sts, work 2 tog.

Next row: Work 2 tog, work to last 2 sts, work 2 tog.

Continue dec at armhole edge on every row until 2 more dec have been worked at armhole edge.

Dec 1 st at both ends of next row.

Continue dec at armhole edge on next and every alt row from previous dec and at neck edge on every 5th row from previous dec until all sts are worked off.

Rejoin wool to remaining group of 66 sts and work to match other half of Front, reversing all shapings.

BACK

Work as Front to ** (132 sts).

Shape raglan armhole by dec 1 st at both ends of every row until 120 sts remain; every alt row until 32 sts remain.

Work 6 rows on these sts.

Cast off.

SLEEVES

Using No 12 needles, Ground Shade, and the through sts method, cast on 66 sts.

Work 12 rows in K 1, P 1 rib.

Work 12 rows in stocking stitch.

Make hem as on Front.

P 1 row.

Work rows 1–11 incl from Chart A, repeating from A to B twice and from B to C once on odd rows; from C to B once and from B to A twice on even rows.

Work 12 rows in stocking stitch.

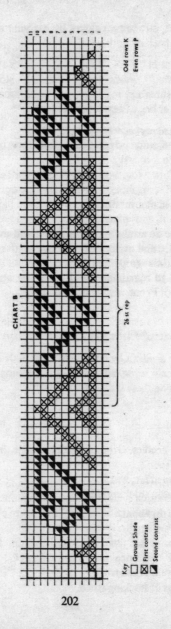

CHART B

Odd rows K
Even rows P

26 st rep

Key
☐ Ground Shade
☒ First contrast
◨ Second contrast

Next row: P6, (inc in next st, P5) 10 times (76 sts).

Change to No 10 needles and proceed in stocking stitch, inc 1 st at both ends of 7th and every following 7th row until there are 112 sts.
Continue on these sts until work measures 18 ins from beg.
Cast off 5 sts at beg of next 2 rows (102 sts).

Shape raglan sleeve as follows:
Dec 1 st at both ends of next and every alt row until 12 sts remain.
Cast off.

MAKE UP

With wrong side of work facing, block each piece by pinning out round edges.
Press each piece using a warm iron and damp cloth.
Using a back-stitch seam, join side and sleeve seams.
Stitch sleeves into position, stitching 6 rows at top of back to 6 sts along cast-off edge at top of sleeve.

NECKBAND

Using set of No 12 needles, and Ground Shade, with right side of work facing, commencing at centre V, knit up 206 sts round neck, turn.
Next row: P, turn.
Work rows 1–11 from Chart B, working 26 sts, rep 6 times and extra sts and dec as shown on Chart.
Next row: P.
Work 12 rows in K 1, P 1 rib, inc 1 st at both ends of every row.
Cast off loosely in rib.

TO FINISH

Fold K 1, P 1 rib round neckband to wrong side of work.
Using a back-stitch seam, join shaped portions of front together.
Neatly stitch down cast-off edge to knitted-up edge on wrong side.
Press neckband and all seams.

Fashion Supplement

LADY'S EVENING JUMPER
Illustrated in Plate 25

Six ½-oz balls Patons Lucelle Fine Ply. Two No 13 needles. 1½ yds of ½-inch ribbon of matching colour. 14 small pearls. 70 dark sequins. 70 light sequins.

Bust, 34–36 ins. Length, 19½ ins.

This garment must be worked at a tension of 10½ sts and 13 rows to one square inch on No 13 needles measured over stocking stitch.

FRONT

Cast on 131 sts and proceed in rib as follows:

1st row: * K1, P1, rep from * to last st, K1.

2nd row: * P1, K1, rep from * to last st, P1.

Rep these 2 rows until work measures 3½ ins from beg.

Proceed in stocking stitch with *dart shapings* as follows:

1st row: K.

2nd row: P.

3rd and 4th rows: As 1st and 2nd.

5th row: K40, M1, K7, M1, K37, M1, K7, M1, K40.

6th row: P.

7th–12th rows: Rep 1st and 2nd rows 3 times.

13th row: K40, M1, K9, M1, K37, M1, K9, M1, K40.

14th row: P.

15th–20th rows: Rep 1st and 2nd rows 3 times.

21st row: K40, M1, K11, M1, K37, M1, K11, M1, K40.

22nd row: P.

Continue in this manner, working dart shapings as before on 7th row following and every following 8th row until there are 183 sts.

Continue on these sts until work measures 11½ ins from beg, finishing at end of a P row (mark each end of last row with a length of coloured wool).

Work 8 rows in stocking stitch.

Shape sleeve edges as follows:

Next row: K7, M1, K to last 7 sts, M1, K7 (185 sts).

Work 5 rows in stocking stitch, thus finishing at end of a P row.

Divide for Right and Left Halves of Front as follows:

1st row: K92, cast off 1 (1 st on needle after cast off), K91.

Still shaping sleeve edge proceed on *first* group of 92 sts for *Right Half of Front* as follows:

1st row: P.

2nd row: K2 tog, K to end.

3rd row: P to last 2 sts, P2 tog.

4th row: K to last 7 sts, M1, K7.

5th row: As 3rd row.

6th row: As 2nd row.

7th row: P.

8th row: As 2nd row.

9th row: As 3rd row.

10th row: K.

Continue in this manner, dec 1 st at neck edge on next 2 rows and every following 2nd and 3rd rows from last dec *at the same time* inc 1 st at sleeve edge as before on 4th row following and every following 10th row until 9 inc *in all* have been worked at sleeve edge (51 sts).

Next row: P to last 2 sts, P2 tog.

Next row: K.

Continue without further shaping at sleeve edge but still shaping neck edge by dec 1 st on next 2 rows and every following 2nd and 3rd rows from last dec until 42 sts remain, thus finishing at end of a P row.

Next row: K.

Shape shoulder as follows:

1st row: Cast off 6, P to last 2 sts, P2 tog.

2nd row: K2 tog, K to end.

3rd row: Cast off 6, P to end.

4th row: As 2nd row.

5th row: As 1st row.

6th row: K.

7th row: As 1st row.

8th row: As 2nd row.

9th row: As 3rd row.

10th row: K.

Cast off.

Rejoin wool to remaining 92 sts at centre of work and proceed for *Left Half of Front* as follows:

1st row: P.

2nd row: K to last 2 sts, K2 tog.

3rd row: P2 tog, P to end.

4th row: K7, M1, K to end.

5th row: P2 tog, P to end.

6th row: K to last 2 sts, K2 tog.

7th row: P.

8th row: K to last 2 sts, K2 tog.

9th row: P2 tog, P to end.

10th row: K.

Continue in this manner, dec 1 st at neck edge of next 2 rows and every following 2nd and 3rd rows from last dec, *at the same time* inc 1 st at sleeve edge as before on 4th row following and every following 10th row until 9 inc *in all* have been worked at sleeve edge (51 sts).

Next row: P2 tog, P to end.

Next row: K.

Continue without further shaping at sleeve edge but still shaping neck edge by dec 1 st on next 2 rows and every following 2nd and 3rd rows from last dec until 42 sts remain, thus finishing at end of a P row.

Shape shoulder as follows:

1st row: Cast off 6, K to end.

2nd row: P2 tog, P to end.

3rd row: Cast off 6, K to last 2 sts, K2 tog.

4th row: P.

5th row: As 3rd row.

6th row: As 2nd row.

7th row: As 1st row.

8th row: As 2nd row.

9th row: As 3rd row.

10th row: P.

Cast off.

Work as for Front.

CHEVRON COLLAR

First half:

Cast on 4 sts.

1st row: Inc in every st (8 sts).

2nd row: Inc in 1st st purlwise, P1, inc in next st purlwise, P1, inc in next st purlwise, P2, inc in last st purlwise.

3rd row: K4, inc in next st, K1, inc in next st, K5.

4th row: P5, inc in next st, P1, inc in next st, P6.

5th row: K6, inc in next st, K1, inc in next st, K7.

6th row: P7, inc in next st, P1, inc in next st, P8.

7th row: K8, inc in next st, K1, inc in next st, K9.

8th row: P9, inc in next st, P1, inc in next st, P10.

Continue in this manner until there are 60 sts.

** **Next row:** K28, K2 tog, sl1, K1, psso, K28.

Next row: P27, P2 tog tbl, P2 tog, P27.

Next row: K26, K2 tog, sl1, K1, psso, K26.

Next row: P25, P2 tog tbl, P2 tog, P25.

Continue in this manner until 20 sts remain.

Next row: K8, inc in next st, K1, inc in next st, K9.

Next row: P9, inc in next st, P1, inc in next st, P10.

Next row: K10, inc in next st, K1, inc in next st, K11.

Next row: P11, inc in next st, P1, inc in next st, P12.

Continue in this manner until there are 60 sts.**

Continue working chevrons in this manner by working from ** to ** 5 times more.

Next row: K28, K2 tog, sl1, K1, psso, K28.

Next row: P27, P2 tog tbl, P2 tog, P27.

Next row: K26, K2 tog, sl1, K1, psso, K26.

Next row: P25, P2 tog tbl, P2 tog, P25.

Continue dec in this manner until 12 sts remain.

Next row: K2 tog, K2, K2 tog, sl1, K1, psso, K2, K2 tog.

Next row: P2 tog, P2 tog tbl, (P2 tog) twice (4 sts).

Cast off.

Work *second half* of chevron collar in same manner.

SLEEVE FACINGS

Using a back-stitch seam join shoulders of back and front.
With right side of work facing *knit up* 150 sts along edge of
    sleeve from coloured thread to coloured thread.
Commencing with a P row work 7 rows in stocking stitch.
Cast off.

MAKE UP

Omitting ribbing, block and press each piece on wrong side using
    a warm iron and damp cloth.
Using a back-stitch seam join side seams up to sleeve facings.
Fold sleeve facings to wrong side of work and stitch into position.
Cut two lengths of ribbon 21½ ins long. Stitch each piece of ribbon
    along inside of shaped neck edges from centre front to centre
    back to keep bias edges firm.
Stitch collar to each side of neck from centre front to centre back.

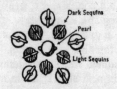

Stitch sequins and pearls to each chevron as shown in diagram.
Press all seams.

LADY'S STRIPED COAT
Illustrated in Plate 27a

7/8/9 oz Dark, 7/8/9 oz Medium, 6/7/8 oz Light, 3 oz Contrast,
Double Knitting. Two No 9 and two No 7 needles. Two stitch-
holders. Eight buttons.
Bust, 34/36/38 ins. Length, 23/23¼/23½ ins. Sleeve, 18 ins.

This garment must be worked at a tension of 5¼ sts and 7 rows
to one square inch on No 7 needles measured over stocking
stitch.

Special Note: As this garment is worked entirely on rows, it is
    essential for the tension to be correct if the final measurements
    are to be obtained.

The *striped patt* used throughout the coat is as follows:
5 rows light, (1 row medium, 1 row light) 3 times, 5 rows medium, (1 row dark, 1 row medium) twice, 7 rows dark.

BACK

Using No 7 needles, the through sts method and Dark, cast on 89/95/101 sts.

Work 14 rows in stocking stitch.

Next row: *Make hem* by knitting tog 1 st from needle and 1 loop from cast-on edge all across row.

Commencing with a P row (wrong side facing), work 27 rows of striped patt 3 times, then rep first 11 rows; 5 rows light, (1 row medium, 1 row light) 3 times.

Keeping striped patt correct, *shape raglan armholes* as follows:
Cast off 3/4/5 sts at beg of next 2 rows.

Dec 1 st at both ends of 3rd and every following 3rd row until 77/81/85 sts remain, every alt row until 23/25/27 sts remain.

Work 3 rows on these sts.

Cast off.

POCKETS (*both alike*)

Using No 7 needles and Dark, cast on 24/25/24 sts.

Work 27 rows in K 1, P 1 rib.

Slip sts on to a stitch-holder and leave.

RIGHT FRONT

Using No 7 needles, the through sts method and Dark, cast on 42/45/48 sts.

Work as Back until first 25 rows of striped patt have been worked.

Keeping striped patt correct, *place pocket* as follows:

Next row: (26th row of striped patt). Work across 9/10/12 sts, work next 24/25/24 sts on to a stitch-holder and leave, work across 9/10/12 sts.

Next row: (27th row of striped patt). Work across 9/10/12 sts, sl sts from top of pocket on to left-hand needle, work across these sts, work 9/10/12.

Continue in striped patt until work matches back up to armhole shaping, finishing at armhole edge.

Shape raglan armhole and front slope as follows:

Dec 1 st at front edge on next and every following 7th/6th/6th row until 9/10/11 dec *in all* have been worked at front edge, *at the same time* shape raglan armhole by casting off 3/4/5 sts at beg of next row, then dec 1 st at armhole edge on 3rd and every following 3rd row until 7 dec have been worked at armhole edge, then every alt row at armhole edge until the 9/10/11 dec have been worked at front edge.

Continue without further dec at front edge but still dec on every alt row at armhole edge until all sts are worked off.

POCKET TOPS (*both alike*)

Slip sts from stitch-holder on to No 9 needle.
Using Contrast, with right side facing, K 5 rows.
Cast off.

LEFT FRONT

Work to match right front, reversing all shapings.

SLEEVES

Using No 9 needles and Contrast, cast on 55/59/63 sts.
K 6 rows.
Next row: K 5/9/13, (inc in next st, K 4) 9 times, inc in next st, K to end (65/69/73 sts).

Change to No 7 needles and repeat 27 rows of striped patt 4 times, then rows 1 to 11, inc 1 st at both ends of 7th and every following 8th row until there are 85/89/93 sts.
Keeping striped patt correct, *shape top* as follows:
Cast off 3/4/5 sts at beg of next 2 rows. Dec 1 st at both ends of every row until 61/63/65 sts remain, every alt row until 5 sts remain.
Cast off.

FRONT BAND

Using No 9 needles and Contrast, cast on 10 sts.
K 6 rows.
Next row: K 4, cast off 2, K to end.
Next row: K 4, cast on 2, K to end.

Continue in garter stitch (every row K), working buttonhole as on last 2 rows on 19th and 20th rows from previous buttonhole, until 8 buttonholes *in all* have been worked.

Continue without further buttonholes until work measures 56/56¼/56½ ins (not stretched) from beg.

Cast off.

MAKE UP

Block and press on wrong side using a warm iron and damp cloth. Using a back-stitch seam join side and sleeve seams and stitch sleeves into position. Using a flat seam, stitch on front band. Attach buttons to correspond with buttonholes.

Press seams.

EVENING STOLE
Illustrated in Plates 25 and 26

6 oz Ground Shade, 2 oz Contrast (for fringe), 4-ply Fingering.
Two No 8 needles. A crochet hook. A cable needle.
Length, 60 ins approx. (with fringe). Width, 16 ins.

Cast on 102 sts.
K 12 rows.
Proceed as follows:

1st row: K5, (KB1, P1, K4, P1, KB1, wf, K5, K3 tog, K5, wf) 4 times, KB1, P1, K4, P1, KB1, K5.

2nd row: K5, (PB1, K1, P4, K1, PB1, P6, K1, P6) 4 times, PB1, K1, P4, K1, PB1, K5.

3rd row: K5, (KB1, P1, C2F, P1, KB1, wf, K3, wf, K3 tog, P1, K3 tog, wf, K3, wf) 4 times, KB1, P1, C2F, P1, KB1, K5.

4th row: As 2nd row.

5th row: K5, (KB1, P1, K4, P1, KB1, wf, K1, wf, K2 tog tbl, K1, K2 tog, P1, K2 tog tbl, K1, K2 tog, wf, K1, wf) 4 times, KB1, P1, K4, P1, KB1, K5.

6th row: As 2nd row.

These 6 rows form the patt.

Rep these 6 rows until work measures 50 ins from beg, finishing at end of a 6th row.

K 11 rows.
Cast off.

To finish:
Block and press on wrong side, using a warm iron and damp
cloth.

To make fringe:
Cut length of cardboard 7 ins wide. Wrap Contrast round cardboard and cut along one edge.

Take 4 lengths, fold at centre, draw loop formed at centre
through edge of stole with crochet hook, draw 8 strands
through loop on hook. Draw up to form tassel fringe. Fringe
all across one end in this manner. Leave 1st 4 strands,
knot 2nd and 3rd 4 strands one inch from end of stole
together.

Rep this action on (5th and 6th), (7th and 8th), etc., sets of
4 strands all across.

Now commencing 1 inch lower down, knot (1st and 2nd), (3rd
and 4th), etc., sets of 4 strands all across.

Complete other end to match.

EVENING SHAWL
Illustrated in Plate 26

9 oz 2-ply Fingering. (In the original, metallic thread was knitted
in with the 2-ply wool but this may be omitted.)
Two No 8 needles. 5¼ yards of silk fringe.
Approximately 48 ins square.

Using 2-ply, cast on 331 sts.
K 8 rows.
Using metallic thread with 2-ply in lace centre *only*, working
5 border sts at each side in 2-ply throughout, proceed as
follows:

1st row: Using 2-ply, K 5, using 2-ply and metallic thread (K 1,
wf, K 2 tog tbl, K 5, K 2 tog, wf) 32 times, K 1, using 2-ply
K 5.

2nd and every alt row: Using 2-ply K 5, using 2-ply and metallic
thread P to last 5 sts, using 2-ply K 5.

Working metallic thread as before on centre 321 sts continue as follows:

3rd row: K5, (K1, wf, K1, K2 tog tbl, K3, K2 tog, K1, wf) 32 times, K1, K5.

5th row: K5, (K1, wf, K2, K2 tog tbl, K1, K2 tog, K2, wf) 32 times, K1, K5.

7th row: K5, (K1, wf, K3, K3 tog, K3, wf) 32 times, K1, K5.

9th row: K5, (K3, K2 tog, wf, K1, wf, K2 tog tbl, K2) 32 times K1, K5.

11th row: K5, (K2, K2 tog, K1, wf, K1, wf, K1, K2 tog tbl, K1) 32 times, K1, K5.

13th row: K5, (K1, K2 tog, K2, wf, K1, wf, K2, K2 tog tbl) 32 times, K1, K5.

15th row: K5, K2 tog, K3, (wf, K1, wf, K3, K3 tog, K3) 31 times, wf, K1, wf, K3, K2 tog, K5.

16th row: K5, P to last 5 sts, K5.

Repeat rows 1–16 until work measures 47 ins from beg.

Using 2-ply K 7 rows.

Cast off.

Block and press on wrong side.

Stitch fringe round shawl as shown in photograph.

EVENING STOLE
Illustrated in Plate 26

5 oz 2-ply Fingering. Two No 9 needles. 6 yards single sequin trimming.

Length, 60 ins. Width, 16 ins.

Cast on 119 sts.

K 10 rows.

Proceed as follows:

1st row: K4, [K1, (wf, K2 tog tbl) twice, K1, (K2 tog, wf) twice] 11 times, K5.

2nd row: K4, P to last 4 sts, K4.

3rd row: K4, [K2, wf, K2 tog tbl, wf, K3 tog, wf, K2 tog, wf, K1] 11 times, K5.

4th row: K4, P to last 4 sts, K4.

Rep rows 1–4 until work measures 56 ins from beg.

213

K 9 rows.
Cast off.

To finish:
Pin out on wrong side (the stole should now measure 60 ins long
    and 16 ins wide). Press lightly using a warm iron and damp
    cloth. Stitch single sequin trimming along garter stitch border at
    sides and ends of stole.

BRUSHED WOOL COAT
Illustrated in Plate 27b

23 oz Double Knitting. Two No 8 needles. Nine buttons.
Bust, 34–36 ins. Length, 25 ins. Sleeve, 18 ins.

This garment must be worked at a tension of 5½ sts and
7½ rows to one square inch on No 8 needles measured over
stocking stitch.

BACK

Cast on 109 sts.
Work in K1, P1, rib for 1½ ins (this portion will form hem when
    coat is completed).
Proceed in *rib patt* as follows:
1st row: * P2, (K1, P1) 8 times, rep from * to last st, P1.
2nd row: * K2, (P1, K1) 8 times, rep from * to last st, K1.
These 2 rows form the patt.
Continue in patt until work measures 17 ins from *top of ribbing*.

Shape armholes by casting off 5 sts at beg of next 2 rows.
Dec 1 st at both ends of next and every alt row until 79 sts
    remain. Continue on these sts until work measures 8 ins from
    beg of armhole shaping.

Shape shoulders by casting off 9 sts at beg of next 6 rows.
Cast off.

RIGHT FRONT

Cast on 55 sts.
Work in K1, P1 rib for 1½ ins.

Proceed in rib patt until work matches back up to armhole shaping, finishing at side edge.

Shape armhole by casting off 5 sts at beg of next row. Dec 1 st at armhole edge on next and every alt row until 40 sts remain.
Continue on these sts until work measures 6½ ins from beg of armhole shaping, finishing at front edge.

Shape neck by casting off 6 sts at beg of next row.
Dec 1 st at neck edge on every row until 27 sts remain.
Continue on these sts until work matches back up to shoulder shaping, finishing at armhole edge.

Shape shoulder by casting off 9 sts at beg of next and every alt row until all sts are cast off.

LEFT FRONT

Work to match right front, reversing all shapings.

SLEEVES

Cast on 73 sts.
Proceed in rib patt until work measures 3½ ins from beg.
Inc 1 st at both ends of next and every following 10th row until there are 83 sts.
Continue on these sts until work measures 18 ins from beg. (Mark this point with length of wool.)
Work 7 rows.

Shape top by dec 1 st at both ends of next and every alt row until 63 sts remain. Cast off 4 sts at beg of next 14 rows.
Cast off.

CUFFS

Cast on 78 sts.
Work in K2, P1 rib for 3 ins.
Cast off.

RIGHT FRONT BAND

Cast on 11 sts.
1st row: K2, (P1, K1) 4 times, K1.
2nd row: (K1, P1) 5 times, K1.

Rep these 2 rows until work measures 1 inch from beg, finishing at end of a 2nd row.

Make buttonhole as follows:
Next row: Rib 4, cast off 3, rib to end.
Next row: Rib 4, cast on 3, rib to end.
Continue in rib, making buttonhole as on last 2 rows 2½ ins from previous buttonhole until 9 buttonholes *in all* have been worked.
Work 4 rows.
Cast off.

LEFT FRONT BAND

Omitting buttonholes, work as right front band.

COLLAR

Cast on 71 sts.
1st row: K2, * P1, K1, rep from * to last st, K1.
2nd row: * K1, P1, rep from * to last st, K1.
3rd and 4th rows: As 1st and 2nd.
5th row: K1, inc in next st, rib to last 2 sts, inc in next st, K1.
6th row: K1, P2, * K1, P1, rep from * to last 4 sts, K1, P2, K1.
7th row: K3, * P1, K1, rep from * to last 4 sts, P1, K3.
8th row: As 6th.
9th row: K2, inc in next st, rib to last 3 sts, inc in next st, K2.
10th row: As 2nd.
11th and 12th rows: As 1st and 2nd.
Continue inc in this manner on next and every following 4th row until work measures 4½ ins from beg.
Cast off in rib.

MAKE UP

Block and lightly press on wrong side, using a warm iron and damp cloth.
Take pieces to your local wool shop who will send them away to be brushed for you, before continuing to make up the garment.
Using a flat seam for K1, P1 rib, and back-stitch seam for remainder, join shoulder, side, and sleeve seams to point marked, and stitch sleeves into position, matching sleeve shaping and armhole shaping. Turn up K1, P1 rib at lower edge and

flat stitch on wrong side to form hem. Using a flat seam, join cuffs, and stitch on to end of sleeves. Using a flat seam stitch front bands and collar into position. Attach buttons to correspond with buttonholes. Press seams.

TWO-PLY SEPARATES
Illustrated in Plate 28a

Skirt

16 oz 2-ply Fingering. Two No 13 and two No 9 needles. Seven-inch zipp. Petersham. 2¾ yds nylon net. Two hooks and eyes. To fit average waist. Length, 31 ins.

This garment must be worked at a tension of 7½ sts and 9½ rows to one square inch on No 9 needles measured over stocking stitch.

First panel

Using No 9 needles, cast on 210 sts.

K 4 rows.

Proceed in pleated and lace patt as follows:

1st row: [P2, (KB1, P3) 4 times, KB1, P2, K1, wf, K3 tog, wf, K2, wf, K2 tog tbl, wf, K3 tog, wf, K1, wf, K2 tog tbl, wf, K3 tog, wf, K2, wf, K2 tog tbl, wf, K3 tog, wf, K2, wf, K2 tog tbl, wf, K3 tog, wf, K1, wf, K2 tog tbl, wf, K3 tog, wf, K2, wf, K2 tog tbl, K1] 3 times, P2, (KB1, P3) 4 times, KB1, P2.

2nd and every alt row: [K2, (PB1, K3) 4 times, PB1, K2, P42] 3 times, K2, (PB1, K3) 4 times, PB1, K2.

3rd row: [Rib 21, K1, K2 tog tbl, wf, K4, wf, K3 tog, wf, K3, wf, K3 tog, wf, K4, wf, K3 tog, wf, K4, wf, K3 tog, wf, K3, wf, K3 tog, wf, K6] 3 times, rib 21.

5th row: [Rib 21, K2, (wf, K2 tog tbl) twice, K3, wf, K2 tog tbl, wf, K3 tog, wf, K3, (K2 tog, wf) twice, K1, wf, K2 tog tbl, wf, K2 tog tbl, K3, wf, K2 tog tbl, wf, K3 tog, wf, K3, (K2 tog, wf) twice, K1] 3 times, rib 21.

7th row: [Rib 21, K3, (wf, K2 tog tbl) twice, K3, wf, K3 tog, wf, K3, (K2 tog, wf) twice, K3, (wf, K2 tog tbl) twice, K3, wf, K3 tog, wf, K3, (K2 tog, wf) twice, K2] 3 times, rib 21.

9th row: [Rib 21, K4, (wf, K2 tog tbl) twice, K7, (K2 tog wf) twice, K5, (wf, K2 tog tbl) twice, K7, (K2 tog, wf) twice, K3] 3 times, rib 21.

11th row: [Rib 21, K5, (wf, K2 tog tbl) twice, K5, (K2 tog, wf) twice, K7, (wf, K2 tog tbl) twice, K5, (K2 tog, wf) twice, K4] 3 times, rib 21.

13th row: [Rib 21, K6, (wf, K2 tog tbl) twice, K3, (K2 tog, wf) twice, K9, (wf, K2 tog tbl) twice, K3, (K2 tog, wf) twice, K5] 3 times, rib 21.

15th row: [Rib 21, K2, wf, K2 tog tbl, K3, (wf, K2 tog tbl) twice, K1, (K2 tog, wf) twice, K3, K2 tog, wf, K1, wf, K2 tog tbl, K3, (wf, K2 tog tbl) twice, K1, (K2 tog, wf) twice, K3, K2 tog, wf, K1] 3 times, rib 21.

17th row: [Rib 21, K3, wf, K2 tog tbl, K3, wf, K2 tog tbl, wf, K3 tog, wf, K2 tog, wf, K3, K2 tog, wf, K3, wf, K2 tog tbl, K3, wf, K2 tog tbl, wf, K3 tog, wf, K2 tog, wf, K3, K2 tog, wf, K2] 3 times, rib 21.

19th row: [Rib 21, K1, wf, K3 tog, wf, K1, wf, K3, K3 tog, wf, K1, wf, K3, K3, wf, K1, wf, K2 tog tbl, wf, K3 tog, wf, K1, wf, K3, K3 tog, wf, K1, wf, K3 tog, K3, wf, K1, wf, K2 tog tbl, K1] 3 times, rib 21.

21st row: [Rib 21, K1, K2 tog tbl, wf, K3, wf, K1, K3 tog, wf, K3, wf, K3 tog, K1, wf, K3, wf, K3 tog, wf, K3, wf, K1, K3 tog, wf, K3, wf, K3 tog, K1, wf, K5] 3 times, rib 21.

23rd row: [Rib 21, K2, wf, K2 tog tbl, wf, K3 tog, wf, K2, wf, K2 tog tbl, wf, K3 tog, wf, K2, wf, K2 tog tbl, wf, K3 tog, wf, K1, wf, K2 tog tbl, wf, K3 tog, wf, K2, wf, K2 tog tbl, wf, K3 tog, wf, K2, wf, K2 tog tbl, wf, K3 tog, wf, K1] 3 times, rib 21.

25th row: [Rib 21, K3, wf, K3 tog, wf, K4, wf, K3 tog, wf, K4, wf, K3 tog, wf, K3, wf, K3 tog, wf, K4, wf, K3 tog, wf, K4, wf, K3 tog, wf, K2] 3 times, rib 21.

27th row: [Rib 21, K1, wf, K3 tog, wf, K3, (K2 tog, wf) twice, K1, (wf, K2 tog tbl) twice, K3, wf, K2 tog tbl, wf, K3 tog, wf, K3, (K2 tog, wf) twice, K1, (wf, K2 tog tbl) twice, K3, wf, K2 tog tbl, K1] 3 times, rib 21.

29th row: [Rib 21, K1, K2 tog tbl, wf, K3, (K2 tog, wf) twice, K3, (wf, K2 tog tbl) twice, K3, wf, K3 tog, wf, K3, (K2 tog, wf) twice, K3, (wf, K2 tog tbl) twice, K5] 3 times, rib 21.

31st row: [Rib 21, K5, (K2 tog, wf) twice, K5, (wf, K2 tog tbl) twice, K7, (K2 tog, wf) twice, K5, (wf, K2 tog tbl) twice, K4] 3 times, rib 21.

33rd row: [Rib 21, K4, (K2 tog, wf) twice, K7, (wf, K2 tog tbl) twice, K5, (K2 tog, wf) twice, K7, (wf, K2 tog tbl) twice, K3] 3 times, rib 21.

35th row: [Rib 21, K3, (K2 tog, wf) twice, K9, (wf, K2 tog tbl) twice, K3, (K2 tog, wf) twice, K9, (wf, K2 tog tbl) twice, K2] 3 times, rib 21.

37th row: [Rib 21, K2, (K2 tog, wf) twice, K3, K2 tog, wf, K1, wf, K2 tog tbl, K3, (wf, K2 tog tbl) twice, K1, (K2 tog, wf) twice, K3, K2 tog, wf, K1, wf, K2 tog tbl, K3, (wf, K2 tog tbl) twice, K1] 3 times, rib 21.

39th row: [Rib 21, K1, (K2 tog, wf) twice, K3, K2 tog, wf, K3, wf, K2 tog tbl, K3, wf, K2 tog tbl, wf, K3 tog, wf, K2 tog, wf, K3, K2 tog, wf, K3, wf, K2 tog tbl, K3, wf, K2 tog tbl, wf, K2 tog tbl] 3 times, rib 21.

41st row: [Rib 21, K2, wf, K3 tog, K3, wf, K1, wf, K2 tog tbl, wf, K3 tog, wf, K1, wf, K3, K3 tog, wf, K1, wf, K3 tog, K3, wf, K1, wf, K2 tog tbl, wf, K3 tog, wf, K1, wf, K3, K3 tog, wf, K1] 3 times, rib 21.

43rd row: [Rib 21, K3, wf, K3 tog, K1, wf, K3, wf, K3 tog, wf, K3, wf, K1, K3 tog, wf, K3, wf, K3 tog, K1, wf, K3, wf, K3 tog, wf, K3, wf, K1, K3 tog, wf, K2] 3 times, rib 21.

44th row: [Rib 21, P42] 3 times, rib 21.

These 44 rows form the patt.

Work rows 1–44 incl 3 times more.

Dec in rib panel as follows:

Next row: [P2, (KB1, P2 tog, P1) 4 times, KB1, P2, patt 42] 3 times, P2, (KB1, P2 tog, P1) 4 times, KB1, P2 (194 sts).

Next row: [K2, (PB1, K2) 5 times, patt 42] 3 times, (K2, PB1) 5 times, K2.

Keeping rib and patt correct, work 42 rows.

Next row: [P2 tog, (KB1, P2 tog) 4 times, KB1, P2 tog, patt 42] 3 times, P2 tog, (KB1, P2 tog) 5 times (170 sts).

Next row: [(K1, PB1) 5 times, K1, patt 42] 3 times, (K1, PB1) 5 times, K1.

Keeping rib and patt correct, work 36 rows.

Next row: K.

Next row: P2, (P2 tog, P1) 56 times (114 sts).

Work 5 rows in stocking stitch.

Next row: P7, (P2 tog, P8) 10 times, P2 tog, P to end (103 sts).

Work 5 rows in stocking stitch.

Next row: P7, (P2 tog, P7) 10 times, P2 tog, P to end.

Work 5 rows in stocking stitch.

Next row: P6, (P2 tog, P6) 10 times, P2 tog, P to end (81 sts).

Work 5 rows in stocking stitch.

Next row: P6, (P2 tog, P5) 10 times, P2 tog, P to end (70 sts).

Change to No 13 needles.

Work 4 rows in stocking stitch.

Cast off.

Work 3 more panels in the same manner.

MAKE UP

Pin out each panel, wrong side facing, the measurements to be:

> Length, 31 ins.
>
> Width at lower edge, 32 ins.
>
> Width at top edge, 9 ins.

Lightly press on wrong side, using a warm iron and damp cloth.

Cut 4 pieces of nylon net to line panels, allowing ½ inch at lower edge for hem.

Make ½ inch hem on lower edge of each piece of nylon net.

Using a back-stitch seam, stitch 3 panels together.

Stitch 4th panel from lower edge to 7 ins from top.

Tack net lining into position and machine along top.

Stitch zipp into opening at top. Cut length of petersham to waist size required. Attach hooks and eyes. Stitch top of skirt on to petersham band, easing in if necessary along top edge.

Press all seams.

Evening Top

3 oz 2-ply Fingering. Two No 12 needles. Set of No 14 needles with points at both ends. Length of elastic.

Bust, 34–36 ins. Length, 15½ ins.

This garment must be worked at a tension of 9 sts and 11 rows to one square inch on No 12 needles measured over stocking stitch.

Using the through sts method and No 12 needles, cast on 128 sts.
Work in K1, P1 rib for 2 ins.

Next row: *Make hem* by knitting tog 1 st from needle and 1 loop
from cast-on edge all across row.

Next row: P11, (inc in next st, P20) 5 times, inc in next st, P to
end (134 sts).

Proceed in stocking stitch with centre panel on 84 sts, the centre
panel being repeats of rows 1–44 of the skirt panel, *noting* that
the bracketed portion is only worked once on every row, the
1st 2 rows placing panel, being as follows:

1st row: K25, [P2, (KB1, P3) 4 times, KB1, P2, K1, wf, K3 tog,
wf, K2, wf, K2 tog tbl, wf, K3 tog, wf, K1, wf, K2 tog tbl,
wf, K3 tog, wf, K2, wf, K2 tog tbl, wf, K3 tog, wf, K2, wf,
K2 tog tbl, wf, K3 tog, wf, K1, wf, K2 tog tbl, wf, K3 tog,
wf, K2, wf, K2 tog tbl, K1] once, P2, (KB1, P3) 4 times, KB1,
P2, K25.

2nd row: P25, [K2, (PB1, K3) 4 times, PB1, K2, P42] once, K2,
(PB1, K3) 4 times, PB1, K2, P25.

Keeping panel correct, continue in this manner, inc 1 st at both
ends of 5th and every following 10th row until there are 154 sts,
working extra sts in stocking stitch throughout.

Continue on these sts until 12th row of 3rd patt from beg on
centre panel has been worked (mark this point with length of
wool).

Continue until 38th row of 3rd patt from beg has been worked.

Shape neck as follows:

Next row: Work across 56 sts, cast off 42, work to end.

Proceed on 1st group of 56 sts as follows:

1st row: P to last 24 sts, P2 tog tbl, P1, rib 21.

2nd row: Rib 21, K to end.

Rep these 2 rows until 33 sts remain.

Shape shoulder by casting off 11 sts at beg of next and every alt
row until all sts are worked off.

Rejoin wool to remaining group of 56 sts at neck edge and complete to match other half of front, as follows:

1st row: Rib 21, P1, P2 tog, P to end.

2nd row: K to last 21 sts, rib 21.

Continue as on these 2 rows until 33 sts remain, thus finishing at side edge.

Shape shoulder as on 1st half.

BACK

Working 84 panel sts in stocking stitch throughout (thus the whole of the back after the ribbing will be in stocking stitch), work to match front until neck shaping is reached.

Work 2 rows.

Next row: K 76, cast off 2, K to end.

Proceed on 1st group of 76 sts as follows:

Dec 1 st at neck edge on every row until 33 sts remain.

Work 1 row, thus finishing at side edge.

Shape shoulder as on front.

Rejoin wool to remaining group of sts and complete to match other half of neck.

NECKBAND

Using a back-stitch seam, join shoulders of back and front.

With right side of work facing, using set of No 14 needles *knit up* 232 sts round neck.

K 5 rounds.

Cast off.

ARMBANDS

Using 2 of the No 14 needles, with right side of work facing, *knit up* 146 sts between points marked.

Commencing with a P row, work 5 rows in stocking stitch.

Cast off.

MAKE UP

Block and lightly press on wrong side using a warm iron and damp cloth. Fold neckband at centre and flat stitch cast-off edge to knitted-up edge on wrong side of work. Complete armbands to match. Using a back-stitch seam, join side and sleeve seams down to hem at lower edge. Join one side of hem with flat seam. Thread length of elastic through hem. Join ends of elastic. Flat stitch edges of hem tog. Press seams.

FOUR-PLY TYROLEAN COAT

Illustrated in Plate 28b

10 oz 4-ply Fingering and oddments of bright colours for embroidery. Two No 12 and two No 10 needles. Twelve buttons. Bust, 34–36 ins. Length, 20 ins. Sleeve, 18 ins.

This garment must be worked at a tension of 7 sts and 9 rows to one square inch on No 10 needles measured over stocking stitch.

RIGHT FRONT

Using No 12 needles, cast on 56 sts.
Proceed in rib patt as follows:
1st row: K1, P2, K8, P2, (KB2, P2, K8, P2) 3 times, K1.
2nd row: P1, K2, P8, K2, (PB2, K2, P8, K2) 3 times, P1.
3rd row: K1, P2, K8, P2, (TW2, P2, K8, P2) 3 times, K1.
4th row: As 2nd row.
Work 1st–4th rows 10 times more. **

Change to No 10 needles and proceed in fancy cable rib patt as follows:
1st row: K1, P2, C2B, C2F, P2, (KB2, P2, C2B, C2F, P2) twice, K15
2nd and 4th rows: P15, (K2, P8, K2, PB2) twice, K2, P8, K2, P1.
3rd row: K1, P2, K8, P2, (TW2, P2, K8, P2) twice, K15.
5th row: K1, P2, K2, C2F, K2, P2, (KB2, P2, K2, C2F, K2, P2) twice, K14, inc in last st.
6th row: P16, (K2, P8, K2, PB2) twice, K2, P8, K2, P1.
7th row: K1, P2, K8, P2, (TW2, P2, K8, P2) twice, K16.
8th row: As 6th row.
9th–16th rows: Omitting inc at end of 5th row, work as on rows 5–8 twice more, working an inc st at end of 11th row, keeping extra st in stocking stitch throughout.
17th row: K1, P2, C2F, C2B, P2, (KB2, P2, C2F, C2B, P2) twice, K16, inc in last st.
18th row: P18, (K2, P8, K2, PB2) twice, K2, P8, K2, P1.
19th row: K1, P2, K8, P2, (TW2, P2, K8, P2) twice, K18.
20th row: As 18th row.
21st row: K1, P2, K8, P2, (KB2, P2, K8, P2) twice, K18.

223

22nd row: As 18th row.

23rd row: K1, P2, K8, P2, (TW2, P2, K8, P2) twice, K17, inc in last st.

24th row: P19, (K2, P8, K2, PB2) twice, K2, P8, K2, P1.

These 24 rows form the cable rib patt, inc having been worked on 5th, 11th, 17th, and 23rd rows.

Keeping patt correct, continue inc on every 6th row as before until 4 more inc (*8 in all*) have been worked and there are 64 sts.

Continue on these sts until work measures 9 ins from *top of ribbing*, finishing so that wrong side of work will be facing when working next row.

Shape armhole by casting off 8 sts at beg of next row. Dec 1 st at armhole edge on next and every alt row until 49 sts remain.

Continue on these sts until work measures 5½ ins from beg of armhole shaping, finishing at front edge.

Shape neck by casting off 7 sts at beg of next row. Dec 1 st at neck edge on every row until 34 sts remain.

Continue on these sts until work measures 7 ins from beg of armhole shaping, finishing at armhole edge.

Shape shoulder by casting off 11 sts at beg of next and following alt row.

Work 1 row.

Cast off.

LEFT FRONT

Work as right front to **.

Change to No 10 needles and complete to match right front, reversing position of front panel and all shapings, the first 2 rows (reversing position of panel) being as follows:

1st row: K15, (P2, C2B, C2F, P2, KB2) twice, P2, C2B, C2F, P2, K1.

2nd row: P1, K2, P8, K2, (PB2, K2, P8, K2) twice, P15.

BACK

Using No 12 needles, cast on 98 sts.

Work as right front to **, *noting* that bracketed portion will be worked 6 times in place of 3 times on every row.

Next row: K8, (inc in next st, K8) 10 times (108 sts).

Change to No 10 needles and P I row.

Proceed in stocking stitch, inc 1 st at both ends of 7th and every following 8th row until there are 120 sts.

Continue on these sts until work matches fronts up to armhole shaping.

Shape armholes by casting off 6 sts at beg of next 2 rows. Dec 1 st at both ends of next and every alt row until 94 sts remain.

Continue on these sts until work matches fronts up to shoulder shaping.

Shape shoulders as follows:
1st and 2nd rows: Cast off 11 sts, work to end.
3rd and 4th rows: As 1st and 2nd.
5th and 6th rows: Cast off 12 sts, work to end.
Cast off.

SLEEVES

Using No 12 needles, cast on 56 sts.
Proceed in twisted rib as follows:
1st row: K1, * P2, KB2, rep from * to last 3 sts, P2, K1.
2nd row: P1, * K2, PB2, rep from * to last 3 sts, K2, P1.
3rd row: K1, * P2, TW2, rep from * to last 3 sts, P2, K1.
4th row: As 2nd row.
Work 1st–4th rows 6 times more, then rep rows 1–3 incl.
Next row: Rib 4, (inc in next st, rib 5) 8 times, inc in next st, rib to end (65 sts).

Change to No 10 needles and proceed in stocking stitch, inc 1 st at both ends of 5th and every following 10th row until there are 91 sts.

Continue on these sts until work measures 18 ins from beg.

Shape top by casting off 3 sts at beg of next 4 rows, 2 sts at beg of next 6 rows. Dec 1 st at both ends of every row until 57 sts remain; every alt row until 47 sts remain; every following 3rd row until 31 sts remain.

Cast off 4 sts at beg of next 6 rows.
Cast off.

RIGHT FRONT BAND

Using No 12 needles, cast on 14 sts.

1st row: K1, KB1, (P2, KB2) twice, P2, KB1, K1.

2nd row: K1, PB1, (K2, PB2) twice, K2, PB1, K1.

3rd row: K1, KB1, (P2, TW2) twice, P2, KB1, K1.

4th row: As 2nd row.

5th row: K1, KB1, P2, KB2, cast off 2 (1 st on needle after cast off), KB1, P2, KB1, K1.

6th row: K1, PB1, K2, PB2, cast on 2, PB2, K2, PB1, K1.

7th and 8th rows: As 3rd and 4th.

Keeping patt correct as on rows 1–4 throughout, continue working buttonholes on 15th and 16th rows from previous buttonhole until 10th row after 11th buttonhole from beg has been worked.

Slip sts on to length of wool and leave.

LEFT FRONT BAND

Omitting buttonholes, work as right front band.

226

NECKBAND

Using a back-stitch seam, join shoulders of back and fronts. Slip sts from top of right front band on to a No 12 needle, right side facing, K I, K B I, patt 10, K B 2 across these sts, using same needle *knit up* 66 sts round neck, slip sts from top of left front band on to No 12 needle, K B 2, patt 10, K B I, K I, across these sts (94 sts). Continue in twisted rib patt on these sts for 8 rows working a buttonhole on 4th and 5th rows to match previous buttonholes.

Cast off in patt.

MAKE UP

With wrong side of work facing, block and lightly press each piece using a warm iron and damp cloth. Using a back-stitch seam, join side and sleeve seams and stitch sleeves into position. Using a flat seam, stitch on front bands. Attach buttons to correspond with buttonholes. Using oddments, work embroidery on welt as shown on photograph (see diagram). Press all seams.

LACE-FRONT CARDIGAN
Illustrated in Plate 29a

12 oz 4-ply Fingering, oddments of coloured wool for embroidery. Two No 13 and two No 11 needles. A cable needle. A stitch-holder. Eight buttons.

Bust, 34–36 ins. Length, 21 ins. Sleeve, 18 ins.

This garment must be worked at a tension of $7\frac{1}{2}$ sts and $9\frac{1}{2}$ rows to one square inch on No 11 needles measured over stocking stitch.

For this pattern:

MB – Make bobble by P I, K I, P I, K I into next st, thus making 4 sts out of next st, turn, K 4, turn, P 4, slip 2nd, 3rd, and 4th sts over first st.

RIGHT FRONT

Using No 11 needles, cast on 60 sts.

Work 4 rows in K I, P I rib, inc I st at end of last row (61 sts).

227

Proceed for lace panel and cable patt as follows:

1st row: K1, P2, K2 tog tbl, KB3, wf, KB1, wf, KB3, K2 tog, P2, K1, (K9, P2) 4 times.

2nd row: (K2, P9) 4 times, K3, PB4, P1, PB1, P1, PB4, K3.

3rd row: K1, P2, K2 tog tbl, KB2, wf, KB3, wf, KB2, K2 tog, P2, K1, (C2F, K1, C2B, P2) 4 times.

4th row: (K2, P9) 4 times, K3, (PB3, P1) twice, PB3, K3.

5th row: K1, P2, K2 tog tbl, KB1, wf, KB5, wf, KB1, K2 tog, P2, K1, (K4, MB, K4, P2) 4 times.

6th row: (K2, P9) 4 times, K3, PB2, P1, PB5, P1, PB2, K3.

7th row: K1, KB1, wf, KB3, K2 tog, P3, K2 tog tbl, KB3, wf, KB1, K1, (K9, P2) 4 times.

8th row: (K2, P9) 4 times, K1, PB1, P1, PB4, K3, PB4, P1, PB1, K1.

9th row: K1, KB2, wf, KB2, K2 tog, P3, K2 tog tbl, KB2, wf, KB2, K1, (C2F, K1, C2B, P2) 4 times.

10th row: (K2, P9) 4 times, K1, PB2, P1, PB3, K3, PB3, P1, PB2, K1.

11th row: K1, KB3, wf, KB1, K2 tog, P3, K2 tog tbl, KB1, wf, KB3, K1, (K4, MB, K4, P2) 4 times.

12th row: (K2, P9) 4 times, K1, PB3, P1, PB2, K3, PB2, P1, PB3, K1.

These 12 rows form the patt.

Work rows 1–12 incl twice more.

Next row: Patt 17, turn and work 11 more rows on these 17 sts, thus completing 4th lace patt from beg.

Break off wool.

Next row: Slip first 17 sts on to stitch-holder and leave.

Rejoin wool to remaining group of sts and *using No 13 needles* work 14 rows in cable patt.

Break off wool (mark this point at side edge with a length of coloured wool). Slip sts from stitch-holder on to needle containing remainder of sts.

Rejoin wool, *noting* that next row will be 1st row of lace panel and 3rd row of cable patt, *using No 11 needles* keeping lace panel and cable patt correct throughout and inc 1 st at outside edge on 5th and every following 8th row until 8 inc *in all* have been worked (69 sts on needle on completion of side inc), proceed for movement of cable panels as follows:

228

Work 12 rows.

Next row: Lace patt 17, cable patt 33, K9, P2, inc in last st.

Next row: P2, (K2, P9) 4 times, lace patt 17.

Keeping lace patt correct and cable patt on 33 sts as on last 2 rows, working remainder of sts in K9, P2 rib throughout, work 10 rows.

Next row: Lace patt 17, cable patt 22, rib patt to end.

Keeping lace patt correct on 17 sts and cable patt on 22 sts as on last row, work 11 rows.

Next row: Lace patt 17, cable patt 11, rib patt to end.

Keeping lace patt correct on 17 sts and cable patt on 11 sts as on last row, work 11 rows.

Next row: Lace patt 17, rib patt to end.

Continue in lace and rib patt until all side inc have been worked and there are 69 sts.

Continue on these sts until work measures $8\frac{1}{2}$ ins from point marked, finishing at side edge.

Shape raglan armhole and front slope as follows:

1st row: Cast off 2, rib patt to last 17 sts, lace patt 17.

2nd row: Lace patt 17, K1, K2 tog tbl, rib patt to last 2 sts K2 tog.

3rd row: Rib patt to last 17 sts, lace patt 17.

4th row: Lace patt 17, rib patt to last 2 sts, K2 tog.

5th row: As 3rd row.

6th row: As 4th row.

7th row: As 3rd row.

Rep rows 2–7 incl until 11 more dec (12 *in all*) have been worked inside 17 st lace panel at front edge (21 sts).

Keeping lace patt correct, continue dec at armhole edge *only* on every alt row as before until 17 sts remain, thus finishing at armhole edge.

Next row: Cast off 8, patt to end.

Next row: Patt all across.

Cast off 9.

LEFT FRONT

Work to match right front, reversing position of cable and lace patts and all shapings, *noting* that neck shaping inside lace

229

panel will be worked K2 tog in place of K2 tog tbl throughout the first 6 rows (after 4 rows in K1, P1 rib) placing position of cable and lace patt being as follows:

1st row: (P2, K9) 4 times, K1, P2, K2 tog tbl, KB3, wf, KB1, wf, KB3, K2 tog, P2, K1.

2nd row: K3, PB4, P1, PB1, P1, PB4, K3, (P9, K2) 4 times.

3rd row: (P2, C2F, K1, C2B) 4 times, K1, P2, K2 tog tbl, KB2, wf, KB3, wf, KB2, K2 tog, P2, K1.

4th row: K3, PB3, (P1, PB3) twice, K3, (P9, K2) 4 times.

5th row: (P2, K4, MB, K4) 4 times, K1, P2, K2 tog tbl, KB1, wf, KB5, wf, KB1, K2 tog, P2, K1.

6th row: K3, PB2, P1, PB5, P1, PB2, K3, (P9, K2) 4 times.

BACK

Using No 11 needles, cast 123 sts.

Work 4 rows in K1, P1 rib.

Proceed in cable patt and lace patt as follows:

1st row: (P2, K9) 4 times, * K1, P2, K2 tog tbl, KB3, wf, KB1, wf, KB3, K2 tog, P2, K1, * K1, rep from * to * (K9, P2) 4 times.

2nd row: (K2, P9) 4 times, * K3, PB4, P1, PB1, P1, PB4, K3, * P1, rep from * to * (P9, K2) 4 times.

3rd row: (P2, C2F, K1, C2B) 4 times, * K1, P2, K2 tog tbl, KB2, wf, KB3, wf, KB2, K2 tog, P2, K1, * K1, rep from * to * (C2F, K1, C2B, P2) 4 times.

4th row: (K2, P9) 4 times, * K3, (PB3, P1) twice, PB3, K3, * P1, rep from * to * (P9, K2) 4 times.

5th row: (P2, K4, MB, K4) 4 times, * K1, P2, K2 tog tbl, KB1, wf, KB5, wf, KB1, K2 tog, P2, K1, * K1, rep from * to * (K4, MB, K4, P2) 4 times.

6th row: (K2, P9) 4 times, * K3, PB2, P1, PB5, P1, PB2, K3, * P1, rep from * to * (P9, K2) 4 times.

7th row: (P2, K9) 4 times, * K1, KB1, wf, KB3, K2 tog, P3, K2 tog tbl, KB3, wf, KB1, K1, * K1, rep from * to * (K9, P2) 4 times.

8th row: (K2, P9) 4 times, * K1, PB1, P1, PB4, K3, PB4, P1, PB1, K1, * P1, rep from * to * (P9, K2) 4 times.

9th row: (P2, C2F, K1, C2B) 4 times, * K1, KB2, wf, KB2, K2 tog, P3, K2 tog tbl, KB2, wf, KB2, K1, * K1, rep from * to * (C2F, K1, C2B, P2) 4 times.

10th row: (K2, P9) 4 times, * K1, PB2, P1, PB3, K3, PB3, P1, PB2, K1, * P1, rep from * to * (P9, K2) 4 times.

11th row: (P2, K4, MB, K4) 4 times, * K1, KB3, wf, KB1, K2 tog, P3, K2 tog tbl, KB1, wf, KB3, K1, * K1, rep from * to * (K4, MB, K4, P2) 4 times.

12th row: (K2, P9) 4 times, * K1, PB3, P1, PB2, K3, PB2, P1, PB3, K1, * P1, rep from * to * (P9, K2) 4 times.

Work rows 1–12 incl twice more.

Next row: *Using No 13 needles* patt 44, turn.

Work 13 rows on these 44 sts.

Break off wool, slip sts on to a length of wool and leave.

Rejoin wool and *using No 11 needles* patt 35, turn.

Work 11 rows on these sts.

Break off wool, slip sts on to a length of wool and leave.

Rejoin wool to remaining group of 44 sts and *using No 13 needles* work 14 rows.

Break off wool, slip all sts on to end of last needle (mark this point with a length of coloured wool).

Rejoin wool, *using No 11 needles* and *noting* that next row will be 1st row of lace patt and 3rd row of cable patt, work 4 rows, thus completing cable patt.

Working sts at each side of lace panel in P2, K9 rib throughout and keeping lace patt correct, inc 1 st at both ends of next and every following 8th row until there are 139 sts, working extra sts into P2, K9 rib throughout.

Continue in patt until work matches fronts up to armhole shaping, finishing so that right side of work will be facing when working next row.

Shape armholes and work *Back Yoke* as follows:

1st and 2nd rows: Cast off 2, patt to end.

3rd row: K2 tog, rib patt 45, K2 tog, K1, lace patt 17, M1, K1, M1, lace patt 17, K1, K2 tog tbl, rib patt to last 2 sts, K2 tog.

4th row: Rib patt 48, lace patt 17, P3, lace patt 17, rib patt 48.

5th row: K2 tog, rib patt 46, lace patt 17, K3, lace patt 17, rib patt 46, K2 tog.

6th row: Rib patt 47, lace patt 17, P3, lace patt 17, rib patt 47.

7th row: K2 tog, rib patt 45, lace patt 17, K3, lace patt 17, rib patt 45, K2 tog.

8th row: Rib patt 46, lace patt 17, P3, lace patt 17, rib patt 46.

9th row: K2 tog, rib patt 41, K2 tog, K1, lace patt 17, M1, K3, M1, lace patt 17, K1, K2 tog tbl, rib patt 41, K2 tog.

10th row: Rib patt 44, lace patt 17, P5, lace patt 17, rib patt 44.

11th row: K2 tog, rib patt 42, lace patt 17, K5, lace patt 17, rib patt 42, K2 tog.

12th row: Rib patt 43, lace patt 17, P5, lace patt 17, rib patt 43.

13th row: P2 tog, rib patt 41, lace patt 17, K5, lace patt 17, rib patt 41, P2 tog.

14th row: Rib patt 42, lace patt 17, P5, lace patt 17, rib patt 42.

Continue dec at side edge on next and every alt row as before, dec and inc outside and between lace panels as before on next and every following 6th row until 10 *more* sets of inc and dec have been worked on centre panel, thus the next row would be 'P25' in centre panel.

Continue without further dec and inc in centre, but still dec at both ends of every alt row as before until 59 sts remain.

Cast off 8 sts at beg of next 2 rows, 9 sts at beg of following 2 rows (25 sts).

Work 3 rows.

Cast off.

SLEEVES

Using No 13 needles, cast on 60 sts.

Work in K1, P1 rib for 3 ins.

Next row: Rib 5, (inc in next st, rib 6) 7 times, inc in next st, rib to end (68 sts).

Change to No 11 needles and proceed in rib patt as follows:

1st row: * P2, K9, rep from * to last 2 sts, P2.

2nd row: * K2, P9, rep from * to last 2 sts, K2.

Continue in rib patt, inc 1 st at both ends of next and every following 7th row until there are 100 sts, every following 6th row until there are 110 sts.

Continue on these sts until work measures 18 ins from beg, finishing so that right side of work will be facing when working next row.

Shape top by casting off 2 sts at beg of next 2 rows. Dec 1 st at both ends of every row until 60 sts remain, then every alt row until 6 sts remain.

Cast off.

Using No 13 needles, cast on 15 sts.

1st row: K2, (P1, K1) 6 times, K1.

2nd row: (K1, P1) 7 times, K1.

3rd and 4th rows: As 1st and 2nd.

5th row: Rib 6, cast off 3, rib to end.

6th row: Rib 6, cast on 3, rib to end.

Continue in rib, working a buttonhole as on 5th and 6th rows on 19th and 20th rows from previous buttonhole until 8 buttonholes *in all* have been worked.

Continue without further buttonholes until work measures 47½ ins (not stretched) from beg.

Cast off in rib.

MAKE UP

Block and press *very lightly* on wrong side using a warm iron and damp cloth. Using a back-stitch seam, join side seams, matching points marked with coloured wool. Join ends of waistband. Join sleeve seams and stitch sleeves into position, matching sleeve and armhole shapings.

Stitch 3 rows at top of back to 3 of cast-off sts at top of sleeve.

Using a flat seam, stitch front band into position. Using oddments of coloured wool work embroidery (as on photograph) at top of each cable patt rib on back and fronts. Attach buttons to correspond with buttonholes. Press seams.

MAN'S CONTINENTAL SWEATER
Illustrated in Plate 29b

12 oz Light, 3 oz Dark 4-ply Fingering. Two No 13 and two No 11 needles.

Chest, 38–40 ins. Length, 23½ ins. Sleeve, 20 ins.

This garment must be worked at a tension of 7½ sts and 9½ rows to one square inch on No 11 needles measured over stocking stitch.

FRONT AND BACK (*both alike*)

Using No 13 needles and Light, cast on 136 sts.

Work in K2, P2 rib for 4½ ins.

Next row: Rib 4, (inc in next st, rib 6) 18 times, inc in next st, rib to end (155 sts).

Change to No 11 needles and proceed in diamond stripe patt as follows:

1st row: * P3, KB2, P3, K6, P1, K6, rep from * to last 8 sts, P3, KB2, P3.

2nd row: * K1, P1, K1, PB2, K1, P1, (K1, P6) twice, rep from * to last 8 sts, K1, P1, K1, PB2, K1, P1, K1.

3rd row: * P3, KB2, P3, K5, P1, K1, P1, K5, rep from * to last 8 sts, P3, KB2, P3.

4th row: * K1, P1, K1, PB2, (K1, P1, K1, P5) twice, rep from * to last 8 sts, K1, P1, K1, PB2, K1, P1, K1.

5th row: * P3, KB2, P3, K4, (P1, K1) twice, P1, K4, rep from * to last 8 sts, P3, KB2, P3.

6th row: * K1, P1, K1, PB2, K1, P1, K1, P4, (K1, P1) twice, K1, P4, rep from * to last 8 sts. K1, P1, K1, PB2, K1, P1, K1.

7th row: * Patt 8, K3, (P1, K1) 3 times, P1, K3, rep from * to last 8 sts, patt 8.

8th row: * Patt 8, P3, (K1, P1) 3 times, K1, P3, rep from * to last 8 sts, patt 8.

9th row: * Patt 8, K2, P1, K1, P1, K3, P1, K1, P1, K2, rep from * to last 8 sts, patt 8.

10th row: * Patt 8, P2, K1, P1, K1, P3, K1, P1, K1, P2, rep from * to last 8 sts, patt 8.

11th row: * Patt 8, (K1, P1) twice, K5, (P1, K1) twice, rep from * to last 8 sts, patt 8.

12th row: * Patt 8, (P1, K1) twice, P5, (K1, P1) twice, rep from * to last 8 sts, patt 8.

13th and 14th rows: As 9th and 10th.

15th and 16th rows: As 7th and 8th.

17th and 18th rows: As 5th and 6th.

19th and 20th rows: As 3rd and 4th.

These 20 rows form the patt.

Work 1st–20th rows 3 times more.

Keeping patt correct, *shape dolman sleeves* as follows:

1st–6th rows: Cast on 2 sts, patt to end.

7th–12th rows: Cast on 3 sts, patt to end.

13th–18th rows: Cast on 4 sts, patt to end.

19th–24th rows: Cast on 5 sts, patt to end.

25th–56th rows: Cast on 6 sts, patt to end (431 sts).

Work 6 rows, thus finishing at end of a 2nd row of patt.

Proceed for *Yoke* as follows:

1st row: P.

2nd row: K.

3rd row: * P2, K8, rep from * to last st, P1.

4th row: * K2, P8, rep from * to last st, K1.

5th row: * K8, P2, rep from * to last st, K1.

6th row: * P2, K2, P6, rep from * to last st, P1.

7th row: * K6, P2, K2, rep from * to last st, K1.

8th row: * P4, K2, P4, rep from * to last st, P1.

9th row: * K4, P2, K4, rep from * to last st, K1.

10th row: * P6, K2, P2, rep from * to last st, P1.

11th and 12th rows: As 1st and 2nd.

13th row: * K3, P2, K5, rep from * to last st, K1.

14th row: * P5, K2, P3, rep from * to last st, P1.

15th row: * K5, P2, K3, rep from * to last st, K1.

16th row: * P3, K2, P5, rep from * to last st, P1.

17th row: * K7, P2, K1, rep from * to last st, K1.

18th row: * P1, K2, P7, rep from * to last st, P1.

19th row: * P1, K8, P1, rep from * to last st, P1.

20th row: * K1, P8, K1, rep from * to last st, K1.

21st and 22nd rows: As 1st and 2nd.

Proceed in stripe patt as follows:

1st row: Using Dark, K.

2nd row: Using Dark, P.

3rd row: Using Light, K.

4th row: Using Dark, P.

These 4 rows form the patt.

Continue in patt until work measures 5¾ ins along end of sleeve.

Shape top of sleeve as follows:

Keeping stripe patt correct, cast off 40 sts at beg of next 6 rows; 43 sts at beg of next 2 rows, 15 sts at beg of next 2 rows (75 sts).

Using Dark, work 6 rows in K I, P I rib on these sts.
Cast off.

CUFFS

Using a back-stitch seam, join top of sleeves and shoulders, omitting 6 rows of K I, P I rib at neck.
Using No 13 needles and Dark, with right side of work facing, *knit up* 64 sts along edge of sleeve. Work in K 2, P 2 rib for 3 ins.
Cast off in rib.

MAKE UP

Omitting ribbing, lightly press on wrong side using a warm iron and damp cloth.
Using a back-stitch seam, join side and sleeve seams.
Using a flat seam, join K I, P I rib at neck edge. Fold K I, P I rib neckband to wrong side of work, and flat stitch into position to form hem.
Press seams.

LADY'S TWO-PLY BUTTON-THROUGH BLOUSE
Illustrated in Plate 30a

5 oz 2-ply Fingering. Two No 13 and two No 12 needles. One stitch-holder. Sixteen small pearl buttons. Length of elastic. Two press studs.
Bust, 34–36 ins. Length, 17½ ins. Sleeve, 5 ins.

This garment must be worked at a tension of 9 sts and 11 rows to one square inch on No 12 needles measured over stocking stitch.

FRONT

Using *two* No 13 needles, cast on 128 sts.
Work in K I, P I rib for 2 ins.
Next row: *Make hem* by knitting tog 1 st from needle and 1 loop from cast-on edge all across row.
Next row: P 9, (inc in next st, P 10) 10 times, inc in next st, P to end (139 sts).
Next row: K 34, (P I, K B 2) 4 times, P 2, K 2, (K 2 tog, wf) twice,

K1, (wf, sl1, K1, psso) twice, K2, P2, K13, P2, K2, (K2 tog, wf) twice, K1, (wf, sl1, K1, psso) twice, K2, P2, (KB2, P1) 4 times, K34.

Change to No 12 needles and *divide* for *Fronts* as follows:

Next row: P34, (K1, PB2) 4 times, K2, P13, K2, P13, slip remaining 63 sts on to a stitch-holder and leave, cast on 12 sts (88 sts), turn, and proceed for *Right Front* as follows:

1st row: K25, P2, K1, (K2 tog, wf) twice, K3, (wf, sl1, K1, psso) twice, K1, P2, (KB2, P1) 4 times, K34.

2nd and every alt row: P34, (K1, PB2) 4 times, K2, P13, K2, P25.

3rd row: K25, P2, (K2 tog, wf) twice, K5, (wf, sl1, K1, psso) twice, P2, (KB2, P1) 4 times, K34.

5th row: (on which 1st set of buttonholes is worked) K8, wf, K2 tog, K6, wf, K2 tog, K7, P2, K2, (wf, sl1, K1, psso) twice, K1, (K2 tog, wf) twice, K2, P2, (KB2, P1) 4 times, K34.

7th row: K25, P2, K3, wf, sl1, K1, psso, wf, sl1, K2 tog, psso, wf, K2 tog, wf, K3, P2, (KB2, P1) 4 times, K34.

9th row: (on which 2nd set of buttonholes is worked) K3, wf, K2 tog, K16, wf, K2 tog, K2, P2, K2, (K2 tog, wf) twice, K1, (wf, sl1, K1, psso) twice, K2, P2, (KB2, P1) 4 times, K34.

10th row: P34, (K1, PB2) 4 times, K2, P13, K2, P25.

These 10 rows form the *lace and tucks* panel, buttonholes having been worked on 5th and 9th rows.

Working sets of buttonholes as before on 22nd rows from previous buttonholes, continue in patt, inc 1 st at end of next and every following 6th row until there are 102 sts on needle, working extra sts into stocking stitch.

Continue on these sts until 2nd row after 10th set of buttonholes from beg has been worked, thus finishing at armhole edge.

Working buttonholes as before and keeping panel correct, *shape armhole* by casting off 10 sts at beg of next row, then dec 1 st at armhole edge on next and every alt row until 81 sts remain.

Continue on these sts until 16 sets of buttonholes from beg have been worked. Work 1 row.

Shape neck by casting off 34 sts at beg of next row. Dec 1 st at neck edge on next and every row until 39 sts remain.

Continue on these sts until work measures 7¼ ins from beg of armhole shaping, finishing at armhole edge.

Shape shoulder by casting off 13 sts at beg of next and every alt row until all sts are cast off.

Rejoin wool to remaining group of 63 sts, *using No 12 needles* cast on 12 sts for *underflap* and proceed for *Left Front* as follows:

Next row: K2, P10, K2, P13, K2, (PB2, K1) 4 times, P34.

Omitting buttonholes, complete to match *Right Front, noting* there will be 13 sts less on needle up to neck shaping and that 21 sts will be cast off in place of 34 on the 1st row of neck shaping, the 1st 2 rows placing the position of tucks and lace panel being as follows:

1st row: K34, (P1, KB2) 4 times, P2, K1, (K2 tog, wf) twice, K3, (wf, sl1, K1, psso) twice, K1, P2, K12.

2nd row: K2, P10, K2, P13, K2, (PB2, K1) 4 times, P34.

BACK

Work *hem* as on front.

Next row: P20, (inc in next st, P22) 4 times, inc in next st, P to end (133 sts).

Change to No 12 needles and proceed in stocking stitch, inc 1 st at both ends of 7th and every following 6th row until there are 163 sts on needle.

Continue on these sts until work matches fronts up to armhole shaping.

Shape armholes by casting off 10 sts at beg of next 2 rows. Dec 1 st at both ends of next and every alt row until 121 sts remain.

Continue on these sts until work matches fronts up to shoulder shaping.

Shape shoulders by casting off 13 sts at beg of next 6 rows.
Cast off.

SLEEVE BANDS AND SLEEVES

Using No 13 needles, cast on 13 sts.

1st row: P1, (P1, KB2) 4 times.

2nd row: (PB2, K1) 4 times, K1.

Rep these 2 rows until band measures 11½ ins from beg.
Cast off in patt.

With right side of work facing, using No 12 needles, *knit up* 100 sts
along P st edge of band.

Commencing with a P row, proceed in stocking stitch, inc 1 st at
both ends of next and every following 4th row until there are
120 sts on needle.

Continue on these sts until work measures 5 ins from lower edge
of band.

Shape top by casting off 3 sts at beg of next 8 rows. Dec 1 st at
both ends of every row until 84 sts remain; every alt row until
64 sts remain, then every following 3rd row until 46 sts remain.

Cast off 6 sts at beg of next 6 rows.

Cast off.

Work another sleeve band and sleeve in same manner.

COLLAR

Using a back-stitch seam, join shoulders of back and fronts.

With right side of work facing, using No 13 needles, cast on 1 st,
commencing at centre of right front band *knit up* 129 sts
round neck to centre of underflap, cast on 1 st (131 sts).

Next row: P.

Next row: K.

Next row: P.

Continue in stocking stitch, inc 1 st at both ends of next and every
following 3rd row until there are 151 sts on needle.

Work 6 rows.

Still working in stocking stitch, dec 1 st at both ends of next and
every following 3rd row until 131 sts remain.

Work 2 rows.

Next row: Cast off 1 st, work to last st, cast off last st.

Break off wool.

Rejoin wool and cast off remaining sts.

MAKE UP

Omitting ribbing, block and press on wrong side using a warm
iron and damp cloth. Fold over buttonhole band to wrong side
of work, and using a flat seam, neatly stitch into position.

Using a flat seam, stitch underflap into position. Using a back-
stitch seam, join sleeve seams and side seams from top of hem.

Stitch sleeves into position, placing sleeve seam $\frac{1}{2}$ inch to front of side seam. Fold collar inside out and using a back-stitch seam, join shaped ends. Turn collar right side out and stitch cast-off edge to knitted-up edge. Stitch round edges of buttonholes. Attach buttons to correspond with buttonholes. Join edges of hem at one side. Thread elastic through slot, join ends of elastic, stitch together then join slots. Attach a press stud to each side of front band at neck. Press all seams.

LADY'S LUCELLE JUMPER, CAP SLEEVE, V NECK
Illustrated in Plate 30b

6 $\frac{1}{2}$-oz balls Patons Lucelle Fine Ply. Two No 13 needles.
Bust, 34 ins. Length, 19$\frac{1}{2}$ ins.

This garment must be worked at a tension of 10$\frac{1}{2}$ sts and 13 rows to one square inch on No 13 needles measured over stocking stitch.

LACE PANEL (worked over 23 sts)

1st row: K8, K2 tog, wf, K1, P1, K1, wf, K2 tog tbl, K8.
2nd row: P7, P2 tog tbl, P2, won, K1, wrn, P2, P2 tog, P7.
3rd row: K6, K2 tog, K1, wf, K2, P1, K2, wf, K1, K2 tog tbl, K6.
4th row: P5, P2 tog tbl, P3, wrn, P1, K1, P1, wrn, P3, P2 tog, P5.
5th row: K4, K2 tog, K2, wf, K3, P1, K3, wf, K2, K2 tog tbl, K4.
6th row: P3, P2 tog tbl, P4, wrn, P2, K1, P2, wrn, P4, P2 tog, P3.
7th row: K2, K2 tog, K3, wf, K4, P1, K4, wf, K3, K2 tog tbl, K2.
8th row: P1, P2 tog tbl, P5, wrn, P3, K1, P3, wrn, P5, P2 tog, P1.
9th row: K2 tog, K4, wf, K5, P1, K5, wf, K4, K2 tog tbl.
10th row: P11, K1, P11.
11th row: K11, P1, K11.
12th row: P11, K1, P11.

These 12 rows form the lace panel referred to as LP throughout instructions.

FACINGS (*two*)

Cast on 34 sts.

Work in stocking stitch for $1\frac{1}{2}$ ins, finishing at end of a P row.

Slip sts on to a safety pin.

FRONT

Cast on 120 sts.

Work in K1, P1 rib for $3\frac{1}{2}$ ins.

Next row: Rib 7, (inc in next st, rib 6) 15 times, inc in next st, rib to end (136 sts).

Proceed in lace panels with centre and side inc as follows:

1st row: K44, work 23 sts as 1st row of LP, K2, work 23 sts as 1st row of LP, K44.

2nd row: P44, work 23 sts as 2nd row of LP, P2, work 23 sts as 2nd row of LP, P44.

Continue in this manner until 6th row of LP has been worked.

Next row: K44, work 23 sts as 7th row of LP, M1, K2, M1, work 23 sts as 7th row of LP, K44.

Next row: P44, work 23 sts as 8th row of LP, P4, work 23 sts as 8th row of LP, P44.

Working 44 sts at beg and end and 4 sts at centre of row in stocking stitch, continuing with lace panels, work 4 more rows.

Next row: Inc in 1st st, K43, work 23 sts as 1st row of LP, M1, K4, M1, work 23 sts as 1st row of LP, K43, inc in last st.

Next row: P45, work 23 sts as 2nd row of LP, P6, work 23 sts as 2nd row of LP, P45.

Keeping lace panels correct throughout, continue in this manner, inc at centre on 5th row following and every following 6th row and at side edges on 11th row following and every following 12th row until there are 172 sts.

Continue without further inc at side edges, but still inc at centre as before until there are 180 sts.

Continue on these sts until work measures 12 ins from beg, finishing so that right side of work will be facing when working next row.

Shape sleeve edges by inc 1 st at both ends of next and every following 6th row until there are 188 sts.

Work 3 rows.

Divide for neck as follows:

1st row: Inc in 1st st, K51, K2 tog, work 23 LP, K17, slip remaining 94 sts on to a length of wool. Slip 1st 17 facing sts on to another safety pin and leave, slip 2nd 17 facing sts on to left-hand needle, with right side of work facing, K across these 17 sts, turn (111 sts).

2nd row: P34, work 23 LP, P to end.

3rd row: (on which shaping on 34 sts is commenced) K to last 57 sts, 23 LP, K2 tog, K14, M1, K2, M1, K14, K2 tog.

4th row: As 2nd row:

5th row: Inc in 1st st, K to last 57 sts, 23 LP, K2 tog, K14, M1, K2, M1, K14, K2 tog.

6th row: As 2nd row.

7th and 8th rows: As 3rd and 4th.

9th row: Inc in 1st st, K to last 59 sts, K2 tog, 23 LP, K2 tog, K14, M1, K2, M1, K14, K2 tog.

** Continue in this manner, shaping 34 sts on every alt row, inc at sleeve edge on every following 4th row and dec at side of lace panel on every following 8th row until there are 117 sts.

Omitting inc at sleeve edge and dec at side of lace panel, but still shaping 34 sts as before, continue until work measures 6 ins from beg of sleeve edge shaping, finishing at sleeve edge.

Still shaping 34 sts as before, *shape top edge* by casting off 5 sts at beg of next and every alt row until 62 sts remain, 4 sts until 38 sts remain.**

Next row: P.

Next row: Cast off 5 sts, K14 (15 sts on needle after cast-off), M1, K2, M1, K14, K2 tog (34 sts).

Next row: P.

Shaping as before on these 34 sts, work 18 rows.

Complete as follows:

1st row: K2 tog, K to last 19 sts, cast off 4, K to last 2 sts, K2 tog.

2nd row: P.

3rd row: Cast off 2 sts, K to last 2 sts, K2 tog.

Work 2nd and 3rd rows 3 times more.

Next row: P.

Cast off remaining 2 sts.

Rejoin wool to 14 sts on needle.

1st row: Cast off 2, P to end.

2nd row: K2 tog, K to end.

Work 1st and 2nd rows 3 times more.

Cast off.

Slip 94 sts left on length of wool on to a needle, point to centre of work, slip 17 facing sts on to end of needle already holding sts, with right side of work facing, K across 17 facing sts, K17, 23 LP, K2 tog tbl, K to last st, inc in last st.

Proceed as follows:

1st row: P to last 57 sts, 23 LP, P34.

2nd row: K2 tog, K14, M1, K2, M1, K14, K2 tog tbl, 23 LP, K to end.

3rd row: As 1st row.

4th row: K2 tog, K14, M1, K2, M1, K14, K2 tog tbl, 23 LP, K to last st, inc in last st.

5th and 6th rows: As 1st and 2nd.

7th row: As 1st row.

8th row: K2 tog, K14, M1, K2, M1, K14, K2 tog tbl, 23 LP, K2 tog tbl, K to last st, inc in last st.

Work as for 1st half from ** to **.

Next row: Cast off 4 sts, P to end (34 sts).

Next row: K2 tog, K14, M1, K2, M1, K14, K2 tog.

Shaping as before on these 34 sts, work 18 rows.

Complete as for 1st half.

BACK

Work ribbing and inc row as on front (136 sts).

Work 4 rows in stocking stitch.

Shape dart as follows:

1st row: K67, M1, K2, M1, K67.

2nd row: P.

3rd row: K.

4th row: P.

Work these last 4 rows 21 times more (180 sts).

Continue on these sts until work measures same as front up to commencement of sleeve edge shaping.

Shape sleeve edges by inc 1 st at both ends of next and every following 6th row until there are 188 sts, every following 4th row until there are 214 sts.

Continue on these sts until work measures same as front up to
top edge shaping.

Shape top edges by casting off 5 sts at beg of every row until
104 sts remain, 4 sts at beg of every row until 48 sts remain.
Cast off.

SLEEVE BANDS

Using a back-stitch seam, join top edges, matching groups of cast-
off sts and leaving 34 facing sts on front free. With right side
of work facing, *knit up* 116 sts round armhole.
Commencing with a P row, work 15 rows in stocking stitch.
Cast off.

MAKE UP

Omitting ribbing, with wrong side of work facing, block and
press, using a warm iron and damp cloth.
Using a back-stitch seam, join side seams and sleeve bands.
Fold sleeve bands in half and stitch cast-off edge to knitted-up
row on wrong side of work.
Using a back-stitch seam, join cast-off edges of 34 facing sts. Fold
34 sts in half and stitch edges into position round neck leaving
34 cast-on sts free
Press all seams.

LADY'S HAT
Illustrated in Plates 29a and 31

2 oz Double Knitting Wool, and oddment of contrasting colour
for embroidery. Set of No 9 and set of No 11 needles with
points at both ends.
To fit an average head.

Using No 9 needles cast on 8 sts, 3 on 2 needles, 2 on 3rd needle.
Join up to form round.
K 1 round into back of every st.
Proceed for *crown* as follows:
1st round: Inc in every st.
2nd–4th rounds: K.

5th round: Inc in every st.
6th–10th rounds: K.
11th round: Inc in every st.
12th round: K.
13th round: Inc in 1st st, K to end (65 sts).

Proceed as follows:
1st round: (P1, KB1, P1, K1, M1, K8, M1, K1) 5 times.
2nd–4th rounds: (P1, KB1, P1, K12) 5 times.
5th round: (P1, KB1, P1, K1, M1, K10, M1, K1) 5 times.
6th–8th rounds: (P1, KB1, P1, K14) 5 times.

Continue inc in this manner on next and every following 4th round until there are 125 sts.

Work 2 rounds.

Next round: *Using No 11 needles* K2, * K2, inc in next st, rep from * to end of round (166 sts).

Using *double wool* work 7 rounds in KB1, PB1, rib.

Cast off in rib.

Embroider each panel as shown on photograph.

Omitting ribbing, lightly press on wrong side.

HAT

Illustrated in Plates 27a and 31

1 oz 4-ply Fingering. 1 ½-oz ball Angora. Two No 11 needles. To fit an average head.

Using 4-ply and the through sts method, cast on 126 sts.

Work in K1, P1 rib for 1¼ ins.

Work in stocking stitch for 1¼ ins, finishing at end of a P row.

Next row: *Make hem* by knitting tog 1 st from needle and 1 loop from cast-on edge all across row.

Proceed as follows:
1st row: * KB1, P1, rep from * to end.
2nd row: * K1, PB1, rep from * to end.
3rd row: * P1, KB1, rep from * to end.
4th row: * PB1, K1, rep from * to end.
5th and 6th rows: As 1st and 2nd.
Next 2 rows: Using Angora, K.

Using Angora work *Ridge* as follows:

Next row: P to last 6 sts, turn.

Next row: K to last 6 sts, turn.

Next row: P to last 12 sts, turn.

Next row: K to last 12 sts, turn.

Next row: P to last 18 sts, turn.

Next row: K to last 18 sts, turn.

Next row: P to last 24 sts, turn.

Next row: K to last 24 sts, turn.

Next row: P to end. **

Next row: K6, (K2 tog, K4) 20 times (106 sts).

Next row: Using 4-ply, K.

Work rows 2–6 as at commencement, 3rd–6th rows, then 3rd and 4th rows.

Next 2 rows: Using Angora, K.

Rep ridge patt to **.

Next row: K5, (K2 tog, K3) 19 times, K2 tog, K to end (86 sts).

Next row: Using 4-ply, K.

Rep rows 2–6.

Next row: K2 tog all across row (43 sts).

Commencing with a P row work 3 rows in stocking stitch.

Next row: K1, K2 tog all across row (22 sts).

Work 4 rows in stocking stitch.

Next row: P2 tog all across row (11 sts).

Work 2 rows in stocking stitch.

Next row: K1, K2 tog all across row (6 sts).

Work 1 row.

Cast off.

MAKE UP

Using a back-stitch seam, join seam. Using Angora make a twisted cord. Attach a tassel to end of cord, stitch cord to top of hat.

HAT WITH PINEAPPLE STITCH
Illustrated in Plate 31

2 oz Dark, 1 oz Light, 4-ply Fingering. Two No 11 needles. To fit an average head.

This garment must be worked at a tension of $7\frac{1}{2}$ sts and $9\frac{1}{2}$ rows to one square inch on No 11 needles, measured over stocking stitch.

Using Dark and the through sts method, cast on 124 sts.
Work 12 rows in K1, P1 rib, 12 rows in stocking stitch.

Make hem by knitting tog 1 st from needle and 1 loop from cast-on edge all across row.

Next row: * P1, inc in next st, rep from * to end (186 sts).
Continue in stocking stitch until work measures $2\frac{1}{4}$ ins from *top of hem* finishing at end of a K row. Break off Dark.
Next row: Join in Light and P all across, inc 1 st both ends (188 sts).
Proceed in pineapple stitch as follows:
1st row: K1, * sl3, K2 tog, pass 3 sl sts over, P into front and back of next st twice and into front again, rep from * to last st, K1 (188 sts).
2nd row: P1, * K5, PB1, rep from * to last st, P1.
3rd row: K1, * KB1, P5, rep from * to last st, K1.
4th row: As 2nd row.
5th and 6th rows: As 3rd and 4th.
7th row: K1, * inc by purling into front and back of next st twice, sl3, K2 tog, pass 3 sl sts over, rep from * to last st, K1 (157 sts).
8th row: P1, * PB1, K4, rep from * to last st, P1.
9th row: K1, * P4, KB1, rep from * to last st, K1.
10th row: As 8th row.
11th row: As 9th row.
12th row: P1, * (K1, P1, K1) into next st, sl2, P2 tog, pass 2 sl sts over, rep from * to last st, P1 (126 sts).
13th row: K1, * KB1, P3, rep from * to last st, K1.
14th row: P1, * K3, PB1, rep from * to last st, P1.
15th row: As 13th row.
16th row: As 14th row.
17th row: K1, * K into front, back, and front of next st, K3 tog, rep from * to last st, K1. Break off Light.
18th row: Using Dark, P.
Work 10 rows in stocking stitch.
Next row: K2 tog all across (63 sts).

Work 7 rows in stocking stitch.
Next row: K1, * K2 tog, rep from * to end (32 sts).
Work 5 rows in stocking stitch.
Next row: K2 tog all across (16 sts).
Work 3 rows in stocking stitch.
Next row: K2 tog all across (8 sts).
Work 1 row.
Cast off.

MAKE UP

Join seam and press lightly.

LADY'S JUMPER WITH V-SHAPED PANEL AND YOKE
Illustrated in Plate 32

10 oz Dark, 1 oz Light, 4-ply Fingering. Two No 12 and two No 10 needles. Set of four No 12 needles with points at both ends. A cable needle. One stitch-holder.

Bust, 34–36 ins. Length, 20 ins. Sleeve, 18 ins.

This garment must be worked at a tension of 7 sts and 9 rows to one square inch on No 10 needles measured over stocking stitch.

FRONT

Using No 10 needles and Dark, cast on 111 sts.
Proceed in rib as follows:
1st row: (K2, P2) 13 times, K2, P3, (K2, P2) 13 times, K2.
2nd row: (P2, K2) 13 times, P2, K3, (P2, K2) 13 times, P2.
Rep these 2 rows until work measures 1½ ins from beg, finishing at end of a 2nd row.

Change to No 12 needles.
Next row: K.
Next row: (P2, K2) 12 times, P6, K1, PB1, K1, P6, (K2, P2) 12 times.
Proceed in rib with centre panel as follows:
1st row: (K2, P2) 12 times, K6, P1, KB1, P1, K6, (P2, K2) 12 times

248

2nd row: (P2, K2) 12 times, P6, K1, PB1, K1, P6, (K2, P2) 12 times.

3rd row: (K2, P2) 11 times, K2 tog, P2, K6, MIP, P1, KB1, P1, MIP, K6, P2, K2 tog tbl, (P2, K2) 11 times.

4th row: (P2, K2) 11 times, P1, K2, P6, K2, PB1, K2, P6, K2, P1, (K2, P2) 11 times.

5th row: (K2, P2) 11 times, K1, P2, C3F, P2, KB1, P2, C3B, P2, K1, (P2, K2) 11 times.

6th row: As 4th row.

7th row: (K2, P2) 10 times, K2, P1, K2 tog, P2, K6, MIK, P2, KB1, P2, MIK, K6, P2, K2 tog tbl, P1, K2, (P2, K2) 10 times.

8th row: (P2, K2) 10 times, P2, K1, P1, K2, P6, (PB1, K2) twice, PB1, P6, K2, P1, K1, P2, (K2, P2) 10 times.

9th row: (K2, P2) 10 times, K2, P1, K1, P2, K6, (KB1, P2) twice, KB1, K6, P2, K1, P1, K2, (P2, K2) 10 times.

10th row: As 8th row.

11th row: (K2, P2) 10 times, K2, K2 tog, P2, K6, MIP, (KB1, P2) twice, KB1, MIP, K6, P2, K2 tog tbl, K2, (P2, K2) 10 times.

12th row: (P2, K2) 10 times, P3, K2, P6, K1, (PB1, K2) twice, PB1, K1, P6, K2, P3, (K2, P2) 10 times.

13th row: (K2, P2) 10 times, K3, P2, C3F, P1, (KB1, P2) twice, KB1, P1, C3B, P2, K3, (P2, K2) 10 times.

14th row: As 12th row.

15th row: (K2, P2) 10 times, K1, K2 tog, P2, K6, MIP, P1, (KB1, P2) twice, KB1, P1, MIP, K6, P2, K2 tog tbl, K1, (P2, K2) 10 times.

16th row: (P2, K2) 11 times, P6, (K2, PB1) 3 times, K2, P6, (K2, P2) 11 times.

These 16 rows form 2 repeats of the cable patt (the rep of cable patt being rows 1-8 incl throughout), movements of cable patt and increases in centre panel patt being worked on 3rd, 7th, 11th, and 15th rows.

Keeping patt correct and working extra sts into centre panel patt throughout, continue dec and inc as before at each side of centre panel on every 4th row from previous set of decreases and increases until work measures 4½ ins from beg.

Change to No 10 needles and continue in patt, working inc and dec on every 4th row as before, *at the same time* inc 1 st at both ends of 3rd and every following 8th row until there are 123 sts, working increased sts at side edge into K2, P2 rib throughout. Keeping movement of panel correct as before, continue on these sts until work measures 12½ ins from beg, finishing so that *wrong* side of work will be facing when working next row. (Mark this point with a length of wool.)

Divide for yoke as follows:

Next row: Patt 33, P next 57 sts on to stitch-holder, patt to end.

Proceed for *armhole and yoke shaping* on first set of sts as follows:

Still dec along side of cable panel on every 4th row as before, but omitting inc on centre panel, *at the same time* dec 1 st at outside edge on next and every following 8th row until 8 dec *in all* have been worked at armhole edge.

Work 2 rows.

Cast off.

Rejoin Dark to remaining group of sts and complete other half of front to match.

YOKE

With right side of front facing, sl 57 sts from stitch-holder on to No 10 needle, join in Light and Dark and proceed in patt as follows:

1st row: * K3L, 3D, rep from * to last 3 sts, K3L.

2nd row: * K3L, P3D, rep from * to last 3 sts, K3L.

3rd and 4th rows: As 1st and 2nd.

5th row: Inc in first st in L, K2L, * K3D, 3L, rep from * to end, inc in last st (59 sts).

6th row: PID, * K3L, P3D, rep from * to last 4 sts, K3L, PID.

7th row: KIL, * K3D, 3L, rep from * to last 4 sts, K3D, IL.

8th row: KIL, * P3D, K3L, rep from * to last 4 sts, P3D, KIL.

9th row: Inc in first st in L, * K3D, 3L, rep from * to last 4 sts, K3D, inc in last st in L.

10th row: K2L, * P3D, K3L, rep from * to last 5 sts, P3D, K2L.

11th row: K2L, * K3D, 3L, rep from * to last 5 sts, K3D, 2L.

12th row: As 10th row.

These 12 rows form the patt, inc having been worked on 5th and 9th rows.

Keeping patt correct, work 6 more rows, working inc as before on next and following 4th row (65 sts).

Slip these sts on to a stitch-holder and leave.

Break off Light.

Using No 10 needles and Dark, cast on 114 sts.

Proceed in *rib* as follows:

1st row: * K2, P2, rep from * to last 2 sts, K2.

2nd row: * P2, K2, rep from * to last 2 sts, P2.

Rep these 2 rows until work measures 1½ ins from beg, finishing at end of a 2nd row.

Change to No 12 needles.

K 1 row.

Next row: As 2nd row of rib.

Continue in rib until work measures 4½ ins from beg.

Change to No 10 needles and continue in rib, inc 1 st at both ends of 5th and every following 8th row until there are 124 sts.

Continue on these sts until work matches front up to point marked.

Work 1 row.

Shape armholes by dec 1 st at both ends of next and every following 8th row until 108 sts remain.

Work 2 rows.

Cast off all across.

Using No 12 needles and Light, cast on 58 sts.

Proceed in rib as on back for 3 ins, finishing so that right side of work will be facing when working next row. Break off Light.

Change to No 10 needles, join in Dark.

Next row: K.

Commencing with a 2nd row, proceed in rib as before, inc 1

st at both ends of 3rd and every following 6th row until there are 90 sts, then every following 4th row until there are 104 sts.

Continue on these sts until work measures 18 ins from beg. (Mark this point with a length of wool.)

Shape top by dec 1 st at both ends of next and every alt row until 92 sts remain, then every row until 2 sts remain.

Cast off.

NECKBAND

Using a flat seam, stitch sides of yoke neatly into position.

Using a back-stitch seam, join shoulders of front to corresponding sts on back.

Using Dark and first of set of No 12 needles, K across 65 sts on front, using two more No 12 needles *knit up* 177 sts round neck (242 sts).

Work 4 rounds in K 1, P 1 rib, dec 1 st at each side of st at front corners of neck on every round.

Cast off in rib.

MAKE UP

Block and press *very lightly* on wrong side using a warm iron and damp cloth. Using a back-stitch seam, join side and sleeve seams up to point marked. Stitch sleeves into armholes. Press seams.

INDEX

Figures in *italics* indicate Plate numbers